Racial Theories

Second Edition

anathema

D0830044

phen- s

This thoroughly revised and updated edition of Michael Banton's classic book reviews historical theories of racial and ethnic relations and contemporary struggles to supersede them. It shows how eighteenth- and nineteenth-century concepts of race attempted to explain human difference in terms of race as a permanent type and how these were followed by social scientific conceptions of race as a form of status. In a new concluding chapter, 'Race as a Social Construct', Michael Banton makes the case for a historically sensitive social scientific understanding of racial and ethnic groupings which operates within a more general theory of collective action and is, therefore, able to replace racial explanations as effectively as they have been replaced in biological science. This book is essential reading for anyone wanting to understand contemporary debates about racial and ethnic conflict.

MICHAEL BANTON is Professor Emeritus of Sociology at the University of Bristol and a former President of the Royal Anthropological Institute of Great Britain. He has written widely on race and ethnicity, and his previous books include *Racial and Ethnic Competition*, *Promoting Racial Harmony* (both published by Cambridge University Press) and *International Action against Racial Discrimination*.

nominalists
idealism
vicissitude
inhering
pillo died
superseding
retrograde
realists

Racial Theories

Second Edition

Michael Banton

CAMBRIDGE
UNIVERSITY PRESS

PUBLISHED BY THE PRESS SYNDICATE OF THE UNIVERSITY OF CAMBRIDGE
The Pitt Building, Trumpington Street, Cambridge CB2 1RP

CAMBRIDGE UNIVERSITY PRESS
The Edinburgh Building, Cambridge CB2 2RU, United Kingdom
  http://www.cup.cam.ac.uk
40 West 20th Street, New York, NY 10011-4211, USA   http://www.cup.org
10 Stamford Road, Oakleigh, Melbourne 3166, Australia

© Cambridge University Press 1998

This book is in copyright. Subject to statutory exception and to the provisions of
relevant collective licensing agreements, no reproduction of any part may take
place without the written permission of Cambridge University Press.

First published 1987. Reprinted 1989, 1990, 1992, 1994
Second edition 1998

Printed in the United Kingdom at the University Press, Cambridge

Typeset in Plantin 10/12 pt [VN]

A catalogue record for this book is available from the British Library

Library of Congress Cataloguing in Publication data

Banton, Michael P.
  Racial theories / Michael Banton. – 2nd edn.
    p.   cm.
  Includes bibliographical references and index.
  ISBN 0 521 62075 9. – ISBN 0 521 62945 4 (pbk.)
  1. Race   2. Race relations.   I. Title.
HT1521.B345   1998   305.8—dc21   97–32115   CIP

ISBN 0 521 62075 9 hardback
ISBN 0 521 62945 4 paperback

Contents

Figures

Preface

In the ten years since the first edition of this book was prepared, bio-medical scientists have recorded astonishing advances in knowledge about the processes of inheritance and the means by which they may be manipulated. During the same period, ethnic conflicts in different world regions have often dictated the headlines in the mass media. The research of social scientists has influenced the ways in which these conflicts have been presented, and has educated the public about the nature of the social changes associated with population differences, but it is difficult to discern any significant theoretical advance during this decade in the understanding of the processes of ethnic and racial alignment. While social scientists dispute among themselves about the kind of theory they should seek (and indeed, about what kinds of theory are possible), most of them recognise that one of their tasks is to find a vocabulary for representing inter-group relations that avoids the misconceptions implicit in nineteenth-century ideas of race and racial relations. This second edition seeks to demonstrate more clearly than its predecessor that its subject matter is not only the older theories but also the contemporary struggle to supersede them. So a title such as *Racial Theories and their Successors* might more accurately have described its content.

One reviewer complained that the first edition, after discussing Race as Class, came to a surprising halt. The author's ideas about the way ahead were to be found not in the conclusion but in the penultimate chapter. They have now been separated from the discussion of Race as Status and elaborated in a new concluding chapter. What were the first three chapters of the first edition have been revised in the light of new material published since 1987 and are preceded by new introductory text. The remaining chapters have been revised to incorporate new material and to bring out more clearly an argument that previously was insufficiently developed. If racial explanations are to be superseded in social science as they have been in biological science, today's social scientists can learn from their predecessors' achievements. Taking a longer perspective should help them find ways of overcoming or circumventing present-day obstacles. Where was the mistake in the belief that the explanation of 'race relations' required a special kind of theory? Can theories about those relations now be superseded by theories of ethnic relations? This book's answer is that whether or not racial relations and ethnic relations are distinguished from one another, they are both forms of social grouping to be explained within a more general theory of collective action.

Professor John Stone kindly commented on a draft of chapter 7, while Professor R. J. G. Savage helped correct an error concerning nomenclature.

MICHAEL BANTON
July 1997

1   Race as designation

In the United States of America in the first half of the nineteenth century it was customary to refer to the three main sections of the population as 'whites', 'negroes' and 'Indians'. In 1866 the legislature passed a Civil Rights Act which declared that all persons born in the United States were citizens thereof, and that 'such citizens, of every race and color . . . shall have the same right . . . to make and enforce contracts' and do various other things. This may have been the first occasion that Congress used the word 'race' to designate groups in this way, and to refer to the protection of constitutional rights 'without distinction of race or color'. Four years later the Fifteenth Amendment to the Constitution provided that the right to vote 'shall not be denied . . . on account of race'. To persons brought up within the English-speaking world this use of the word 'race' to designate human groups or sections of the population is unremarkable, but to persons brought up in other language worlds it can seem highly questionable. Some French people would even call it 'racist' in the modern sense of that word, because it misrepresented the nature of the differences between the groups.

Others might not carry their objections as far as this, but still express deep concern over a trend in English usage which has gathered strength since 1866. For example, it has been announced that the British population census in 2001 will include a question on ethnic group that will include 'Mixed-race' as one of the optional answers. To speak of people as 'mixed-race' implies that there are pure races, a notion known for over a century to have no scientific justification. All human populations have diverse genetic origins, so any mention of mixture is misleading without a reference to the time period in which it is thought to have occurred. The Coloured people of South Africa are at present frequently described as 'mixed-race', although they have been a distinctive group, or set of groups, for many generations. In the United States a person whose genetic origins are 5 per cent from continent A and 95 per cent from continent B, may be assigned to the race identified with continent A. How have the millions of people who speak the English

1

language got themselves into such a conceptual mess? And how can they get out of it?

Any search for an answer must begin with a history of popular classifications. In the mid-nineteenth-century United States 'whites', 'negroes' and 'Indians' were culturally different. They could also be distinguished by their outward appearance, but the relation between culture and appearance was accidental. Though the white group was characterised by a higher level of literacy than the others, there was no necessary relationship between whiteness and literacy. Outward appearance was not a sign of an inward difference that explained why more whites were literate, as if the word 'race' explained why they were more advanced; therefore it was not a good name to use for the difference. Members of the three groups had been brought together in a new economic and political system in which they occupied unequal positions. To identify someone as 'white', 'negro' or 'Indian' was to employ a proper name, a name that was unique to the group so designated (a capital letter for 'Negro' came later). To identify the groups as 'races' was to imply that the biological differences were the key ones. Today it might be said that the three should have been designated not races but ethnic groups, a designation that is not without its problems but which does not encourage so much confusion.

There is now a whole family of expressions centred upon the conception of race, including racial discrimination, racial group, racial prejudice, racial segregation and racism; used together they can make up a racial idiom. One of the most questionable is 'race relations', an expression that first came into use in the United States in 1910 to denote relations between blacks and whites. Its most objectionable feature is its implication that the relations between persons thought (rightly or wrongly) to belong in different 'races' differ in some important respect from the relations between persons thought to belong in the same race. Secondly, its use is said to legitimise an obsolete and dangerous conception of race. The belief that there were pure and mongrel races, and that races were unequal, was central to the ability of the National Socialist movement in Germany to mobilise so much popular support. Beliefs about the special biological characters of Jews, Gypsies, mentally handicapped persons and sexual deviants resulted in unprecedented atrocities. The ideas which made such things possible must now be anathema. On the other hand it is said, firstly, that members of the English-speaking public are accustomed to think of people as belonging in races and that anyone who wishes to correct their misunderstandings must address them in language that they can easily follow. Secondly, the idiom of race has been used internationally to render racial discrimination illegal, while in Britain 'race relations' is the name of the principal law giving effect to this obligation. These laws play a vital part in reducing the likelihood of any repetition of the Nazi experience. Their dependence upon the idiom of race is too important a usage for anyone to ignore.

The disadvantages inhering in the expression 'race relations' have been recognised for at least half a century (see Hodson, 1950: 305), but there is a genuine dilemma, since the proposed alternatives are little better than the original expression. The idiom of race is used in so many different contexts, both popular and technical, that what might replace it in one context would be unsatisfactory in another. Rather than trying to cut the knot by insisting on a particular replacement, it may be better to begin by untying the knot of past errors to find the sources of the problem. If so, it is necessary to pay close attention to questions of language. The biologists got into difficulties as soon as they changed from a Latin nomenclature and tried to fit the vernacular word 'race' into their classificatory scheme. They escaped from the linguistic trap by developing a theoretical language which is suited to their special purposes, and it looks as if social scientists will have to do the same. There is a growing recognition (e.g. Miles, 1982: 3,19; Banks, 1996:180–90) that part of the present problem is the existence, side by side, of two modes of discourse. One is the practical language of everyday life, employing what are sometimes called folk concepts. The other is a theoretical language in which scientists employ analytical concepts to designate things that the public know under other names. Analytical concepts have to serve purposes different from those served by the words which form part of the practical language of everyday life and therefore may have to be defined differently. When the same word is used in both languages, this can cause confusion. The language now used by those who study the biology of human variation is a technical one with merits that can be appreciated only by those who have studied its foundations. It also makes it easier to neutralise any influence that political passions may exert upon the conduct of research. Social scientists will meet one frustration after another if they do not learn these lessons or if they try to develop schemes tied too closely to the popular conceptions current in one country or one language. Economists and psychologists have progressed further in this respect than sociologists, partly because many sociologists have felt a moral obligation to address as wide a readership as possible and have allowed their political opinions to decide their approach.

Any attempt to untie the knot has to start from the observation that the most serious source of misunderstanding was the theory of permanent racial types, and that this was, among other things, an error in the science of the immediately pre-Darwinian era. By maintaining that every human had distinctive talents inherited as a member of a particular race, some writers set forth a plausible interpretation not only of individual behaviour and of group relations, but of the course of history itself. It had a special appeal in the newly industrialising societies of Europe and North America which were experiencing much more rapid economic growth than other parts of the world. Thus in 1847, a future British prime minister, Benjamin Disraeli, had a character in his novel *Tancred* declare that 'All is race; there is no other truth'. Disraeli used the idiom of race to celebrate Jewish achievement in spite of persecution rather than to disparage other races, but fundamentally he assumed that to think racially was to be modern and scientific (Vincent, 1990: 27–37). In both its scientific and its historical pretensions the theory was new, as can be seen when it is set alongside its predecessors.

The first two phases

In different cultures humans expect different kinds of explanation. For example, if a man falls sick with malaria, Europeans may accept as an adequate explanation the proposition that he had been bitten by a disease-carrying mosquito. In some African cultures people might not be satisfied with this as an explanation. They would ask why did the mosquito bite this man rather some other person who was nearby? It is in this context that propositions about the effect of witchcraft, or destiny, or divine punishment, are put forward to explain connections that most modern Europeans are content to attribute to chance.

Expectations about what constitutes a satisfactory explanation influence the ways in which words are used as terms in an explanation. It seems as if in the sixteenth–eighteenth centuries most Europeans were satisfied that differences between humans, animals, and plants were explained by showing their place in God's creation, and that one of the motivations for studying natural history was to come closer to an understanding of God's design for the universe. At this time the word 'race' was mostly used to designate a set of persons, animals or plants connected by common descent or origin. It was part of a conceptual scheme in which the distinctive characteristics of specimens were explained genealogically, by showing where they belonged in God's creation.

When it came to humans, the main dispute was whether or not all humans were descended from Adam and Eve. Some authors attempted to account for racial differences by relating them to events in the Biblical narrative. For example, the story (in *Genesis* 10: 25–6) of Noah's curse upon his son Ham, declaring that he would be a 'servant of servants' to his brothers, was used to account for the Negro's blackness although there was no reason to believe that Ham was black. The diversity of races was

attributed to God's decision to confound the language of the children of
men after they built the tower of Babel and to scatter them upon the face
of all the earth (*Genesis* 11: 1–9).

During these centuries knowledge about variation in living forms was
increasing rapidly and much effort went into the description and classification of specimens. Just as birds and plants were identified by Latin
names, so were the various classes (like *genus*, *species* and *varietas*) to
which they were assigned. Much of the confusion started from attempts
to find a place for the word 'race' in a classificatory scheme which did not
need it. Was it a synonym for variety or for species? And if it was only a
synonym for an existing term, why should it be introduced?

In this first phase, which is described in chapter 2 on Race as Lineage,
natural historians collected, described and classified specimens. The
Biblical view allowed for occasional catastrophes, like the deluge which
occasioned the construction of Noah's ark, and occasional volcanic eruptions; these might be sources of change, but basically the universe was
perceived as harmonious and static.

Two recent volumes of readings have sought to illustrate the origins of
the idea of race. One started with a 1762 review of Buffon's *History*
(Augstein, 1996); the other with an extract from Linnaeus' work of 1735
(Eze, 1997). In the eighteenth century authors tried to account for the
differences between humans, such as those in skin colour. Sometimes
they used the word 'race' to designate a group of people, but they could
equally well have used some other word. A conception of race as later
generations have come to know it was not essential to any of their
explanations; it had no analytical value, so in this sense there was no idea
of race in the eighteenth century.

The work of geologists forced the natural historians to reconsider their
time-scale and to confront the evidence for change in all living forms.
This opened a second phase in which research workers struggled to come
to terms with the evidence of evolution in nature and the unequal development of human societies. New problems required new explanations.
To start with, there was a preoccupation with the influence of the environment and a readiness to account for change in human societies in
terms of 'moral' causes, in particular with the greater success of some
humans in creating social institutions that enabled them use to their
talents productively. These explanations were then challenged by others
which traced the differences to the operation of supposed physical causes,
such as those of biological inheritance.

It began to look as if the differences between whites, blacks and yellows
were persistent and of long standing. Chapter 3 on Race as Type shows
how, starting with Cuvier, there was increasing sympathy for the view that

racial differences had been constant for as far back as there was evidence. Those who relied on the Old Testament story could offer no reason why God might have created different races, so a genealogical explanation satisfied fewer people. The word 'race' came to signify a permanent category of humans of a kind equivalent to the species category. The first doctrines which were truly racial theories claimed to explain relations *between* groups as the outcome of the properties of species. They appealed to principles different from those used for explaining relations *within* races, just as relations between, say, tigers and antelopes were different from relations between tigers or relations between antelopes.

The more systematic typological theorists, like Nott and Gliddon, recognised that the races of the contemporary world were historical creations assembling people of mixed origin, but they maintained that appearances were deceptive. Though men could migrate and mate with stranger women, humans could not overcome the anthropological laws of permanence of type, the infertility of hybrids, and the limits to acclimatisation; it was these which determined the ultimate outcome. Others did not draw so clear a distinction between race and type. For example, Robert Knox asserted that race was the key to the interpretation of history, but his argument depended upon a definition of race that made it a synonym for type as this word was used by Nott and Gliddon. This assumption of permanent difference is the capital error and the central issue with which the history of racial thought must be concerned. It must explain how the error came about, why it has been so difficult to overcome, and why the elaboration of better explanations had to depend upon the establishment of new modes of analysis.

Since later generations have pilloried some of those who elaborated typological explanations as evil-minded or personally prejudiced individuals, it can be better to take an example from the writing of a much-respected figure: from Gilbert Murray, the classical scholar, humanitarian, and devoted supporter of the League of Nations. At one point he observed (as if this needed no demonstration) that

> There is in the world a hierarchy of races . . . those nations which eat more, claim more, and get higher wages, will direct and rule the others, and the lower work of the world will tend in the long run to be done by the lower breeds of men. This much we of the ruling colour will no doubt accept as obvious. (1900: 156)

Unquestionably, whites were at this time superior to blacks and yellows in political and economic power, but Murray's explanation of this was wrong. It failed to distinguish between nations, as political units, and races, as biological units. The position of white people at the top of the hierarchy was attributed to their biological inheritance and the predicted future division of labour throughout the world was represented as an expression of this hierarchy. The political and economic sources of white power developed over the previous five centuries merited no attention. The text also failed to follow up an interesting line of argument of its own, namely the claim that development was driven by the tendency of certain nations to consume more, and in particular by their demand for more food. Why some groups consumed more was an interesting question to which the racial theories offered a highly speculative biological answer. One of the tasks for the next phase of thought was to separate the sorts of question that could be answered biologically from those which required a different kind of answer.

The third phase

The third phase is one in which racial theories have been superseded by more powerful explanations which do not need any concept of race. Where the typologists regarded racial characteristics as the properties of species, population genetics in the 1930s demonstrated that the unit of selection was not the species but the gene, and more recently was popularised in the title of a best-selling book, *The Selfish Gene* (Dawkins, 1976). How the mistaken theories were superseded in biology is described in chapter 4 on Race as Subspecies. The accumulation of specimens and their classification did not lead to generalisation or to any explanation of their diversity. New theories were necessary for that. In distinguishing the questions addressed by a new generation of research workers, and the kinds of answer they proposed, it can be useful to employ two words of Latin origin. The *explanandum* (plural, *explananda*) is the thing that is to be explained, and *explanans* (plural, *explanantia*) is that which explains it. With the growth in knowledge research workers lost interest in the old explananda and moved on to new ones, but, to take a very simple illustration, the explanans for the problem 'why is the Negro's skin black?' changed from 'because of a Biblical curse', to 'because it has always been black', and then to 'because it confers a selective advantage in certain environments'.

One of the merits of representing the history of racial theories as falling into three phases is that the various contributors can be seen as having a place in an intellectual structure. Some of them are representative of a particular phase or viewpoint; others are transitional from one to the next; yet others are simply confused or are opportunists who put together incompatible elements to construct an unconvincing thesis. Dividing up the subject and distinguishing different uses of the word 'race' in these phases can also help the commentator avoid falling into the trap of presentism. This is the tendency to interpret other historical periods in terms of the concepts, values and understanding of the present time. Many writers about racial thought have failed to notice that when their predecessors wrote about groups distinguished in racial terms they did not conceive of race in the way that is implicit in subsequent uses of the word.

Anyone who seeks to explain how it is that some contributions led to a growth of knowledge, and helped to move racial thought on from one phase to another, must draw upon some philosophy of science. Up to the middle of the present century the dominant view was the inductivist one formulated by Francis Bacon. It represented research as a procedure whereby people collected specimens, classified and named them, and then noted the generalisations that emerged. According to Bacon, the chief obstacle to the growth of knowledge was excessive self-confidence among research workers unable to recognise how they were blinded by their own prejudices and superstitions; to avoid error, they should purge their minds of preconceptions. Bacon's successors maintained that the scientific procedure was to express the generalisations as explanatory hypotheses and try to verify them. The challenge to this prescription came from Karl Popper, who maintained that the mind could not be purged of preconceptions. Hypotheses occur to investigators as, working within particular intellectual traditions, they attempt to account for new as well as old observations. Discoveries come from the refutation of conjectures. Mistakes are made continuously: the task is to learn from them. In the study of racial thought the Baconian philosophy revealed itself in the representation of race as 'a modern superstition' and in the claim that doctrines of racial superiority expressed the racial prejudices of their authors. Those who followed Popper's view of the matter stressed the relative inability of scientific institutions in the nineteenth century to regulate claims to scientific authority, especially when the political climate in Europe and North America encouraged the growth and dissemination of the doctrines.

Popper's interest was in the discoveries which ushered in major scientific advances, the revolutions which feature in the title of Thomas Kuhn's book *The Structure of Scientific Revolutions* (1962). Yet Kuhn's work attracted more attention for what it had to say about the paradigms, or patterns, of 'normal science' in between the revolutionary upsets. It accompanied the revival of interest in the sociology of knowledge which encouraged historians to examine what Kuhn called the 'external social, economic and intellectual conditions' when analysing changes in science. Kuhn wrote (1968: 76) of the 'internal approach' to the history of science as being concerned with the substance of science as knowledge. It concentrated upon the problems with which scientists grappled and their attempts to resolve them. Kuhn contrasted this with the 'external approach' which is concerned with the activity of scientists as a social group within the larger culture and looks at ways in which their problem selection and their search for explanations are influenced by the social and political conditions of their time. Both are legitimate ways of writing history. The tension between them is not in the answers they offer, but in their choice of questions.

Ernst Mayr in his magisterial account of *The Growth of Biological Thought* (1982: 28–31) has pictured that growth as driven by the hypothetico–deductive method. By simply collecting specimens and recording observations science could never have progressed from systematic botany to plant genetics. As Mayr says: 'Progress in many branches of science depends upon observations made in order to answer carefully posed questions.' Darwin's ability to identify good questions was crucial to the scientific revolution he inspired.

The concepts of population genetics made possible a reliable explanation of the physical differences between human populations which had intrigued the typologists. So although the typological doctrine had never been accepted by the more respected scientists of the era, it is reasonable to see the new concepts as superseding the concept of race in biological science. Geneticists could examine the underlying relations which determined the process of speciation. Instead of trying to identify a subspecies by drawing a line round a collection of individual specimens, they selected samples in order to study the frequency of particular genes within them, and examined the processes of change in gene frequencies.

Population genetics provided explanations of the physical inheritance of characters, but did not attempt to explain cultural inheritance or the social relations between people assigned to groups and categories on the basis of their physical characteristics. Some other kind of science had to find how to supersede the erroneous mid-nineteenth-century explanations of the relation between race and social affairs. A comparison of the present position with that when Gilbert Murray was writing suggests that over this period a very great deal has been learned about the relations between peoples, and that the general public is now much better informed about the relative significance of biological and social causes of human variation. Indeed, no one need spend long studying the publications of the 1950s to see that there has been continuing progress.

Much of this improved understanding is to the credit of biological and social scientists who have addressed popular audiences. Nevertheless, some would think it hubristic were they to compare their work with that of biological scientists because they cannot offer explanations of the same quality. They might say that the subject matter of social science is just too different – that, for example, social forms cannot be classified like plant species, and that there are no underlying determinants of social variety that can be compared with genes. Some would argue that social science is fundamentally political and that much of the apparent intellectual progress is only a reflection of the political changes from an era of imperial expansion and bellicose nationalism to one in which whites are a dwindling proportion of the world's population. They now have to try harder to understand the views of others. According to some of these critics the social sciences can never attain to objective knowledge.

When they first ventured onto the academic stage, all the social sciences received a critical, if not hostile, reception which was to their eventual benefit. In the debates about the kinds of explanation they might be able to offer, a distinction was sometimes drawn between generalising and historical sciences. The former seek causal explanations of more limited aspects of events, accounting for them in terms of general principles. The latter seek historical explanations which set out to account for events in terms of previous events, highlighting their unique character (Popper, 1945/66, ii: 263–4 and 362 n.7). Economics and psychology, which early in the twentieth century were seen as historical sciences, have developed general theories which subsume the subject matter of nineteenth-century racial theories within conceptual schemes that make no reference to race. They have developed their own theoretical languages.

One of the reasons why developments in sociology have been different lies in that subject's history. Many of its nineteenth-century precursors took a very general view of their vocation, frequently attempting to interpret the course of history in terms of predominating factors. They often looked at societies as wholes: thus John Stuart Mill, writing 'on the logic of the moral sciences', distinguished two kinds of sociological inquiry. He favoured study of 'the causes which produce, and the phenomena which characterise, States of Society generally. In the solution of this question consists the general Science of Society' (1843: 594). This led later to a conception of sociology as a synthesis of the special social sciences, like economics, political science, psychology, human geography, etc. In the early years of the twentieth-century other writers, and most notably Durkheim and Weber, the 'founding fathers of sociology', laid the foundations for a more modest (if still very ambitious) intellectual enterprise, as a special social science of the same order as the others, though a tension between the two conceptions of the subject continues. The more limited conception is reflected in chapter 5 of this book, the more ambitious one in chapter 6. The difference centres not upon whether sociologists should make use of historical material but upon the kinds of questions that are asked of it, or the kinds of explanation attempted.

Some of the obstacles to the advancement of the social sciences are inherent in the complications of their subject matter. There are other obstacles which derive from the social scientist's own socialisation into a particular society and the near-impossibility of standing apart from it. Yet some difficulties, such as those embodied in language, can be greatly reduced even if not overcome.

As has already been suggested, the process by which more powerful explanations are developed (within both biological and social science) comes from the development of a theoretical language by vesting ordinary words with special meanings, coining new words for these meanings, or agreeing to use mathematical symbols to denote factors in an equation. The process is sometimes slow, and some proposals to give words special meanings and make them into concepts never succeed. Thus in his *History of the Conquest of England by the Normans* (1825), Augustin Thierry took the word 'class' and attempted to use it for explaining the kinds of conflict occasioned by that conquest. In everyday English 'class' is now used in a variety of ways, often to identify what sociologists prefer to call differences of status. Though Karl Marx hailed Thierry as 'the father of the "class struggle" in French historical writing', only a minority of sociologists believe that it has the explanatory power Marx attributed to it. Thierry's book also stimulated W. F. Edwards, the founder of the *Société Ethnographique* in Paris, to develop ideas about race as something that could explain the course of history, and it was this proposal which was developed by the racial typologists to advance what they considered a scientific theory. Any suggestion that 'race' can serve as an analytical concept is now almost universally rejected. The word continues to be used in everyday language in a variety of senses, notably as a name for categories constituted by reference to the outward physical differences of complexion, hair form and bone structure, and it is this usage, given official endorsement in the United States in 1866, which has often encouraged the belief that cultural differences can be explained by physical ones.

A specialist on the history of Greece, writing about the use of the Greek-origin word 'ethnicity', concludes that it was 'a somewhat retrograde step that ethnicity should ever have entered into the *analytical* vocabulary of the social sciences' (Just, 1989: 76). His regret is premature, because social scientists use a great many words which have, or have had, theoretical pretensions, but have not gained acceptance as analytical concepts and probably never will. To give but one example from another sphere altogether, the word 'kinship' has practical value in ordinary language and is much used by anthropologists, but it is too general to have any place in the explanation of special relations between persons who are kin to one another. 'Ethnicity' is presently used in a similar way to kinship but it might one day earn a place in the analytical vocabulary of the social sciences.

It is sometimes convenient to write as if there were two languages, paralleling the distinction between the world of appearances and the world of determining relations in which the appearances are manufactured, but for other purposes it can be more accurate to envisage a continuum. At one end, the practical language uses folk concepts which change with the growth of knowledge – for example, the concepts of witchcraft and possession, once used to explain misfortune and mental illness, have now been succeeded by better ones. Folk concepts are modified in line with popular experience; ideas about other peoples change in step with the frequency and character of the encounters from which that experience is derived. There can also be two-way traffic between the two languages, some concepts elaborated for theoretical purposes being taken into everyday speech (like 'role model', 'electoral swing', 'charisma', etc.). So in the course of time folk concepts acquire additional meanings which increase their serviceability in everyday communication while at the same time introducing ambiguities. The various meanings are then identified in dictionaries. Furthermore, folk concepts are limited to the societies which fashion them. The word 'race', for example, is not easily translated into non-European languages because of the multiple associations it has acquired in English. Analytical concepts must be capable of international, or transcultural, use.

The difference between folk and analytical concepts, or between words in the practical and the theoretical languages, does not lie in the words themselves but in the use which can be made of them. Where folk concepts are ordinary language names of things, analytical concepts are names necessary to explanations. Theories are built with analytical concepts defined as precisely as possible in order to reduce ambiguities and make the meaning of propositions more certain. Concepts are sharpened by promoting those which have most explanatory power, but an ordinary dictionary definition cannot adequately convey their meanings. For example, a dictionary entry which says that an allele is 'one of two alternative Mendelian characters' is only a beginning. Anyone who wants to understand what explanations the concept renders possible will have to consult a textbook.

Concepts like allele, antigen, antibody, agglutination, and so on, have contributed to the development of a battery of concepts which supersede 'race' in the explanation of the physical aspects of human variation.

Differences in outward appearance are best described as phenotypical variation, for where 'race' suggests that individuals may be classed as belonging in a relatively few discontinuous categories, phenotypical variation more readily implies a continuous variation in which differences of appearance shade into one another with no sharp lines of differentiation.

The unequal development of societies across the world is best explained not by postulated differences in genetic inheritance but by deploying the concepts of economics. As a means of accounting for differences within societies the results of intelligence testing are much disputed, but psychologists can now account for some of the differences that used to be associated with race by calling upon technical expressions developed to account for variations between populations in perception, in the acquisition of useful skills, and so on. The progress of sociologists in elaborating a set of concepts that will supersede in their subject (in which social anthropology may be included) any reliance upon a concept of race forms the subject matter of chapters 5–7 of this book. It may be that eventually the analysis of processes of the creation and dissolution of group boundaries, of inclusive and exclusive processes in group maintenance, and the concepts associated with them, will constitute a theoretical language. The working sociologist has to concentrate on developing the theory; consideration of the status of its component concepts is more a matter for philosophers.

To understand which questions scientists and scholars seek to answer, it is helpful to see each individual research worker as standing within an intellectual tradition. They have received training which has directed their attention to particular problems and to what is interesting about them. They have come to regard particular previous investigations as exemplars of the best way to conduct research, and on the other side, have come to believe that other procedures are unproductive or retrograde. In this way research traditions are built up which incorporate ideas about good and bad practice. They are driven forward by internal controversy and new knowledge so that they change over time. They also vary from one country to another, and sometimes from one university to another. Popper and Kuhn took their examples from physical science where intellectual revolutions have been fairly clear-cut and there has been least opportunity for research in different countries to pursue idiosyncratic interpretations (the Lysenko affair in Soviet genetics is an illuminating example of these constraints). Biological science, so Ernst Mayr (1982: 36–45) argues, differs from physical science. General laws are less important and have to allow for exceptions that are not refutations. The study of evolution necessitates the use of concepts of a special kind. Social science differs even more, since the people who are being studied are constantly changing their behaviour in the light of what they have learned about the principles governing the operation of their societies. Social science traditions differ greatly from one country to another, partly for this reason, partly because of political constraints, and partly because the research workers concentrate upon what are perceived as the important problems of their own societies. The study of ethnicity and ethnic relations in Russia today is very different from that in the United States, while that in western Europe has yet another character.

When the first edition of this book was in preparation there were two chief intellectual traditions in the study of the social aspects of racial relations. They were reviewed in chapters 4 and 5, entitled Race as Status and Race as Class, which may have suggested too simple a contrast; they feature again, somewhat revised, in this second edition (chapters 5 and 6), in order to designate traditions which draw on different philosophies of society as well as of science. The first assumed that sociology, following in the course of economics and psychology, could develop as a generalising science. The second, with its sources in Hegelian philosophy and Marxist materialism, maintained that the whole of social science was a historical enterprise bound to the conditions of the epoch which had made it possible. These differences influenced the selection of problems for study and the kinds of question posed. Those pursuing the goal of a generalising science believed that the individual scholar should be free to study the kinds of problem he or she found interesting, and that intellectual advances had often come from the study of unfashionable problems. They often concerned themselves with the ideas people held, and were therefore likely to interest themselves in the sorts of questions that characterise the internal history of science. Those who, like the Marxists, subscribed to a theory about the course of historical change, maintained that scholars had a moral obligation to study the kinds of problem that would help politically progressive people select the sorts of strategy beneficial to the population. When it came to the history of science, they were more likely to study the influence of external conditions. Yet before the end of the 1970s this second tradition was starting to divide. One branch held to a severely structural interpretation of the Marxist model, another started to explore its microsociological assumptions, while other writers, although continuing to seek historical explanations, abandoned any adherence to the tenets of historical materialism and shifted to the analysis of developments in the cultural sphere, such as the influence of the mass media and the character of popular culture.

A long debate may lead to a conclusion that can be stated quite shortly, which is convenient for teachers seeking to introduce a subject. It can be valuable to lead new students through some of the classical analyses, like the studies of communities in Mississippi in the 1930s by Lloyd Warner and Dollard, even if black–white relations in the Deep South have been transformed since that time. But when summarising the current state of theory it is possible leave to one side, without any disrespect to their authors, many valuable contributions to the study of ethnic and racial relations that have not improved the general theory and may not have been directed to this end. The first edition of this work was criticised by some reviewers for what it omitted. This was partly the author's fault for failing to make it sufficiently clear that the book was offered as a contribution to the philosophy of social science that utilised a historical approach, rather than as a contribution to the history of racial theorising. It was intended to state a case that the dilemma about what use to make of the word 'race' in social science could be resolved only by severing an improved theoretical language from the practical language. By contrast, a history of racial theorising would have required attention to some writers who were historically important in the period prior to the Second World War because of their public influence, but whose work was of little theoretical relevance because it lacked philosophical originality. A history would also have required the sort of research that distinguishes Elazar Barkan's *The Retreat of Scientific Racism* (1992) or Saul Dubow's *Scientific Racism in Modern South Africa* (1995), and have necessitated writing a much longer book.

The typological theory started from the presumed properties of so-called 'permanent types'. The capacities of every human were thought to be decided by the type (or mixture of types) which had gone into his or her constitution. In this respect the theory had a 'top-down' character in that the properties of the species were thought to determine the capacities of the individual. In biology, this was replaced by a 'bottom-up' theory which started from individual genes and worked upwards to show how they determined inherited behaviour patterns. In social science few problems are as important as those relating to the interaction of the 'macro' and the 'micro'. To follow the formulation of Theodor Geiger (1967: 147–50), some of its theories are katascopic (top-down), while others are anascopic (bottom-up). In economics, any macro theory is supposed to state the micro assumptions upon which it relies. In psychology, most theories are bottom-up, whereas sociologists have for a long time concentrated on the top-down approach.

Jon Elster (1989: 97) challenged sociologists by contrasting Adam Smith's *homo economicus* to Durkheim's *homo sociologicus*:

The former is supposed to be guided by instrumental rationality, while the behaviour of the latter is dictated by social norms. The former is 'pulled' by the prospect of future rewards, whereas the latter is pushed from behind by quasi-inertial forces. The former adapts to changing circumstances, always on the lookout for improvements. The latter is insensitive to circumstances, sticking to the prescribed behaviour even if new and apparently better options become available. The former is easily caricatured as a self-contained, asocial atom, and the latter as the mindless plaything of social forces or the passive executor of inherited standards.

There is enough truth in the suggestion that sociological theory has neglected 'pull' in order to emphasise 'push' to recommend that the potentialities of the alternative approach be explored seriously.

The top-down approach (stressing push) has seemed to offer the chance of quickly discovering important influences on social trends, and it has offered opportunities for the elaboration of political philosophies. A bottom-up strategy (concentrating on pull) has not been for the faint-hearted because tracing a path from the individual actor through the maze of social institutions would require a scheme much more complicated than programming a computer to play chess. Tasks like this are not completed within the life-work of a single scholar.

This book reaches somewhat pessimistic conclusions about the possibilities of a top-down theory which could replace the idiom of race in social science. It suggests that social scientists should consider more carefully recent work that lays the foundations for a bottom-up approach.

2 Race as lineage

diff. bet poly + monogenisis why not widely accepted in a time when Bible was the authority on human affairs

The word 'race' entered the English language in 1508 in the poem *The Dance of the Sevin Deidly Sins* by the Scotsman, William Dunbar. Among those who followed the sin of Envy he listed:

> And flatteris in to menis facis;
> And bakbyttaris of sindry racis,
> To ley that had delyte.

It was introduced into an intellectual world in which the Bible was accepted as the authority on human affairs. All humans were descended from Adam and Eve. To understand what had happened to the various sections of humanity subsequently it was necessary to trace their histories back genealogically through the links in the ancestral chain. People were differentiated because they had migrated to different regions and because God had guided the course of events. He had punished some, as by putting the mark upon Cain and by permitting the curse upon Ham and his descendants. Different groups had doubtless been dispersed after the Flood and after the fall of the Tower of Babel. Yet the Bible was obscure in places and its answers seemed to be hidden, so it had to be studied with intelligence and faith. How was it possible to reconcile stories of people in distant lands with a Bible that made no mention of these lands? One possible solution was to maintain that Adam was the ancestor of the Jews alone, and that other peoples' nature and history could be traced back to separate ancestors. Such an explanation, later called that of polygenesis, was first advanced by Paracelsus in 1520. It was taken up again in 1655 by the luckless Isaac de Peyrère, who wrote 'I would that St Augustine and Lactantius were now alive, who scoffed at the Antipodes. Truly they would pity themselves if they should hear and see those things which are discovered in the east and west in this clear-sighted age . . .' Yet his book was burned and its author forced to recant. Isaac de Peyrère was a man of Jewish descent who professed to be a Christian; his claim of separate origins seems to have been intended as testimony to the greater glory of the Jews (Poliakov, 1974: 132–4).

The supposition that the differences between the various groups were fundamental and could be traced back to separate origins, whether or not of divine creation, could be discussed only allusively. The power of organised religion supported the alternative doctrine of monogenesis, which insisted that all humans descended from Adam and Eve and that therefore any differences were superficial. Ideas of race developed within this opposition.

Classification

Though 'race' came into increasing use in the sense of lineage during the sixteenth and seventeenth centuries (as in the 1570 reference in Foxe's *Book of Martyrs* to 'the race and stocke of Abraham') its future significance was being decided in another realm of discourse, that of natural history. People looked to the Bible for explanations not of human origins only, but of all living things. One of the first to offer a systematic natural history was John Ray (1627–1705), a founder of the Royal Society, who in 1690 wrote *The Wisdom of God Manifested in the Works of the Creation*. John C. Greene (1959: 17) describes this as a reaffirmation of the Christian doctrine of the creation infused with the hopefulness generated by the scientific revolution of his time. Ray maintained that 'the number of true species in nature is fixed and limited and, as we may reasonably believe, constant and unchangeable from the first creation to the present day'. In the beginning God had created a limited number of animals and plants. The study of nature could bring humans to an understanding of the wisdom, power and benevolence by which the Creator ministered to their intellectual and spiritual as well as physical needs. Still, it was not always easy to discern God's design or to sort out the diversity of living forms. Ray's guiding principle was that what God had created was the species, and that 'a species is never born from the seed of another species', that is, it consisted of individual specimens linked by descent. His criteria for distinguishing the essential features of plant species from 'accidents' of variation in size, colour and number of leaves, were subjective and open to dispute. Just as Ray would not accept that a black cow and a white cow, or two similar fruits with a different taste, were necessarily separate species, so he would make no such distinction between a Negro and a European. But while he could experiment by sowing the seed of a plant and seeing whether it gave rise to a similar variety, when it came to the bigger animals he had to class together specimens whose common descent he could not verify.

This leads straight to the central problem of racial thought, one that runs through from the seventeenth century (if not earlier) to the present

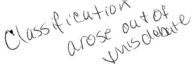
Classification arose out of unisdebate

time, and is far from settled yet: What is the nature of species? There is nothing wrong in classifying humans according to their appearance. The problems revolve around the nature of the classes from which a classification is constructed and the significance of the differences between them. In this they reflect one of the oldest and most fundamental disputes in philosophy. In the Middle Ages a major battle was fought between the nominalists and the realists. According to Popper (1957: 27) the former held that universal terms like 'energy', 'velocity', 'carbon', 'whiteness', etc., differed from singular terms or proper names like 'Alexander the Great', 'Halley's Comet' and 'the First World War', in that the former were labels for sets or classes of individual things. The nominalists regarded the universal term 'white' as identifying a set composed of things as different as snowflakes, tablecloths and swans. The realists contended that whiteness was an intrinsic property; snowflakes shared this property along with tablecloths and swans. They believed that universal terms denoted universal objects (called 'forms' or 'ideas' by Plato) just as singular terms denoted individual things. The doctrine traditionally called realism has also been called idealism (which might seem to be its opposite) and so Popper concluded that it would be less confusing to speak of an opposition between nominalism and essentialism. Nominalists regard words as instruments of description which permit scholars to generalise about the behaviour or relations of individuals which are classed separately or together. Essentialists believe that research must seek the essence of things in order to explain them. Nominalists regarded the classification of individuals to constitute a species as a matter of convenience. Different classifications could be used for different purposes. In biology, Robinet, Buffon and Lamarck at all various times gave their assent to the view that 'there are only individuals, and no kingdoms or classes or genera or species'. Essentialists started from the Bible story and believed that the task of classification was to grasp the essential character of the original form which explained the diversity of outward appearances.

Categories just a toolkit

The number and variety of forms was daunting. Were all dogs, for example, to be accounted one species? They inter-breed, but the differences between the spaniel, the terrier and the bulldog were striking. One scheme which assisted simplification was the notion of a Great Chain of Being, a *scala naturae*, to which Linnaeus referred when in 1754 he wrote:

If we consider the generation of animals, we find that each produces an offspring after its own kind . . . so that all living things, plants, animals, and even mankind themselves, form one chain of universal being from the beginning to the end of the world. Of all the species originally formed by the Deity, not one is destroyed. (quoted in Bendyshe, 1865: 435)

The ambiguities of this conception can be seen in the passage quoted, for while it refers to a vertical or temporal chain in which individuals are linked to their ancestors and descendants of different generations, it also implies that plants, animals and humans are linked to one another in a horizontal or classifactory chain such that the individuals of each species shaded into those of the next, or inter-graded, as if sharp differentiation was impossible. *Natura non facit saltum* (nature makes no leap) was the slogan expressing the view that there were no discontinuities or breaks in natural variation. Linnaeus' dogmatic assertion that no species was ever destroyed was an attempt to eliminate a serious problem. John Ray had earlier been troubled by the discovery of the fossils of apparently extinct shell fish. He decided that such shell fish might still be lodged so deep in the seas or on rocks so remote that they had not been noticed. For why would God have created them if they were not necessary to his design? The natural historian felt obliged to assume that God's creation was perfect; to do otherwise would be to suggest that God was a poor craftsman. When in 1706, 1739, and later, the skeletal remains of mammoths were discovered in New York state, in Ohio, and in other parts of North America, it was inferred that there must somewhere be living mammoths because, in the words of Thomas Jefferson (in 1785), 'Such is the economy of nature, that no instance can be produced, of her having permitted any one race of her animals to become extinct' (Greene, 1959: 96–120).

Linnaeus (1707–78) is famous for his classifactory system, sometimes called binomial because he identified creatures by the names for the genus and the species. To these is now added another division, once called the variety but now known as the subspecies. Thus gulls belong to the genus *Larus* and the Herring Gull is *Larus argentatus* or *Larus argentatus argentatus*. The third name is not normally repeated unless there are two or more subspecies. Thus the British subspecies of the Lesser Black Backed Gull is named *Larus fuscus britannicus* to differentiate it from *Larus fuscus antelius*. In the tenth edition of his *Systema Naturae* (1758) Linnaeus divided the species *Homo sapiens* into six diurnal varieties: *ferus* (four footed, mute, hairy); *americanus* (red, choleric, erect); *europaeus* (white, ruddy, muscular); *asiaticus* (yellow, melancholic, inflexible); *afer* (black, phlegmatic, indulgent); *monstrosus* (further subdivided to include deviant forms from several regions). The diurnal varieties were compared with a single nocturnal one, the troglodytes or cave-dwellers, exemplifed by *Homo sylvestris* (man of the woods, or Orang Utan). Right up to the early years of the nineteenth century there were doubts about where the line was to be drawn between men and apes, and which side of that line Pygmies, Hottentots and Orang Utans belonged. Many travellers' tales

problems arose Latin to vernacular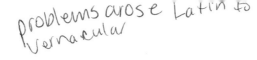

asserted that the last-named was 'equally ardent for women as for its own females'. Believing that apes were men in a primitive stage of development, the whimsical Scottish judge and author Lord Monboddo maintained that Orang Utan–human matings might be fertile; his views were satirised by Thomas Love Peacock in his 1817 novel *Melincourt* which tells how the central figure, Sir Oran Haut Ton, comes to be elected a Member of Parliament.

Linnaeus was too honest to deal with other problems as dogmatically as he dealt with that of extinct species. He encountered a striking mutation of flower structure in the plant *Linaria*, which he believed to be a new species. He also studied some hybrids which seemed to be new species. This led him after a while to the conclusion that perhaps only genera had been created in the beginning and that species were the product of hybridisation among them (Mayr, 1982: 259).

The Linnaean classifactory enterprise depended upon the assumption that the various sets of individuals to be classified were stable, for how could they be classified if they were changing? Some new principle had to be incorporated into the scheme to deal with change. Linnaeus' great French contemporary Buffon (1707–88) moved further in this direction and there was, of course, a Biblical warrant for a change in the story of the expulsion of Adam and Eve from the Garden of Eden. If they had been sent to live in inferior environments might it not be expected that they would degenerate? In the first volume of his *Histoire Naturelle* (1749) Buffon rejected the concept of species, contending that only individuals existed. The idea of a species could be rendered intelligible only 'by considering Nature in the succession of time, and in the constant reduction and renovation of beings'. Yet Buffon abandoned this view in his second volume, asserting that two animals belong to the same species 'if by means of copulation they perpetuate themselves and preserve the likeness of the species'. The horse and the donkey were separate species because the product of their mating was sterile (the offspring of a male donkey and a mare is called a mule; that of a stallion and a female donkey is called a hinny). In the first volume Buffon also elaborated an environmental view of human variation, suggesting that after being diffused over the whole surface of the earth mankind 'underwent divers changes, from the influence of climate, from the difference of food, and of the mode of living, from epidemical distempers, as also from the inter-mixture, varied *ad infinitum*, of individuals more or less resembling each other'.

fertile species

How environments might occasion organic change was far from clear. The philosopher Immanuel Kant (1724–1804) supposed that the ancestral human stock had been endowed with latent powers which could be evoked or suppressed in new circumstances. Like the other authors of his time, Kant had to base his generalisations on the often unreliable reports of travellers. A recent commentator (Eze, 1997: 57) has taken a harsh view of what looks like a sarcastic comment on one of these stories. An interpretation of the causes of change which resembled Kant's was developed at much the same time by Johann Friedrich Blumenbach (1752–1830), the German anatomist who has been called the father of anthropology. It was he who first advanced the five-fold classification: Caucasian, Mongolian, Ethiopian, American, Malayan, and maintained that the different kinds of humans differed only in degree. Blumenbach was puzzled by the way that acquired characters (in particular peculiarities of appearance made by accident or by intention, such as the binding of children's head or feet) were not handed down to the next generation when other 'marks of race', organic disorders and deficiencies of speech were so transmitted. He concluded that there must be some hidden agencies which operated to change the bodies of animals. This change he called degeneration, but seems to have meant by it not deterioration so much as the kinds of modification that arise as one generation succeeds another (though cf. Sloan, 1973). He wrote of degeneration as an explanation of variation within a species and as opposed to separate creation. In his view the genital liquid interacted with other material to produce a formative force which resulted in the normal reproduction of the animal or plant unless it was deflected in some way; in which case it produced monsters, hybrids, or greater variation. Climate had great influence in 'diverting the formative force from its accustomed path'. Domestic animals showed greater variation than wild ones, because they had been subjected to more varied conditions, especially of food. All hogs, for example, descended from the wild boar. Yet endless differences could be seen between the kinds of domestic hogs to be found in various European countries. The original wild condition of man was not known, but in spreading over the earth he had exposed himself to so many different stimuli that he had developed even more variation than the hog.

If forms were changing, this complicated the problem of classification. It also had implications for the use of the word race. Kant distinguished between *Naturbeschreibung* (nature-description) and *Naturgeschichte* (natural history). The former was static, a classification at a moment in time which was based upon similarities between specimens ordered into genera, species and varieties. The latter dealt with relations between varieties, species and genera over time. What was species in *Naturbeschreibung* must in *Naturgeschichte* often be called only race since it was impossible to distinguish species from genus in the historical dimension (see especially Greene, 1959: 363n/15.). Johann Gottfried von Herder also in 1784 protested about the use of the word race to denote classes when it was properly used to designate a difference of origin; since all humans were of the same origin no racial difference existed in their species.

External conditions

The discovery of the hidden agencies of evolution is a story that belongs with the internal history of biology. Before sketching its outlines it will be appropriate to comment upon the external conditions of racial thought from the sixteenth to the eighteenth centuries. The first of these conditions must be the power of organised religion to prevent speculation coming to any conclusions which could not be fitted into the monogenetic view of humanity as the descendants of Adam and Eve. This conception was threatened by the new ideas arising from discoveries overseas. Contemplating reports about the life of peoples in the newly discovered regions of America, Europeans were bound to ask, 'Why are they not like us?' Trying to identify what was distinctive about these other peoples, Europeans were forced into a new self-consciousness. They had to ask what was distinctive about themselves, and why their own way of life was to be preferred. Thus the French essayist Montaigne (1533–92) described what he had learned about the customs of the peoples near the bay of Rio de Janeiro and suggested that there was no more barbarism in their eating men alive than in some of the things he and his readers had lately seen in France. Three men of this foreign nation, he wrote, visited Rouen in the times of Charles IX, who talked with them a great while. Montaigne also did his best to question them on many points and reported: 'I find that there is nothing in that nation that is either barbarous or savage, unless men call that barbarism which is not common to them.' In 1721 Montesquieu's *Persian Letters* started a new fashion when it held up to a European nation a picture of itself as it might appear in the eyes of people from another culture.

The early explorers in the Pacific had only fleeting contacts with the islanders, who often received them in friendship. Their accounts were favourable, but the European writing inspired by them went further and built the myth of the Noble Savage. This was of importance politically, for to believe that the savage is noble is to believe than man is naturally good. If evil does not have its origin in human nature, it must spring from the faulty organisation of society. As Rousseau urged: 'God makes all things good; man meddles with them and makes them evil.' To believe that man is naturally good is to believe that under another regime he could lead a better life, and such an outlook must therefore be a powerful spur to the radical reorganisation of society. This kind of romanticism was an important influence in the changes of opinion leading up to the French Revolution in 1789. After the Revolution the myth disappeared and, as missionary activity in the Pacific increased, it was replaced, first by 'the evangelistic picture of an ignoble and degraded brute' and then by a conception of the savage as 'representative of the childhood of man, interesting because he possessed the unrealised accomplishments of the child' (Smith, 1960: 22–2, 108, 251).

Montesquieu's great work *The Spirit of Laws* (1748) was important for its elaboration of environmental explanations of cultural and physical variation. 'Cold air constringes the extremities of the external fibres of the body', he wrote; 'this increases their elasticity, and favours the return of the blood from the extreme parts to the heart.' He himself had frozen half of a sheep's tongue and examined it under a microscope to study these changes. Such processes meant that people were more vigorous in cold climates; national character was shaped by environmental influences, while forms of government had to suit the character of the country's inhabitants. 'The people of India', he wrote, 'are mild, tender and compassionate. Hence their legislators repose great confidence in them.' Montesquieu also referred to 'countries where excess of heat enervates the body, and renders men so slothful and dispirited that nothing but the fear of chastisement can oblige them to perform any laborious duty; slavery is there more reconcilable to reason'. While acknowledging that in such environments slavery could be founded on natural reason, he still insisted that it had to be rejected since 'all men are born equal' and he deployed his heaviest sarcasm against those who thought they were justified in going off and enslaving Negroes (though Cedric Dover, 1952: 125–6, took another view of this passage). Montesquieu's message was that each people was adapted to its own environment and therefore everyone should stay where they were. The same lesson was taught by Voltaire's story of Candide whose misadventures while travelling abroad led him to decide that he should stay at home and cultivate his own garden. It was widely believed that Europeans who migrated to North America were liable to degenerate because they were not suited to that climate (Echevaria, 1957). Indeed, the mortality from new diseases that travellers encountered was often frightening.

In the eighteenth century Europeans wondered why their nations had recently made such great technological progress and were able to spread their influence. Why could not other peoples do likewise? What were the causes of progress? The environmentalist view stressed what were called the moral causes of progress, as in the work of Adam Ferguson, a sociological forerunner who maintained that progress depended upon having a social organisation suited to the people's environment (cf. the contrast between physical cause and moral cause explanations in Curtin, 1964: 227–58).

Though there was a substantial literature in the seventeenth and eighteenth centuries about Africans and other non-Europeans, the word 'race' was rarely used either to describe peoples or in accounts of differences between them. Anthony J. Barker has combed through this literature. In 1748 David Hume, in a footnote to his essay *Of National Characters*, stated that since, among the races of the world, only the Negro race has never developed any major civilisation, he suspected that Negroes might be 'naturally inferior to the Whites'. Noting that this remark had attracted attention because of Hume's eminence as a philosopher, Barker (1978: 77) replied that the very rarity of such comments was symptomatic of a pervasive apathy about problems of racial and cultural difference among the more innovative thinkers of the period. He overlooked the discussion of cultural variation in connection with the moral causes of progress, but this is not the main issue. Barker contended that there was a contemporary theory of African inferiority even if it was not to be found in the works of the intellectuals. It could be reconstructed piecemeal from the writings of more obscure authors. This reconstruction revealed a theory of the cultural inferiority of West Africa; of the African as shaped by a culture that was to be condemned, but with a human potential to be salvaged. They were black because the African environment had made them so; they were neither natural slaves nor were they especially well equipped to work in the tropics (Barker, 1978: 100, 62). Little use was made of the image of the black man in the romantic writing about the noble savage because people knew so much more about Africans than about Pacific Islanders and had formed an unfavourable estimate of African society as incapable of developing the region's potential wealth (cf. Curtin, 1964: 95). Therefore, when the agitation against the slave trade began (this can be dated from the formation in 1787 of the Committee for the Abolition of the Slave Trade) it started a debate that was conducted within a framework of existing knowledge. For the abolitionists, the central issues were the morality and necessity of the trade. Only a handful of pro-slavery writers asserted that blacks were inferior; most of them pointedly rejected such views except in so far as they contended that only Negroes could work in extreme heat. The traders themselves formed a third party. They rationalised the problems they had experienced in their dealings with West Africans in mutually contradictory charges of native incompetence and sharp practice. The detailed information which many of them provided came from a context of mistrust and ethnocentric contempt and not from assumptions about racial inferiority.

Those who disputed about the slave trade agreed on some fundamental

points, foremost among them being that the Negro was no more amen-
able to the regimentation of slavery than any other man. In 1730 Ralph
Sandiford had complained that one of the great injustices of the slave
trade lay in taking Africans to 'unnatural climates which is hard for them
to bear whose Constitutions are tendered by the Heat of their Native
County; for God that made the World, and all Man of one Blood, that
dwelt upon the Face of the Earth, has appointed them Bound of their
Habitations'. In so saying he was repeating the text of the Acts of the
Apostles 17: 26. Some had argued that whites could work in the West
Indies as well as anyone else, but the British Government refused to
transport white convicts to the islands and the belief that only blacks were
suited to tropical drudgery gained ground. The idea of divinely ordained
racial zones could be interpreted either way. The contending parties were
united in the belief that because of their bad environment and their
cultural backwardness, it could be to the Africans' advantage to be
removed from their existing society provided that it could not be reor-
ganised along European lines (and the vicissitudes of the attempted
resettlement of blacks in Sierra Leone from 1787 onwards did not encourage any optimism on that score). What they disputed was whether
the slave trade was a proper means for enabling Africans in some other
setting to realise their full human potential.

The contrary view has often been sustained by a superficial reading of a
passage in Eric E. Williams' *Capitalism and Slavery* in which he wrote:

Slavery in the Caribbean has been too narrowly identified with the Negro. A racial
twist has thereby been given to what is basically an economic phenomenon.
Slavery was not born of racism: rather, racism was the consequence of slavery.
Unfree labor in the New World was brown, white, black and yellow; Catholic,
Protestant and Pagan. (1944: 7)

The thrust of this argument was in the first sentence. There was no reason
for Williams to deny that there were white prejudices against blacks
before New World slavery. (On Williams' thesis about abolition, see
Temperley, 1987). There is now no reason for anyone else to deny that
such prejudices were increased by slavery. The argument is about the
interaction between racial attitudes and structures of exploitation. It is
important because twentieth-century writers recognise in their own societies doctrines or practices they call racism and they ask when these
originated. The first difficulty is that of defining sufficiently clearly just
what it is whose origin is to be discovered; the second that of separating it
from the various other beliefs and forms of behaviour with which it is
associated. It has also to be remembered that an ideology is likely to be a
synthesis of ideas, some of which will have been familiar for a long period.

It may be a long time in the making before it is formulated in a way that commands widespread assent. One view sees racism as an ideology generated to defend the interests of whites who made great profits from sugar production in the West Indies; this ideology was then developed to serve the interests of the capitalist classes. The main alternative view relates the prejudices of whites towards blacks to status distinctions drawn within white society and sees it as starting to increase greatly after the middle of the nineteenth century.

A straightforward statement of the first position is to be found in a history of black people in Britain entitled *Staying Power* (Fryer, 1984), which dates English racism as originating among Barbados planters in the eighteenth century. They told one another that Negroes were beasts without souls who should not be baptised lest this encourage rebellion. Their attitudes were then brought home and adopted by whites in England who deplored marriages between black men and white women as polluting English blood. Since only a few people (perhaps four or five) wrote to this effect it is necessary to assess their representativeness and influence. The author most frequently quoted is Edward Long, son of a Jamaican planter who served there as a judge and who in 1774 published a *History of Jamaica* which shows that he hated colonial governors almost as much as he hated blacks. Long's views are said to demonstrate the existence and appeal of racism in England in the 1770s, but Barker (1978: 162) reports that other pro-slavery writers repudiated Long's views about race and that Long 'produced criticisms of the slave system so fundamental that his work, for all its racialism, came to be used far more by abolitionists than by pro-slavery writers'. William Wilberforce, the leader of the abolitionists, when speaking in Parliament, frequently quoted Long. It was his criticisms of slavery that were influential and not his views about race. So if Long's arguments are to be interpreted as an ideology advancing material interests these could not have been the interests of the slave-owners.

In the section of his *History* dealing with Negroes, Long begins with an unacknowledged extract from the most unfavourable contemporary description of Africa and then goes on to organise observations about the various kinds of apes and men in accordance with the postulate of a Great Chain of Being. Those who believed in such a chain regarded it as a static hierarchy, the links of which were the various species whose distinctiveness was proven by their inability to produce fertile offspring. Long knew well that in the West Indies blacks and whites did produce fertile offspring, and so did interested members of the British public who could observe the results of inter-racial mating in their own country, who heard reports of black–white liaisons in West Africa and the West Indies, and who could occasionally observe blacks and whites. So Long maintained that while blacks and whites could inter-breed the results of such unions were of diminishing fertility: if two mulattoes had children they would not survive to maturity. This was scarcely a contribution to the development of a theory of racial inequality. There were such contributions but they came not from writers identified as spokesmen for economic interests, but from within the internal history of racial thought as represented by serious scholars like Charles White and Georges Cuvier whose works are discussed later. The view that the main increase in racial consciousness occurred in the latter part of the nineteenth century will be outlined on p. 78.

One of the major eighteenth-century changes in the external conditions likely to influence racial thought was the declaration of the independence of the United States in 1776. A majority of the whites chose to break away from the country with which they had previously identified themselves. To create a new state was difficult. To create a new nation to support that state, more so. For what was to bind together the members of the new nation and distinguish them from the British with whom they shared language, religion, culture and physical appearance? They decided, in effect, that it should be their political institutions. They would form a more perfect union to establish a higher standard of justice and insure domestic tranquility, as their constitution was to declare. There are here some connections which may surprise those who expect doctrines of racial inferiority to have arisen from black–white encounters, for the circumstances in which both the French and English first came to use the word race in a political context were remarkably similar and they had their echo in late eighteenth-century North America.

From the sixteenth to the eighteenth centuries there were historians of France who maintained that their country's history was that of the interaction of two races. At the end of the fifth century, they said, a small Frankish Kingdom had conquered Gaul, but the Franks and the Gauls had remained distinct. The nobility were the descendants of the Franks whose name was supposed to mean 'free' and who derived their claim to privilege from the right of conquest. These claims were contested by other historians who asserted that the Gauls had invited the assistance of the Franks to help expel the Romans. Historians searched the writings of Caesar and Tacitus to see what they had to say about the earliest Frenchmen, as if that would decide the entitlements of their successors. In England, Richard Verstegan opened his book *Restitution of Decayed Intelligence*, first published in 1605, with the proclamation that 'Englishmen are descended of German race and were heretofore generally called Saxons'; he went on to explain why 'the Germans are a most noble nation' and to stress that according to Tacitus the authority of their kings was limited.

This Germanic race had settled in England from AD 449. Such a history was advanced to challenge the ambitions of the Stuart monarchs who wanted to weaken the power of Parliament and to rule by divine right. It asserted that the royal claims had not been acknowledged in the past and that they ran contrary to the nature of the people. It was suggested that the Anglo-Saxon centuries, before the arrival of Norman rulers in 1066, had been a golden age. An ancestral myth was created which derived the chief English virtues from their Anglo-Saxon forebears. Sir Walter Scott got this idea from a play about Runnymede and used it in one of the best-selling novels of the century, *Ivanhoe*, published in 1820. Scott presents it as a struggle between two races. It is probable that no single book or event did more to introduce the word race into popular use than Scott's historical romance (Banton, 1977: 15–26).

By 1776 many whites in the United States aligned themselves with the English radicals who had been demanding constitutional change in order to cleanse their country of religious and political abuses stemming from the Norman Conquest and to restore Anglo-Saxon institutions. This trans-atlantic affinity is seen most vividly in the writings of Thomas Jefferson, the principal author of the Declaration of Independence and the third president of the United States. He thought the study of the Anglo-Saxon language so important for his fellow countrymen that he wrote a simplified grammar to make it more accessible, and included the subject in the curriculum of the University of Virginia. Like de Tocqueville, later, Jefferson stressed the fundamental importance of a country's institutions; since in his view Anglo-Saxon freedom had been based on the holding of land in fee simple, nothing gave him greater pleasure than his work for the abolition of primogeniture and entail in the law of Virginia (Horsman, 1981: 21). Jefferson is noted for advocating the abolition of slavery but his *Notes on the State of Virginia* (written in 1781–2 though not generally available before 1787) show that he found environmentalist explanations of black–white differences unpersuasive. He noted that slavery among the Greeks and Romans had produced slaves of talent and achievement – but they had been whites. As for Negroes, he concluded, 'It is not their condition then, but nature, which has produced the distinction.' Though uncertain whether blacks were 'originally a distinct race, or made distinct by time and circumstance' the difference between them and the whites was equated with the difference between species (see Jordan, 1968: 429–90).

Such theories evoked the disapproval of the president of what is now Princeton University. Samuel Stanhope Smith published in 1787 *An Essay on the Causes of the Variety of Complexion and Figure in the Human Species, to Which Are Added Strictures on Lord Kaims's Discourse, on the*

Original Diversity of Mankind. Though it is the Scots jurist whose doctrines are singled out, Smith had his targets nearer home as well. His starting point was the belief that Christians were not at liberty to question the Biblical account. His principal argument then, as in the second edition of 1810, was that all conceptions of morality would be confused if it were thought that the different kinds of men were different species:

> The rules which would result from the study of our own nature, would not apply to the natives of other countries who would be of different species; perhaps, not to two families in our own country, who might be sprung from a dissimilar composition of species. Such principles tend to confound all science, as well as piety; and leave us in the world uncertain whom to trust; or what opinions to frame of others . . . The doctrine of one race, removes this uncertainty, renders human nature susceptible of system, illustrates the power of physical causes, and opens a rich and extensive field for moral science.

Smith would not accept any division between the reasoning of religion and that of science. As Jordan writes, he marshalled Linnaean classification and the power of environmental influence to support the book of Genesis. Stanhope Smith and Jefferson both started from assumptions of human equality. Smith's assumption came from a religious belief that constrained the significance attributable to physical differences. Jefferson's assumption came from a scientific belief that acknowledged fundamental similarities, allowed for the possibility that Negroes might be unable ever to equal whites, but added 'whatever be their degree of talent, it is no measure of their rights'. Stanhope Smith was

> inclined to ascribe the apparent dullness of the negro principally to the wretched state of his existence first in his original country . . . and afterwards in those regions to which he is transported to finish his days in slavery, and toil . . . The abject servitude of the negro in America . . . must condemn him, while these circumstances remain, to perpetual sterility of genius.

In the twenty-three years that passed before publication of the second edition of Smith's book, the objections to the monogenetic explanation of diversity increased. In particular, evidence had accumulated which pointed to inherited differences in the capacities of individuals of different race. Arguments had to address themselves to the nature and significance of those inequalities. One author whose work, though not widely read in the United States, had impressed some influential people, was the Manchester surgeon Charles White. So Stanhope Smith had to study White's slender volume *An Account of the Regular Gradation in Man, and in different Animals and Vegetables; and from the former to the latter* (1799). White had measured the anatomical features of over fifty Negroes, compared them with figures for whites, and concluded that in respect of 'bodily structure and economy' the Negro was closer to the ape than was the European. In seeing, hearing, smelling, memory, and the powers of mastication the European was 'least perfect, the African more so, and the brutes most perfect of all'. As the title indicated, White's thought was dominated by the idea of the Great Chain of Being. He wanted to see 'the pernicious practice of enslaving mankind . . . abolished throughout the world' and held that 'the negroes are, at least, equal to thousands of Europeans, in capacity and responsibility; and ought, therefore, to be equally entitled to freedom and protection'. By the same measure they were not equal to even more thousands of Europeans. Where the line might be drawn between men and apes needed further investigation and infertility could not be accepted as a sufficient criterion of species. Stanhope Smith believed that he must combat this unbiblical notion of a chain of being and to do so he changed his ground; abandoning his presumption of the unity of religion and science, he contested arguments from science with counter arguments from science alone. He made his own measurements of Negro anatomy and skin temperature, arguing that the American environment was producing changes, especially among domestic slaves (as opposed to field hands) and among free Negroes. Among other things, their complexions were becoming whiter. The effect of heat was to thicken the skin and to free the bile which had deposited a dark residue such 'that colour may be justly considered as a universal freckle'. If the temperature was reduced, then complexions lightened; just as the complexions of Europeans varied from the Mediterranean up towards the Arctic, so could physical differences between Negroes and Caucasians be explained by reference to universal causes. Stanhope Smith could deny neither the facts of physical difference nor those of present racial inferiority. His answer to the measurements of facial angle, for example, was not to declare them irrelevant but to assert that the Negro form was changing so as to resemble the higher form of the Whites. As Jordan has observed, 'his whole book shouted that the Negro was going to be the equal of the white man only when he came to look like one' (Jordan, 1968: 486–8, 507–17).

Chronology

If all men and women were descended from Adam and Eve, as the Bible seemed to say, then it was possible to calculate how many generations had passed from Adam through the line of David down to the period of recorded history, and discover for how many years humans had lived on the earth's surface. One who attempted this was a vice-chancellor of Cambridge University, John Lightfoot, who in 1644 came to the conclusion that 'Man was created by the Trinity about the third hour of the day, or nine of the clock in the morning' in the year now identified as 3928 BC. Six years later Archbishop James Ussher decided that 'the beginning of time fell upon the night before the twenty-third day of October in the year of the Julian calendar 710' which was 4004 BC. Ussher's date was widely accepted and printed in some English translations of the Bible, though there were many other studies that came to somewhat different conclusions. One of the obstacles to any formulation of a theory of evolution was the resulting belief that the earth was only about 6,000 years old and that therefore any explanation of change would have to show how the contemporary diversity could have been produced in such a period of time. As late as 1886 Sir Samuel Baker, the African explorer, concluded that there could be no doubt as to the rapidity with which races became differentiated, for the differences between Englishmen and the Africans of the White Nile must have been the work of only 5,870 years.

The debates about the age of the earth which started within geology, especially with a paper by James Hutton delivered before the Royal Society of Edinburgh in 1785, were therefore of very wide importance. On the one hand were ranged the Neptunists who held that all rocks were formed as precipitation from the water of a primitive universal ocean which had held in solution great quantities of mineral matter. Granite was one of the oldest of rocks; softer rocks, like sandstone, had been created more recently, but in any event the earth must be of great antiquity. The Neptunists were opposed by the Plutonists (or Vulcanists) who held that many rocks were of igneous or volcanic origin. Hutton's theory was important to the latter school. He maintained that natural agents now at work and within the earth had operated with general uniformity throughout long periods of time. There was also a third position, called catastrophism, which contended that God for his own purposes (such as to punish a sinful humanity) had from time to time caused dramatic changes by ordaining great floods and volcanic eruptions; this was the only doctrine that could easily be harmonised with a Biblical chronology.

If the claim that the earth was of great antiquity was accepted, it became possible to contemplate an evolutionary explanation of natural diversity. The great chain of being could represent a process whereby higher forms had developed from lower. The centre of intellectual advance in this respect was Paris, and the three most important names were those of the botanist Lamarck (1744–1829), the comparative anatomist Cuvier (1769–1832), and the morphologist Geoffroy (1772–1844), whose full name was Etienne Geoffroy Saint-Hilaire. According to Lamarck, all animals could be ordered so as to show a graded series of 'perfection'. There was such an amazing diversity of organisms that 'anything which it is possible to imagine has effectively taken place'. Transformations could occur within lines of descent but change was so slow as to be imperceptible, the evidence for this being available in the fossil record. Evolutionary change explained why some forms had died out, and by studying it scholars could learn more about the harmony of nature and the wisdom of the creator. Since environments change, there must be some process enabling a species to remain in balance with its environment. By introducing a time factor, says Mayr (1982: 349), Lamarck had discovered the Achilles' heel of the old theology. Change occurred because God had given all species the power to develop towards greater complexity and a capacity to react to special conditions in the environment. There was a sequence whereby a changing environment created new needs, which altered the animals' habits and these changed its use of its various parts or organs so that over time, they changed too. Cuvier (whose influence is discussed in chapter 3) opposed such theories of organic development. He interpreted the geological record as showing the stability of the major animals over long periods of time, while the drastic breaks in geological strata seemed to support the possibility of rapid change in connection with natural catastrophes. Geoffroy's views were in some ways less sophisticated than Lamarck's, for he thought that the environment might influence the animal embryo directly. Where Cuvier believed that function determined structure, Geoffroy maintained the reverse: 'animals have no habits but those that result from the structure of their origins'. Cuvier stressed correlation, asserting that all herbivores have hoofs and no carnivores have horns. Geoffroy stressed connection and composition, maintaining that all animals were built according to a single plan which could be seen in the relative position of organs: the hoof of the ruminant became the claw of the lion, the paw of the monkey, the wing of the bat, the fin of the sea mammal, and so on. He challenged the conventional distinction between vertebrates and non-vertebrates but could make little impression against Cuvier's more cautious, well-grounded arguments. It was thought unsatisfactory to argue for the unity of composition, as Geoffroy did, by pointing to correlations between the parts of animals; if one form was to develop from another, the intermediate forms had also to be viable creatures who could feed and survive; otherwise they would not be able to pass on their characters. It is doubtful whether Geoffroy is properly regarded as an evolutionist (Mayr, 1982: 362–3, 462–3) but his work added substantially to interest in the ways in which environmental influences might explain variation. Any explanation of racial differences among humans had to be part of a more complex explanation of the origin and nature of species of all kinds. Those who favoured an evolutionary explanation were inclined to see races as intergrading rather than as distinct, but this still left room for the possibility that some were naturally superior.

There was a striking parallel between an ordering of species from simple to complex and the development of the embryo from its initial simplicity in the egg to its complexity in the adult form. If there was an evolution of species it had to be transmitted through the embryo. This might be the place to look for the 'hidden agency' whereby environment altered species. From the early 1820s it was argued that 'ontogeny recapitulates phylogeny'. According to this view the higher forms had to pass through the earlier phases of evolution before reaching their own stage. None of the earlier stages could be left out. Ontogeny, by which is meant the life history of an individual, had to repeat phylogeny, that is, the evolutionary history which had produced the species to which the individual belonged. It was thought that while in the embryo each individual went through the earlier phases including the adult stages. Every human while in the womb recapitulated the development of a fish, a reptile, a bird, and a mammal, before it emerged as a human. In this form the theory was demolished in 1828 by von Baer, who showed that the embryo of a higher animal is never like the adult form of a lower animal but only like its embryo (Gould, 1966: 52–7). Nevertheless, modified in certain particulars, the theory of recapitulation remained influential throughout the nineteenth century, being revived by Ernst Haeckel in 1866 so that it stimulated discoveries which remain important today (Mayr, 1982: 474–5).

Naturphilosophie

While the laboratory work flourished in Paris, German biology succumbed to a romantic movement called *Naturphilosophie* which sought a unification of all knowledge about nature through such transcendental beliefs as that which saw the history of the universe as the history of spirit, beginning in primal chaos and striving upward to reach its highest expression in man. Thus L. Oken in 1847 divided natural phenomena into four categories based on earth processes (nutrition), water processes (digestion), air processes (respiration), fire processes (motion). He classified mammals in varying ways including their sensory systems: so the sense of feeling was represented by carnivores; taste by seals; smell by bears; hearing by apes; and sight by men. Humans could be distinguished as black, yellow and white, but why where there no blue or green races? Their absence suggested to Oken that colour was an unsatisfactory basis for classifying humans and he advanced a five-fold classification based on the organs of sense, so that there were eye men, nose men, ear men, and so on. This kind of approach reached its highest point in the work of Carl Gustav Carus. To the modern reader his arguments often sound absurd but *Naturphilosophie* was an important influence upon nineteenth-century racial thought.

Carl Gustav Carus (1789–1869) was a man of talents almost as varied as Goethe's. A physician to the royal family, privy counsellor, professor at Dresden, friend of Goethe, art critic and landscape painter, he also published important works on medical topics, on psychology, on the symbolism of the human form and an account of his travels in England and Scotland. In nine of the books he published between 1835 and 1861 Carus had something to say about race but it occupied a relatively small place in the mass of his writing and he is rarely remembered for his racial theory. Carus was impressed by the influence of great men on the course of history and wondered whether their prominence revealed anything about more general differences in human capacity. This explains why his 100-page essay *On the Unequal Capacity of the Different Divisions of Mankind for Higher Spiritual Development* (his chief statement about race) was published as a memorial to Goethe on the centenary of his birth. Carus was acquainted with earlier racial classifications and the work of Klemm and J.C. Prichard, but he was dissatisfied with classifications based solely on external physical form. He thought he had found a better basis in the relation of the divisions of mankind to the earth as a planet, and in particular to the sun. This separated the earth's peoples into those of the day, of the eastern twilight, of the western twilight, and of the night. He referred to a recognised but not yet explained law that progress follows a path from east to west; the great human migrations had gone in this direction and so had epidemic diseases. But no argument was advanced as to how the sun could have had a differential effect upon humans: the terminology was metaphorical. Carus himself represented it on occasion as dealing with symbolic relationships and made no attempt to deal with the obvious difficulties inherent in such a theory. He drew on Morton's measurements of cranial capacity but instead of maintaining that physique determined culture, he regarded them both, physique and culture, as manifestations of the whole entity.

Carus wrote, 'The day peoples, who achieve a specially pure form in the region of the Caucasus, have spread out their type, sometimes in greater, sometimes in lesser perfection, over all Europe . . .' but this is the only time he used the word 'type'. The eastern twilight peoples were the Mongolians, Malayans, Hindus, Turks, and Slavs; the western twilight peoples were the American Indians; the night peoples were the Africans and Australians. Carus opened his discussion of the day people with a statement of the recapitulation theory, listing the most notable twelve: Caucasians, Persians, Armenians, Semites, Pelasgians, Etruscans,

Thracians, Illyrians, Iberians, Romans, Celts and Germans. Apparently the last named recapitulated in their embryonic development not only their eleven forebears but also certain peoples from the other three-quarters of humanity. From this, Carus said, emerged an important phenomenon 'that the big movements in the history of peoples, if they stem from a special stock, always demonstrate the special energy of this stock . . . in the childhood of peoples the material force is dominant but in more developed circumstances the spiritual principle comes to the fore' (1849: 81–2; see also Poliakov, 1974: 250). It was the duty of the day peoples to guide and help the less favoured ones. Though he was not explicit on this point, Carus implied that in the right circumstances a people could civilise itself and in this he provoked Gobineau's dissent.

The other great German racial theorist of this period also lived in Dresden. This was Gustav Klemm (1802–67) who spent most of his life in charge of the royal library in that town. In the years 1843–52 he produced a ten-volume study, *Allgemeine Cultur-Geschichte der Menschheit*, synthesising ethnographic accounts of the peoples of the world; in it he distinguished three stages of cultural evolution: savagery, domestication and freedom. He divided mankind into active and passive races, stating that peoples differed in mentality and temperament. Much of the argument was summarised in an address of his on the fundamental ideas of a general science of culture (Klemm, 1851). Klemm's conception of culture history was of a philosophy of history of the kind envisaged by Herder and Kant; it emphasised environmental and cultural influences upon human development and was opposed to the more idealistic orientation deriving from Fichte in which different aspects of culture were subordinated to political evolution (Voegelin, 1993b: 159). In politics Klemm was a liberal democrat who found the decline of the ancient regime congenial, while the rise of egalitarian democracy appeared to him as the crowning peak of history.

One problem is to decide whether Carus and Klemm were advancing a conception of races as permanent human types or were using the terminology of race in a metaphorical fashion. There are many passages in the original sources that favour the second interpretation but their intention is often obscure to the modern reader. Moreover, the two leading authorities, Erich Voegelin (the refugee from Nazi Germany) and Hermann Blome (who wrote in an intellectual milieu sympathetic to the typological conception of race) are not in complete agreement. Blome is adamant that Carus' conception of race had nothing whatsoever in common with those definitions that were rooted in biological categories; his four races were appearances of similarity which existed only as symbolical manifestations of planetary relations. Whereas Klemm's conception of race was free from romantic influences in its ethnological and culture–historical foundation, his theory of race bespoke the romantic spirit and philosophy (1943: 221, 253). Blome wrote:

Just as Klemm thought it was from the 'marriage of peoples' and from the penetration of the passive by the active peoples that humanity starts upon a general cultural development, so Carus saw the inequality of human races as Nature's summons to interaction, to give-and-take, whereby humanity as a total organism might be served. The tribe of day peoples was 'entitled to regard itself as the true flowers of humanity', but for Carus that signified not only that this tribe was the bearer of civilization but also that, because of its superiority, power, resoluteness and perseverance, it had the duty to lead the weak and less favoured tribes by lighting their path and assisting them along it; in so doing it would prove true to itself [quoting Carus, 1849: 85]. To the question exactly how this task was given to the day peoples or active tribes, both Carus and Klemm give extensive answers. They see the whole of humanity as one great organism; its unequal parts, the races, have to stand in an inter-acting relationship of exchange and progress, so that under the leadership of the white race the 'idea' of humanity can be realized. (Blome, 1943: 254–5)

The pictures of Caucasian and Ethiopian skulls in Blumenbach's volumes were unsatisfying because the author could not say what their peculiarities meant. In the new romantic visions these pictures became alive. Men belonged no longer to abstract categories, but to races whose distinctive physical and cultural characters were related to the basic principles of Creation.

Voegelin also emphasised the way in which Carus' theory brought body and mind together. He believed that in Christian theology there must be a sharp distinction between these two realms and deplored the way in which biological differences could be used to divide the human community. Consequently he looked more anxiously at Carus' basic philosophy and pictured his synthesis as important to the later development of more ominous racial theories. Voegelin was unimpressed by Klemm's interpretations, describing his racial theory as a rather banal conglomeration of all the suggestions which an industrious research worker could receive from his generation, but he went on to conclude that Klemm and Gobineau were at one in their major theses, namely: (1) all important cultures in history have as their basis a symbiosis of races; (2) there are distinct human types called by Gobineau the strong and the weak, by Klemm the active and passive; (3) the races migrate, or at least the active do; (4) migration leads to the conquest of the weak by the strong; (5) as a result of conquest the races enter into a symboisis which, by mixture or extermination, ends with the dissolution of the active conquering race as a distinct unit; (6) when the active race dissolves, political tension disappears and an egalitarian society is established (an occasion for Klemm's satisfaction and Gobineau's despair).

This does not do full justice to the differences between the two writers. Klemm did not employ the concept of type; nor is it evident that he did regard racial characteristics as innate and permanent. He wrote of humanity as divided into two kinds of races analogous to the division into two sexes and to the division of the atmosphere into oxygen and nitrogen, so the argument seemed to lie on a metaphorical plane. Though he selected Caucasians as exemplifying the active races, and coloured peoples the passive races, and though he paid considerable attention to the expansion of the former, any conception of them as superior was left implicit. Explicitly he emphasised the complementary nature of the two halves. Active races isolated from their passive partners (like the nomadic Mongols) were incomplete and could not achieve true culture. On occasion he referred to the active and passive castes. 'First through the mixture of the two races, the active and the passive, I would like to say through the marriage of peoples, does humanity become complete; in this way it first springs to life and nourishes the blossoms of culture' (1843 i: 192–204; 1851: 169, 179).

The romantic world-view of a writer like Carus needs to be explored with the care of a social anthropologist trying to discover the conceptual structure of a strange culture. Its representation of race has more in common with the biblical story of the creation than with the approach of the modern scientist. Though Carus clearly formulated a theory of European superiority, it was within a conception of races as forming a symmetrical whole, and led to conclusions about how people ought to behave rather than to interpretations of their actions as pre-determined.

Nature and culture

The most respected writer on questions of race after Blumenbach was an Englishman, James Cowles Prichard (1786–1848). As a boy in Bristol he liked to visit the docks and speak with foreign sailors; indeed he chose medicine for his profession primarily because it afforded him opportunities to pursue his anthropological inclinations. For his MD in Edinburgh in 1808 he wrote a dissertation entitled *De Generis Humani Varietate* and he went on to expand this into a book written in English entitled *Researches into the Physical History of Mankind* which in successive editions 1813, 1826, 1838, 1851, expanded from one volume into five. It was complemented by another, *The Natural History of Man: comprising inquiries into the modifying influence of physical and moral agencies on the different tribes of the human family* which, published in 1843, 1845, 1848 and 1855, expanded into two volumes. The former dealt with man's physical nature, the latter with his culture, but Prichard saw no opposition between the two any more than he could contemplate a conflict between his science and his religious belief. In his first work Prichard was concerned both to defend the Mosaic account by criticising suggestions that human diversities have been constant from the very beginning, and to argue that there was no good evidence to indicate that acquired characters could be transmitted by heredity to the next generation. Both these arguments returned again and again in his later books. First came the question whether the races of mankind 'constitute separate species or are merely varieties of one species'. Species were to be identified by 'peculiarities of structure which have always been constant and undeviating'. Prichard used race to refer to physically distinctive nations but was equally content to write of 'the tribes of men' (cf. 1826: 90). Faithful to the traditional interpretations of Genesis Prichard believed that the Creation occurred some 6,000 years earlier; his problem was to explain the appearance of racial differences within this period by some hypothesis other than that of the inheritance of acquired characteristics and, in the current state of knowledge he could not do this. Always he was led back to antecedents, as when he wrote, 'in some instances . . . the forms of several animals seem to be so modelled on a particular type, that they have all been imagined to have arisen from the same race' (1826: 91).

While rejecting the claim that acquired characters could be inherited, Prichard was conscious that children do not resemble their parents in any predictable manner; he contended that the more accurate our researches into the ethnography of the world became, the less ground could be found for the opinion that the characteristics of human races were permanent. So he enquired:

has man received from his Maker a principle of accommodation by which he becomes fitted to possess and occupy the whole earth? He modifies the agencies of the elements upon himself; but do not these agencies also modify him? Have they not rendered him in his very organization different in different regions? (1843: 3–4)

At one time Prichard came quite close to what we now know to be the answer. He remarked that whole colonies of individuals may perish when moved to climates for which they are not adapted. Horses and cattle when transported to Paraguay and allowed to run wild underwent an alteration, but domesticated breeds did not. Perhaps, he said, there was an analogy with the races of man, and that once varieties were newly established in a stock they might continue there long after the race had been removed from the climate in which they originated (1826: 581–3).

From his anatomical studies Prichard concluded, tentatively, that there were three types of skull: prognathous, pyramidal and oval. Every type showed deviations and shaded into the others by insensible gradations. All three types of cranium were found amongst Negroes and the types seemed to be associated with degrees of civilisation rather than geographical populations. Each species, said Prichard, had a psychological character, but the type was preserved in the individual varieties, so he studied the psychological make up of human races and concluded that this supported the evidence of external characters, and that mankind constituted a single species (cf. Stocking, 1973).

The industry with which Prichard assembled evidence from so many sources, and the sobriety of his judgements, gave his books a special authority, but much turned on the definition of species, which was problematic. Usage varied. In 1826 Desmoulins, a Paris anatomist, was putting forward a classification of man into sixteen species; certain of these were divided into races, which made race a subspecific category. More than two decades later a cautious English ethnologist was writing 'a race is a class of individuals concerning which there are doubts as to whether they constitute a separate species or a variety of a recognized one. Hence the term is subjective . . . the present writer . . . has either not used the word race at all, or used it inadvertently' (Latham, 1850: 564).

Implications of error for racial thought

The relevance of the argument which started in embryology is illustrated by some of the fall-out from a controversy generated by Robert Chambers (1802–71). His personal story bears upon his work, for both he and his brother were born hexadactyls, with six fingers on each hand and six toes on each foot. While adolescents, they were operated upon to have the extra fingers and toes removed. Afterwards Robert ailed and may have employed his time while convalescent to read and reflect upon the possible causes of his unusual inheritance. Later he wrote a book *Vestiges of the Natural History of Creation* (1844) in which he set forth the 'Principle of Progressive Development' as an explanation of evolution. Knowing that it would be regarded as a scandalous work, especially by the religious folk of Edinburgh, he had his wife copy out his manuscript in her handwriting and then sent it to a friend in Manchester to arrange for its publication. It appeared and attracted the very disapproval he had anticipated. The book was widely read and went through ten editions in ten years. His responsibility for the work was not acknowledged until thirteen years after his death but the suspicion that he might be the author was such that when, late in life, he was being considered as a candidate for the post of Lord

Provost of Edinburgh, he felt obliged to withdraw for fear of further controversy.

The most distinguished British scientists of the time, including T.H. Huxley, attacked *Vestiges* ferociously, but Ernst Mayr (1982: 383–5) considers that despite all the faults Chambers saw the forest where the others could see only the trees. Chambers marshalled the evidence for a slow and gradual process of evolution in no way correlated with environmental catastrophes, even though he could not explain quite how it came about. Among other things, he drew attention to the reasons for believing that embryos go through stages resembling their more primitive relations: 'in the reproduction of the higher animals, the new being passes through stages in which it is successively fish-like and reptile-like. But the resemblance is not to the adult fish or the adult reptile, but to the fish and reptile at a certain point in their foetal progress' (1844: 212). Later on he came back to the hypothesis of recapitulation in more striking terms:

Our brain . . . after completing the animal transformations, it passes through the characters in which it appears in the Negro, Malay, American, and Mongolian nations, and finally is Caucasian. The face partakes of these alterations . . . The leading characters, in short, of the various races of mankind, are simply representations of particular stages in the development of the highest or Caucasian type . . . The Mongolian is an arrested infant newly-born. (1844: 306–7)

The notion of recapitulation was widely accepted in the middle and latter part of the century. It appeared in one of Tennyson's poems. It was parodied by Benjamin Disraeli in his novel *Tancred* (1847) when he had Lady Constance say:

It is all explained . . . First there was nothing, then there was something; then, I forget the next, I think there were shells, then fishes. Then we came . . . Again the next stage will be something very superior to us, something with wings . . . this is development. We had fins: we may have wings.

It is not surprising then if it was in the mind of a superintendent of a London mental hospital when, in 1866, he tried to classify the various kinds of mental disorder among patients in his care. Did some disorders stem from environmental causes, he asked? Has the nurse dosed the child with opium? Has the little one met with any accidents? Did instruments cause injury in childbirth? Did the mental disorder stem from congenital or developmental causes? Those who suffered from the congenital disorders of idiocy and imbecility could be classified by reference:

to one of the great divisions of the human family other than the class from which they have sprung. Of course there are numerous representatives of the great Caucasian family. Several well marked examples of the Ethiopian variety have

come under my notice . . . some arrange themselves around the Malay variety . . .
The great Mongolian family has numerous representatives, and it is to this
division, I wish, in this paper, to call special attention. A very large number of
congenital idiots are typical Mongols. So marked is this, that when placed side by
side, it is difficult to believe that the specimens are not children of the same
parents . . . They are, for the most part, instances of degeneracy arising from
tuberculosis in the parents.

The superintendent was Dr John Langdon Down and the condition he
was describing (Down, 1866: 259–62) is now known to be caused by
triploidy of the twenty-first chromosome which prevents the normal
development of some organs of the body. For at least a century this
condition was called Mongolism, but it is now identified as Down's
syndrome. Down thought that his argument told against the contemporary supposition that human races represented distinct and permanent
types. If it was the case, as he maintained, that disease could destroy the
features which distinguished races, then such examples of degeneracy
'furnish some argument in favour of the unity of the human species'.
Down's underlying proposition is that disease causes retrogression to a
form occurring earlier in the developmental sequence. Proper development depended on the correct environmental conditions. Thus Down,
who favoured the admission of women to higher education, later supported this policy by asserting 'if there is one thing more certain than
another about the production of idiocy it is the danger which arises from
the culture of only one side of a woman's nature' (1887: 89).
   Another example of the implications of error is provided by the history
of telegony, the hypothesis that offspring sometimes inherit characters
from a previous mate of their dam. It began with a letter written by Lord
Morton to the Royal Society in 1820, and published by them. Morton
reported that he had mated an Arab mare with a quagga (a now extinct
zebra-like creature) and obtained a foal with faint stripes. Later he mated
the mare with an Arab stallion, producing three foals, all with rather more
marked stripes, presumably as a result of the prior mating. This phenomenon was given the name telegony to denote inheritance from a step-
father. Darwin in 1868 was prepared to accept that such things could
happen and telegony was later debated by such eminent authorities as
Spencer, Romanes and Weismann. It was falsified by experiments conducted outside Edinburgh in the 1890s by J. Cossar Ewart, who wrote the
article on telegony in the eleventh edition of the *Encyclopaedia Britannica*.
The belief in telegony nevertheless lingered. For another fifty years some
English sheep-breeders would not allow a pure-bred ewe that had once
been mated with a ram of another breed to remain in the Flock Book.
Among humans it has given rise to what in the United States used to be

called the 'black baby myth': the belief that if a white woman has sexual intercourse with a black man there is always the possibility that any baby she may subsequently bear, perhaps years after the incident in question, will have black physical characteristics. The persistence in this belief in England was investigated by Veronica Pearson (1973). She interviewed two samples of elderly women. Sample A was of twenty-five women, average age 77.4 years, many living in a poor innter city neighbourhood of Bristol with a significant proportion of black residents; Sample B was of twenty-five women, average age 68.8 years, all of whom had previously been school teachers. In Sample A, ten women said they believed that if a white woman has sexual relations with a black man any child she subsequently bore might be black; another woman had heard of this belief but thought it unlikely to be true. In Sample B, four accepted the belief, four though it unlikely and two had heard of it in connection with animal breeding.

Explanations of physical variation among humans cannot be separated from explanations of similar features among animals. Only in the 1760s did Europeans begin to breed farm animals systematically to produce the characteristics they valued. It was from the study of controlled breeding, or domestication as it was called, that Prichard and Darwin got their ideas about natural selection. (Whereas in China the idea of race was associated more with that of seed, Dikötter, 1992:165.) It is only to be expected that when Europeans in the twentieth century profess beliefs about inheritance and intelligence among humans, they will be influenced by their beliefs about inheritance among animals and *vice versa*. So the story of telegony teaches a lesson about the dangers of treating beliefs about race in isolation, as well as showing that it can take a long time to overcome the effects of past mistakes.

3   Race as type

A new phase in the history of racial thought was inaugurated in the chronologically convenient year of 1800 by Georges Cuvier when he submitted a memorandum for a French expedition to the Pacific, advising on 'the researches to be carried out relative to the anatomical differences between the diverse races of man' (Stocking, 1968: 13–41). Cuvier's career prospered and under Napoleon he became one of the dominant figures in French science.

Cuvier was a Protestant who accepted the Biblical story of man's common descent but did not believe that Genesis provided a complete chronology. He took up the questions of Creation and classification in a more open-minded manner than his predecessors, believing that a scientist should concentrate on problems where sufficient evidence was available or could be accumulated, and should not concern himself with those that were for the time being beyond reach. Within zoology Cuvier continued Linnaeus' work by compiling a magisterial study of the animal kingdom. He distinguished four principal branches within this kingdom, the vertebrates, molluscs, articulates and zoophytes, which were further divided into genera and subgenera. Cuvier put great reliance on the concept of biological type, believing that if that had been grasped the essentials of the category could be understood. He emphasised the importance of type in opposition to those who considered that the various forms shaded imperceptibly into one another. Genera and species were both discrete, morphologically stable units, and therefore examples of types. In his extensive study of fishes each volume deals with one genus and the first chapter is devoted to a description of the specimen chosen to represent the type. Cuvier is probably better known, however, for his geological theory that there had been a series of natural catastrophes (such as floods) which had killed off large numbers of species and divided natural history into some eight separate epochs. A biographer (Coleman, 1964) has concluded that Cuvier did not believe, as was often very understandably thought, that each epoch began with a new creation. He thought that some individuals survived the catastrophes; migration and the mutual exchange of species between territories could then account for subsequent diversity. In this way Cuvier could accept that all men were descended from Adam, suggesting at the same time that the three major races escaped in different directions after the last catastrophe, some 5,000 years before, and had developed in isolation. A variant of this theory, sometimes associated with Cuvier (e.g. Prichard, 1843: 133) regarded the three major races as stemming from particular mountain slopes: whites from the region of Mount Caucasus, yellows from the neighbourhood of Mount Altai, and blacks from the southern face of the chain of Mount Atlas.

Lineage and variety confused

For Cuvier *Homo sapiens* was a division of the vertebrates and was split into three subspecies: Caucasian, Mongolian and Ethiopian. Each of these three was further subdivided on geographical, linguistic and physical grounds. Malays, Eskimos and American Indians remained outside these subdivisions but, being inter-fertile, all mankind was one species. Near the beginning of Cuvier's *Le Règne animal* of 1817 is a section entitled 'Variétés de l'espèce humaine' which starts:

Quoique l'espèce humaine paraisse unique, puisque tous les individus peuvent se mêler indistinctement, et produire des individus féconds, on y remarque de certaines conformations héréditaires que constituent ce qu'on nomme des *races*.

The italics are in the original. Although Kant and Herder had warned about the dangers of confusing a name for a class and a reference to origin, Cuvier made race and variety synonymous. Cuvier's first English translator took it upon himself to reduce some of the confusion, for in the 1827 London translation the last sentence appears as 'which constitute what are called *varieties*'. In several of the passages where Cuvier put 'race' this translator put 'variety'. Yet in the next English translation (published in New York in 1831) the sentence runs 'which constitute what are termed *races*' and 'race' is used thereafter.

Prichard regretted any failure to distinguish race from variety, and he may have had Cuvier in mind when he wrote (1836: 109) that:

races are properly successions of individuals propagated from any given stock; and the term should be used without any involved meaning that such a progeny or stock has always possessed a particular character. The real import of the term has often been overlooked, and the word race has been used as if it implied a distinction in the physical character of a whole series of individuals. By writers on anthropology, who adopt this term, it is often tacitly assumed that such distinctions were primordial, and that their successive transmission has been unbroken.

If such were the fact, a race so characterised would be a species in the strict meaning of the word, and it ought to be so termed. (1836: 109)

This is such an important issue, and the ambiguity in the word race so easily taken for granted, that it seems desirable to pause and use a very simple example of the difference between race as lineage and as variety. Let the reader recall the first use in English of the word 'race' in the sense with which this book is concerned. Foxe referred to 'the race and stocke of Abraham'. A later member of that stock was Moses, who was classified as a Levite. Moses had a brother and sister, Aaron and Miriam. He first married a Midionite woman, Zipporah, who bore him two sons, Gershon and Eliezer. Later he married an Ethiopian woman (Aaron and Miriam 'spoke against him' for this). Imagine that this wife bore him a son. That son would be just as much of 'the race and stock' of Levi as would Gershon and Eliezer. But if some contemporary anthropologist had set out to classify the individuals, Moses would have been accounted a Semite and his son a hybrid; he would not have been assigned to the same race as Levi and Moses. The ambiguity arises because individuals of similar 'race' look alike and similarity of appearance is attributed to common descent. Since the processes of descent are complicated, and were ill understood at the time, it would have been better had the warnings of Kant and Prichard been heeded and the vocabulary of classification kept separate from that of descent.

Two features of Cuvier's conception of human varieties deserve attention. The first was his representation of them as forming a hierarchy with whites at the top and blacks at the bottom. The second was his contention that differences in culture and mental quality were produced by differences in physique. 'It is not for nothing,' he wrote, 'that the Caucasian race has gained dominion over the world and made the most rapid progress in the sciences.' The Chinese were less advanced. They had skulls shaped more like those of animals. The Negroes were 'sunken in slavery and the pleasures of the senses' yet they 'were rational and sensitive creatures', while 'slavery was degrading for both slave and master and must be abolished' (Coleman, 1964: 166).

To argue that man was an animal was scarcely daring. The key question was whether he was just an animal. Man could create his own world, could build a civilisation, and study himself. Could this be explained by the same principles as those which accounted for his physical being? Cuvier's affirmative answer to this question is one of the biggest steps leading to the doctrine of racial types. It can also be seen as a criterion for distinguishing between two paradigms in the study of man: the anthropological approach which sought to explain both physique and culture in a unified theory that found the causes of differentiation in biological laws; and the ethnological approach which drew a sharp distinction between man's physical nature and his culture, believing that the latter demanded explanations of a different kind (cf. Stocking, 1973: c). This was not the way in which most nineteenth-century writers saw the distinction. Latham, for example, saw anthropology as studying the relations of man to other mammals, ethnology as studying the relations of the different varieties of mankind to each other; both were concerned with physical influences and not with the study of moral causes, which was the province of history (1850: 559). Others drew the dividing line in different places still, but it became ever clearer that the key question was whether culture was independent of physical character, so it is not unreasonable to label the two kinds of answer to it as 'anthropological' and 'ethnological'.

The notion of type was a convenient one because it was not tied to any particular classificatory level in zoology, so that it was easy to refer to the physical types characteristic of particular nations, to 'types of cranial conformation', or to say that a skull 'approximates to the Negro type' without having to establish just what that type was. This was appreciated at the time, for W.F. Edwards in his important essay of 1829 observed:

In identifying a combination of well defined characters as a type–a word which has the same sense in ordinary speech and in natural history – I avoid all discussion about the rank which a group so characterized will occupy in general classification, since it suits equally well the distinctions between variety, race, family, species, genus, and other categories yet more general. (1829: 125)

As the evidence about the diversity of human forms accumulated, more and more writers tended to refer to various kinds of type and, indeed, the construction of typologies of various kinds became a characteristic of nineteenth-century scholarship. It was used in the analysis of poetry, aesthetics, biography, personality and culture. In sociology it contributed to the concept of an ideal type. In anthropology and ethnology the concept of racial type was central to the debates about race for more than a century. It appealed to many, like Edwards, because it could be used at any taxonomic level; this was one of the main objections to it from writers like Prichard who believed that the problems of classification were confused by the introduction of a new kind of class which did not have a definite place. Prichard used the word 'type' himself, but he would have been only consistent had he rejected it as redundant. Writers who were impressed by the differences between blacks and whites but were reluctant to call them separate species sometimes called them races and implied a species difference (see, for example Jordan's comment on John Augustine Smith in his introduction to S. Stanhope Smith, 1965: xxxix).

On two counts, therefore, Cuvier must bear a heavy responsibility for the nineteenth-century confusion about the meaning of the word race. Firstly, because he blurred the distinction between the earlier sense of race and the concept of a variety. Secondly, because his use of a concept of type made it easier for his successors to discuss natural differences without facing up to questions about whether these were differences at the level of genus, species or variety.

The American school

The conception of race as type was developed most systematically in the United States. The external conditions of the society in which the authors lived and the reasoning internal to their field of study both influenced the course of the development, but the two kinds of influence cannot be separated and weighed against one another. Any writings about racial differences were immediately scrutinised to see what implications they might have for the conflict over Negro slavery. The authors themselves could not but hold opinions about slavery which were likely to influence any attempt they made to study human variation dispassionately. Yet at the same time there were many features of daily life in the New World arising from the relations between blacks, whites and native Americans which encouraged genuinely intellectual speculation about the causes of variation. Nor can there be any doubt that Cuvier's works were studied and that he was regarded as one of the greatest authorities.

Slave owners had been aware from an early period that it was desirable for slaves to be allowed a period of acclimatisation; they knew, too, that it took time for a European to adjust to the new conditions. Though acclimatisation might help, it did not confer immunity to new diseases, and when cholera came to North America in 1832 fear galvanised Southern planters into seeing that slave cabins were scrubbed and cleaned, that buildings were white-washed, and that slave bedding was aired. The following year cholera cost the planters of Louisiana $4 million, for the disease hit blacks much harder. In Charleston, for example, where the population was evenly divided, 80 per cent of the deaths were of blacks. Medical students were told that slave medicine was the most profitable speciality because planters were so anxious to protect their investments. When cholera came to the Mississippi delta in 1849 a physician could be paid up to $500 a day to remain on the plantation and attend to slaves (Kiple and King, 1981: 148–66).

Other diseases affected Europeans but not blacks. In the late seventeenth and early eighteenth centuries half of the English who went to West Africa died in their first year and only one in ten were able to return to England (see Curtin, 1964: 58–87, 483–7). In the late eighteenth-century slave ships more of the English sailors died than did slaves. The slave dealers in Bristol and Liverpool tried to conceal the evidence that about 20 per cent of the crew died each voyage. In West Africa in the nineteenth century white troops died at rates varying between 48 and 67 per cent per annum, mostly from yellow fever and malaria, while black troops, who had some inherited immunity for these diseases, died at 3 per cent per annum. European armies could not fight in the Caribbean. Between 1803 and 1816 white soldiers there died at a rate of 13.8 per cent per annum, blacks at 6.4 per cent. While both blacks and whites contracted yellow fever, the relative immunity of blacks meant that they recovered when whites did not. Thus in Memphis in 1878, 78 per cent of blacks were infected and 9 per cent died as a result, whereas 70 per cent of the infected whites succumbed. These differences (and the susceptibility of Native Americans to smallpox, measles and mumps) can now be explained. In West Africa genes which conferred immunity to the fevers has been favoured by natural selection. The diet of people there was rich in carbohydrates but deficient in protein, calcium, iron and vitamins C and D. With plenty of sunlight the lack of vitamin D did not matter; nor did the inability to digest milk products which was associated with a genetic adaptation to that environment. Transported to North America, however, these deficiencies became more important. A slave diet which was good relative to the dietary requirements of whites, did not give the blacks the nutrients they needed; the practice of soil-eating (which slave-owners feared as a cause of death and sought to prevent) may very well have arisen as a response to nutritional deficiencies. Blacks suffered more than whites from cholera, tuberculosis, whooping cough, tetanus, scrofula and pellagra (Kiple and King, 1981). These differences could reasonably sustain the belief that there were actual and inherited differences between the people of different races.

White people in the United States met blacks and reds almost exclusively in situations in which whites were the superior party in terms of power and knowledge. In any unequal relationship the superior party is likely to stereotype members of the inferior party, and when inherited differences of outward appearance are added this tendency is all the stronger. So a report from a leading historian, George M. Fredrickson (1971: 43) is of particular interest. He writes that prior to the 1830s, although black subordination was widespread and whites commonly assumed that Negroes were inferior, 'open assertions of *permanent* inferiority were exceedingly rare'. One of the first such published assertions was a pamphlet by Richard Colfax, published in New York in 1833, which assembled a whole series of negative evaluations of Negro capacity and concluded that their disadvantages were unalterable since despite 'their proximity to refined nations' they had 'never even *attempted* to raise themselves above their present equivocal station in the great zoological chain'. This was, as Fredrickson says, an assertion; it lacked a scientific explanation of the causes of inequality.

The kind of explanation that was to appeal to people who thought like Colfax was already in the making, for in 1830 a Philadelphian doctor, Samuel George Morton (1799–1851), chose to deliver a lecture on the skulls of the five races of Blumenbach's classification. Being unable to buy or borrow any Mongolian or Malay skull, he decided to start his own collection. By 1839 he had enough for him to publish a book *Crania Americana*. As the title indicates, most of his skulls were American, but he found sufficient of other kinds to add a footnote to the last page of his text (see figure 3.1). In it he reported the results of measurements of their internal capacity, suggesting that whites had the biggest brains, blacks the smallest, and that brown people came in between. Difference in brain size, he implied, explained differences in the capacity for civilisation. This footnote was historically of the greatest importance, for the table was reproduced in 1849 by Carus who, while he did not accept Morton's view, regarded both brain size and cultural differences as manifestations of some, as yet ill understood, law of development. The table was then copied from Carus by Gobineau and given much greater publicity. Can it be said that the course of history would have been much different had Morton's footnote been overlooked? Or would these measurements have been repeated by some other scholar much as, say, Mendel's paper on the genetics of garden peas was overlooked and then its principles redis-covered?

It could be argued that it did not matter very much whether Mendel's laws were discovered in 1866 or in 1900. It was just a matter of time before someone discovered them and the laws would be the same who-ever did it. But for Morton's findings, it could be said, matters were otherwise, since Morton's table of measurements was misleading; had the measurements been carried out by someone lacking Morton's racial bias the resulting table would not have seemed to support Gobineau's claims. This argument would make much of the report that when Stephen Jay Gould (1978, 1981: 50–69) re-examined Morton's skulls in 1977 using better techniques of measurement and newer statistical procedures, he concluded that the internal capacity of Mongolian and Modern Cau-casian skulls should have been reported as 87 cubic inches, Amerindian 86, Malay 85, Caucasian skulls from Ancient Egyptian tombs 84, and African 83. Yet Gould's own evidence has been called into question by a further study of the material and yet another set of measurements

Note. – *On the Internal Capacity of the Cranium in the different Races of Men.* – Having subjected the skulls in my possession, and such also as I could obtain from my friends, to the internal capacity measurement already described, I have obtained the following results. The Mean of the American Race, (omitting the fraction) is repeated here merely to complete the Table. The skulls of idiots and persons under age were of course rejected.

Races	No. of skulls	Mean internal capacity in cubic inches	Largest in the series	Smallest in the series
Caucasian	52	87	109	75
Mongolian	10	83	93	69
Malay	18	81	89	64
American	147	82	100	60
Ethiopian	29	78	94	65

1. The *Caucasians* were, with a single exception, derived from the lowest and least educated class of society. It is proper, however, to mention that but three Hindoos are admitted in the whole number, because the skulls of these people are probably smaller than those of any other existing nation. For example, seventeen Hindoo heads give a mean of but seventy-five cubic inches – and the three received into the table are taken at that average. To be more specific, we will give in detail the number of individuals of each nation as far as ascertained.

Anglo-Americans	6
Germans, Swiss and Dutch, ...	7
Celtic Irish and Scots, ...	7
English, ...	4
Guanché (Libyan), ...	1
Spanish	1
Hindoo, ...	3
Europeans, nation not ascertained, ...	23
	52

2. The *Mongolians* measured, consist of Chinese and Eskimaux – and what is worthy of remark, three of the latter give a mean of eighty-six cubic inches, while seven Chinese give but eighty-two.

3. The *Malays* embrace Malays proper and Polynesians, thirteen of the former and five of the latter – and the mean of each presents but a fractional difference from the mean of all.

4. The *Ethiopians* were all unmixed Negroes, and nine of them native Africans, for which I am chiefly indebted to Dr. McDowell, formerly attached to the colony at Liberia.

5. Respecting the *American* Race I have nothing to add, excepting the striking fact that of all the American nations the Peruvians had the smallest heads, while those of the Mexicans were something larger, and those of the barbarous tribes the largest of all, viz:

Toltecan nations	{	Peruvians collectively, ... 76 cubic inches
		Mexicans collectively, ... 79 cubic inches
		Barbarous tribes, as per Table, ... 82 cubic inches

An interesting question remains to be solved, viz: the relative proportion of brain in the anterior and posterior chambers of the skull in the different races; an inquiry for which I have hitherto possessed neither sufficient leisure nor adequate materials.

Figure 3.1 Morton's footnote

(Michael, 1988). This concluded that Morton's research had been conducted with integrity and that its errors were not to be attributed to racial bias. The overriding reason for rejecting his tables was that they relied on an undefined and unsound conception of race. (Incidentally this further re-measurement reported the following mean cubic capacities: American, 80, Caucasian 83, Malayan 85, Mongolian 85, and Negro 82.)

Like other anthropologists of his time, Morton failed to appreciate the association between brain size and stature. Big people have bigger brains. Men are bigger than women; men have bigger brains. There are ethnic differences in stature, for reasons of environment and nutrition, and so there are ethnic differences in brain size, but no association between the differences in intelligence between men and women. The association between cranial capacity and stature could have been deduced from Morton's skulls but though he made remarks suggesting a partial awareness of it, Morton never recognised this explicitly or allowed for it. Nor had anyone else at that time recognised it. Morton's partial awareness can be seen in his reference to Hindoo skulls in paragraph 1 of his footnote. Why include only three of the seventeen in his measure? He gave no proper reason. The effect of his doing so was to make the Caucasian average higher than it otherwise would have been. In paragraph 5 he remarked that Peruvians had small heads, but he left them out of the average for American skulls in the table, basing this entry solely upon the so-called 'barbarous tribes'. What Morton should have done was to prepare separate tables for male and female skulls and, to allow for his having more skulls from some groups than others, he should have taken averages for each group by sex in order to calculate for each race an average of the averages for the subgroups. If this is done, the differences between the races turn out to be very small, while the differences within the races are substantial. It will be noticed that in paragraph 2 Morton attached no significance to the figure for Eskimos being almost as high as that for Caucasians; he failed to observe that some American skulls were large, those for the Iroquois returning an average of 91.5, well above the Caucasian; small errors of measurement and the rounding out of decimal points all seem to have gone in the direction of reinforcing his prior expectation that the skulls of white people would be larger than those of black people. Yet Gould, who is a severe critic, found no evidence of fraud or conscious manipulation. Morton made no attempt to cover up his errors.

Morton's views about racial differences among humans should not be seen in isolation from contemporary attempts to account for variation in forms of life generally. One possible explanation was that which, following Cuvier, emphasised the stability of species over time. Applied to humans it was almost certain to produce a theory that differences in the ways of life and levels of attainment of races stemmed from permanent physical differences. The most obvious and best understood physical differences were the anatomical ones so those, and particularly anything associated with possible differences in the brain, were bound to attract attention. Craniological studies were stimulated by Morton's findings but they were not dependent upon them and they would have flourished in any event. Seen from this standpoint, Morton's errors appear less momentous.

Those who, like Stanhope Smith and Prichard, believed that humans constituted one species stemming from an original pair, had to explain how it was that the descendants of this pair varied in so many ways. Three kinds of explanation were open to them (1) divine intervention, like a curse upon the descendants of Ham; (2) congenital or accidental variations arising naturally had been selectively preserved (the explanation Prichard entertained in 1826 but from which he retreated); (3) the effect of climate. The critics scoffed at the first and brought forward persuasive arguments against the second and third. Congenital variations were not uncommon and a parent might transmit one (like, say, being cross-eyed) to a child but thereafter they seemed to die out. Whoever heard of a cross-eyed race, it was asked. Climate could certainly exert an influence, just as Europeans became sunburned, but how could an acquired character be transmitted to offspring? Prichard himself had denied that such transmission occurred. The examples of change he cited all seemed to have happened long ago. Why could such changes not be observed in the present? Prichard acknowledged that many types remained unchanged after centuries in new environments, so why should one stock change and not another (see Nott and Gliddon, 1854: 57–9)? If, on the other hand, the use of fertility as the criterion of species was abandoned, it became possible to regard the various kinds of humans as different species separately created. Diversity could then be regarded as having existed, unchanged from a much earlier period; perhaps, indeed, from the creation. This led on to the view that each race was adapted to a particular climate and a particular zone of the earth. If that was the case then inherited characters had to be understood in relation to different environments. In this form, the theory of permanent racial differences provided no justification for believing one race superior to another. Each was superior in its own zone or province.

This fourth explanation of diversity can be traced back to the sixteenth century, but it was given new life and persuasiveness by Cuvier, reinforced by Morton, and then developed most explicitly in Nott and Gliddon's book *Types of Mankind* (1854). At much the same time people in France, Britain and Germany were working along similar lines and they produced similar statements, so that racial typology constituted an international school of thought. If Nott and Gliddon had not elaborated upon the Cuvier–Morton line of argument, then someone else would have done. The Typological Theory can be summarised as holding that:

1 Variations in the constitution and behaviour of individuals are the expression of differences between underlying types of a relatively permanent kind, each of which is suited to a particular continent or zoological province.
2 Social categories in the long run reflect and are aligned with the natural categories that produce them.
3 Individuals belonging to a particular racial type display an innate antagonism towards individuals belonging to other types, the degree of antagonism depending upon the relationship between the two types.

Morton moved steadily towards an acceptance of these propositions. On the first page of *Crania Americana* he declared, 'from remote ages the inhabitants of every extended locality have been marked by certain physical and moral peculiarities, common among themselves, and serving to distinguish them from all other people. The Arabians are, at this time precisely what they were in the days of the patriarchs.' The concept of type did not appear (though he used it in 1841) and he presented races as subspecific classes. Morton introduced some doubts about the orthodox view, as when he referred to calculations that Noah and his family left the Ark 4,179 years previously whereas Ethiopians were known to exist 3,445 years ago; recent discoveries, he added, made it clear that only by a miracle could the Negro race have developed out of the Caucasian in the course of 734 years (1839: 1, 88). But the general effect was very restrained. Having obtained a collection of Egyptian skulls, he was willing to go a little further five years later, and in *Crania Aegyptica* (1844: 66) reached the conclusion that 'Negroes were numerous in Egypt, but their social position in ancient times was the same as it now is, that of servants and slaves.' Negroes had a natural social position as well as a geographical position and gave evidence of being a permanent type.

In later publications Morton's attack on orthodoxy became more explicit. He criticised the view that infertility of hybrids was the best test of separate species for creatures that had become domesticated, and emphasised 'the repugnance of some human races to mix with others'. By this time Morton had acquired allies, and they were men of a more combative temperament. The first was George Robins Gliddon (1809–57), the English-born vice-consul for the United States in Cairo, who collected ancient Egyptian skulls for him. Then came Josiah Clark Nott (1804–73) a physician in Alabama, Ephraim George Squier (1821–88), the first authoritative voice in American archaeology, and Louis Agassiz (1807–73), a professor of natural history in Switzerland who moved to the United States in 1846 and became a professor at Harvard. Nott was the first of this new school to argue that the various races, being permanent and lacking in adaptability, had been created separately in their several environments. The others followed quite quickly.

All versions of the monogenetic theory depended upon the assumption that human life on earth was to be counted in several thousands of years. Religious orthodoxy presumed a chronology of about 6,000 years. The anthropologists gave reasons for concluding that natural causes could not have produced the existing range of racial diversity within so short a time period. They began with the evidence, already mentioned, which, they claimed, indicated that Negroes and Caucasians were as distinct physically 4,000 years ago as they were at the present time. Then, with the excavation of Native American burial mounds in the Mississippi valley by Squier, a skull was found which Morton pronounced 'a perfect type' of its race, the race which was 'indigenous to the American continent, having been planted there by the hand of Omnipotence'. To determine the age of the mounds was difficult, but some calculations could be based upon the levels of land which constituted terraces in the valley and testified to a process by which the river had subsided. They proved that the burial mounds were of 'no inconsiderable antiquity'; the reader could deduce that the time period was many times greater than 6,000 years. The chronology therefore supported the claim that Native Americans were indigenous to the continent and not the result of some earlier immigration. As Stanton wrote in his excellent study (1960: 88), Squier had done for the Indian what Gliddon had done for the Negro. The archaeological evidence contradicted the claims of the orthodox, like Samuel Stanhope Smith, that environmental influence could bring about enough change within historical time to account for the diversity of races. It greatly strengthened earlier criticisms such as that of Charles White, who objected that if the environment could produce different species, then the entire animal kingdom could derive from a single ancestral pair and a more 'degrading notion' could not be imagined. John Augustine Smith, the critic of his namesake, had also objected that if environmental change affected complexion this did not explain why different individuals living in the same environment could have such different complexions. Why, too, if the Creator had originally adapted the Indians for the various American climates, did Morton think there was a single Indian type?

The anthropological school was greatly strengthened by the support received from Agassiz. Before leaving Switzerland he had delivered lectures in which he maintained that 'all organised beings, plants as well as animals, are confined to a special area' but this principle did not apply to humans who could spread across all the regions of the earth. Agassiz had not, apparently, considered the evidence for human diversity with any care. In the United States he encountered Negroes for the first time and his response showed little of the caution to be expected of a scientist. Their appearance shocked him. He wrote home to his mother that the Negro could not be of the same species as the white man. Any one could easily see that the Negro was not the white man's equal, and almost all white men did. Four years later, in 1850, Agassiz declared that the races shared the distinguishing attributes of humanity in differing degrees. Like other animals, the races of men occupied distinct zoological provinces and 'did not originate from a common centre, nor from a single pair'. This became the foundation of the argument underlying Nott and Gliddon's 1854 book *Types of Mankind*. Near the beginning was a nineteen-page 'Sketch of the Natural Provinces of the Animal World and their Relation to the different Types of Man contributed by Prof. L. Agassiz, L.L.D.' with a coloured lithographic Tableau and Map. On the map eight provinces were distinguished: the Arctic, Asiatic, European, American, African, East Indian, Australian and Polynesian realms. In the tableau Agassiz called the second realm Mongol; he added an extra division after the African to catalogue the fauna of the Cape-lands and its 'distinct race of men, the Hottentots', and left out the races and animals of Polynesia. Agassiz drew attention to flora and fauna characteristic of particular provinces (as, for example, marsupials and Australian Aborigines were distinctive of the Australian realm), but there were many errors in his scheme (see Quatrefages, 1879: 163–7). He wrote, 'I am prepared to show that the differences existing between the races of men are of the same kind as the differences observed between the different families, genera and species of monkeys or other animals' and concluded that there were only two possible explanations of organic diversity. One was that mankind originated from a common stock, which would mean that their present diversity had arisen since the creation and was not part of any plan operating at that time. The other was that diversity was determined by the will of the Creator and the present geographical distribution of animals was part of God's plan, demonstrating the great harmonies established in Nature.

In Part I of *Types of Mankind*, the hand of Dr Nott is very evident. In 1843 a medical journal had published an article of his entitled 'The Mulatto a Hybrid – Probable Extermination of the Two Races If the Whites and Blacks Are Allowed to Intermarry' in which he testified that mulattoes did not live so long as members of the parent races. The union of mulattoes was less prolific than the union of mulatto with White or Negro. After reading this article, Morton had written to its author and collaboration ensued. In *Types of Mankind*, Nott repeated his earlier claims. Morton had defined a species as 'a primordial organic form'. There were remote species, of the same genus, among which hybrids were never produced; allied species, which produced infertile offspring; and proximate species which could produce fertile offspring. Nott followed this, but added a fourth category in between the first two: this consisted of those cases in which hybrids could not reproduce between themselves but could do so when mated with the parent stock. Morton had maintained that what at that time were called the five races, could be better designated five groups, each of which could be divided into proximate races. Nott argued that hybridity was not a unitary phenomenon but something to be studied in terms of degrees of hybridity, and that this demonstrated the wisdom of Morton's definitions. The observations in Nott's 1843 article were based largely upon his knowledge of mulattoes in South Carolina. In 1854 he added that further observations in Mobile and New Orleans had introduced some modifications to his views, since had had there witnessed many examples of great longevity among mulattoes and of manifestly prolific marriages among them. His conclusion was that around the Mexican Gulf the blood of the white population was preponderantly drawn from French, Italian, Spanish, Portuguese and other dark-skinned whites. Their blood mixed more easily with that of African peoples than did that of the people of Anglo-Saxon origin on the Atlantic coast of North America. Nott went on to maintain that the smallest admixture of Negro blood conferred immunity to yellow fever; to discuss the evidence for telegony and its implications; and to assert, in an anticipation of Darwin's theory, that 'Nature marches steadily towards perfection; and that it attains this end through the consecutive destruction of living beings'.

At the end of Part I of *Types of Mankind* is printed a list of 'deductions' or conclusions (reproduced in figure 3.2). They show an intellectual commitment to environmental relativism. Elsewhere in the text Nott and Gliddon declared:

Every race, at the present time, is more or less mixed [but] there is abundant evidence to show that the principal physical characters of a people may be preserved throughout a long series of ages, in a great part of the population, despite of climate, mixture of races, invasion of foreigners, progress of civilization, or other known influences; and that a *type can long outlive its language, history, religion, customs, and recollections.* (p. 95)

They could maintain that present-day races were mixed because they distinguished between the type, which was immutable, and the contemporary expression of it in a population which could diverge from that type

1. *That the surface of our globe is naturally divided into several zoological provinces, each of which is a distinct centre of creation, possessing a peculiar fauna and flora; and that every species of animal and plant was originally assigned to its appropriate province.*

2. *That the human family offers no exception to this general law, but fully conforms to it: Mankind being divided into several groups of Races, each of which constitutes a primitive element in the fauna of its peculiar province.*

3. *That history affords no evidence of the transformation of one Type into another, nor of the origination of a new and* Permanent *Type.*

4. *That certain Types have been* Permanent *through all recorded time, and despite the most opposite moral and physical influences.*

5. *That* Permanence *of Type is accepted by science as the surest test of* Specific *character.*

6. *That certain Types have existed (the same as now) in and around the Valley of the Nile, from ages anterior to 3500 years B.C., and consequently long prior to any alphabetic chronicles, sacred or profane.*

7. *The the ancient Egyptians had already classified Mankind, as known to them, into* Four Races, *previously to any date assignable to Moses.*

8. *That high antiquity for distinct Races is amply sustained by linguistic researches, by psychological history, and by anatomical characteristics.*

9. *That the primeval existence of Man, in widely separate portions of the globe, is proven by the discovery of his osseous and industrial remains in alluvial deposits and in diluvial drifts; and more especially of his fossil bones, imbedded in various rocky strata along with the vestiges of extinct species of animals.*

10. *That* Profligacy *of distinct species, inter se, is now proved to be no test of* Common Origin.

11. That those Races of men most separated in physical organization – such as the Blacks and the Whites – do not amalgamate perfectly, but obey the Laws of Hybridity. Hence

12. *It follows, as a corollary, that there exists a* Genus Homo, *embracing many primordial Types or 'Species.'*

Figure 3.2 Nott and Gliddon's 'conclusions'

to a certain degree. Their distinction lived on in the twentieth century in the notion of pure types or pure races. The racial thought of the Nazis was close to this way of thinking and when, in the period following upon the Second World War, attempts were made to correct mistaken popular beliefs about race, it was common to stress that science offered no warrant for any conception of pure races. Both the first and second UNESCO statements on the nature of race (in 1950 and 1951) included the sentence, 'Vast social changes have occurred that have not been connected in any way with changes in racial type.' Such references to type can still be noticed. In a 1961 presidential address to the American Anthropological Association (Washburn, 1963), the speaker said:

If we look back to the time when I was educated, races were regarded as types. We were taught to go to a population and divide it into a series of types and to re-create history out of this artificial arrangement. Those of you who have read *Current Anthropology* will realize that this kind of anthropology is still alive, amazingly, and in full force in some countries; relics of it are still alive in our teaching today.

It is also necessary to look out for occasions on which, though the word type is not employed, the word race is used in the sense of a pure or permanent type underlying the diversities of modern populations. The sense of race as type is still significant.

Discussing the Mongolian group, Nott wrote that the facts confirm 'the only rational theory: viz., that races were created in each zoological province, and therefore all primitive types must be of equal antiquity'. Despite this environmental relativism, there are many passages witnessing to the author's belief in white superiority:

The higher castes of what are termed Caucasian races, are influenced by several causes in a greater degree than other races. To them have been assigned, in all ages, the largest brains and the most powerful intellect; *theirs* is the mission of extending and perfecting civilization – they are by nature ambitious, daring, domineering and reckless of danger – impelled by an irresistible instinct, they visit all climes, regardless of difficulties; but how many thousands are sacrificed annually to climates foreign to their nature!

Caucasians 'have in all ages been the rulers', while 'none of the fair-skinned types of mankind' have hitherto been able to realise the Germanic style of democracy described by Tacitus. Dark-skinned races, on the other hand, were 'only fit for military governments', and Negroes, as Jefferson said had never produced a thought above the level of plain narrative (Nott and Gliddon, 1854: 67, 79, 404–5, 456). In a separate article Nott maintained that race mixture could be beneficial. A 'small trace of white blood in the Negro improves his intelligence and moral character, and a small trace of Negro blood, as in the quadroon, will protect the individual against the deadly influence of climate'. The Caucasian was a happy blend of the best qualities of several species, a true 'cosmopolite' (Stanton, 1960: 160). It would seem as if Nott was not so persuaded by the typological doctrine of zoological provinces that he felt he should adhere to it consistently. Nott also collaborated with Henry Hotze (on whom see Lorimer, 1978: 149–50) in publishing a one-volume edition of translated selections from Gobineau's *Essay*. Nott testified, 'I have seldom perused a work which has afforded me so much pleasure'; he contributed a fifty-page appendix which updated Morton's cranial measurements, set out to correct Gobineau on the matter of hybridity, and observed that Gobineau had been hindered by 'religious scruples'. In reality, wrote Nott, the first chapter of Genesis gave an account entirely in accordance with the teachings of science, but the passage in Acts, 17: 26 misled readers because the translator had taken liberties with the original text.

In 1854 Nott referred to the claim that white Europeans would degenerate in the North American environment, but did not commit himself to it. Three years later in another volume edited by the same authors, Nott reviewed the statistics of morality and morbidity and concluded 'races . . . have their appropriate geographical ranges, beyond which they cannot go with impunity'. He commented sardonically on man that 'although boasting of *reason*, as the prerogative that distinguishes him, he is, in many respects, the most unreasonable of animals'. One respect was that 'he forsakes the land of his birth, with all its associations, and all the comforts which earth can give, to colonise foreign lands – where he knows full well that a thousand hardships must await him, and with the certainty of risking his life *in climates that nature never intended him for*' (1857: 399–400). If each type was suited to its own province, none could be superior to the others. Unwilling to break with this principle, Nott could not develop his inclination to maintain that the Caucasian was the highest type.

The easiest way of reconciling typology with a belief in white superiority would have been to add an extra proposition to the list set out (p. 58). This might have stated that zoological provinces could overlap, and that where, as in the Valley of the Nile, European and African provinces overlapped, Europeans would rule. Nott and Gliddon never made such a claim though it would have resolved an apparent conflict between their first and sixth conclusions and strengthened the grounds for their statement (1854: 79) that 'no two distinctly-marked races can dwell together on equal terms'. Nor did they, like Knox, identify what later came to be called race prejudice and claim that it was an inbred characteristic of some or all types. This seems not to have been something which they regarded as requiring explanation. Nevertheless their doctrine of race included a theory of race relations, for they asserted that the natural order determined what kinds of social relations would be harmonious. If the permanent types had distinctive attributes then any social relationship which did not permit these attributes to obtain natural expression would eventually fail.

Part I of *Types of Mankind* was critical of the monogenetic theory, but in

Part II Gliddon carried the fight into the critics' camp. Since many who appealed to the authority of the Bible knew it only in the translation authorised by King James, Gliddon stressed that this was based on the Latin and Greek translations of the Old Testament and not on the Hebrew originals. He selected the 10th chapter of Genesis, which lists the generations of Noah, to explain the features of the Hebrew text, and followed an Italian scholar to maintain that the series of names of Noah's descendants could be interpreted as a geographical recital of the various parts of the earth known at the time the manuscript was first prepared. He discussed the structure of the first three chapters of Genesis, quoting the views of some fathers of the church on matters of exegesis, and reviewed some of the 120 or so attempts to calculate the date of the creation using the Biblical evidence. How good his scholarship was would be a matter for expert assessment, but it must surely have astonished those who rejected racial typology on the simple grounds that it was contrary to Bible truth.

It should not be thought that the typological theory was welcomed by Southern whites as a justification for the prevailing pattern of racial inequality. White Southerners were divided along class lines but both sections defended slavery on Biblical grounds, leading Stanton (1960: 194) to assert that 'the South turned its back on the only intellectually respectable defence of slavery it could have taken up'. This requires some qualification. For decades there had been a Southern Bourbon tradition which defended slavery as an institution independently of the question of racial difference. Non-slave holding whites, of course, disliked it. Some aspired to become slave-owners themselves and many were anxious to protect and increase their privileges at the expense of black workers. With the extension of the suffrage in the 1830s to white males by the weakening of property-owning qualifications, the white workers' influence grew and the planter class had to adjust to their beliefs, demands and phobias. The shift in opinion was reflected in the views of George Fitzhugh, a spokes-man for the Bourbon philosophy. In 1854 he had declared, 'We deplore the doctrine of the *Types of Mankind*, first, because it is at war with scripture . . . secondly, because it encourages and incites brutal planters to treat negroes, not as weak, ignorant and dependent brethren, but as wicked beasts without the pale of humanity.' Other wirters over the decades had equally insisted that the facts of inequality could just as well be taken to indicate that blacks should be treated with extra kindness. Dr Charles Caldwell of North Carolina (on whom see Erickson, 1981), criticising Stanhope Smith in 1830, maintained that Caucasians were not justified in enslaving the Africans or destroying the Indians 'merely be-cause their superiority in intellect and war enable them to do so. Such practices are an abuse of power.' Sir William Lawrence, lecturing on medicine in London in 1819 declared, 'Superior endowments . . . should be employed to extend the blessings of civilization . . . not as a means of oppressing the weak.' William Jay, a relatively conservative supporter of abolition in the United States, in 1853 addressed those who favoured sending blacks back to Africa and asked if it was conceivable that Christ would have commanded men to love one another had they not been given the power to do so? Yet the reader is apt to conclude that arguments from physical difference were increasingly being taken as guides to morality. In 1861 Fitzhugh announced his conversion to the view that blacks and whites were separate species and that 'the habitudes, instinct, moral and intellectual qualities and capabilities of all animals are the universal and necessary concomitants (if not the consequences) of their physical conformation'. If the white South had turned its back on racial typology to start with, it soon found a way of accepting it (Fredrickson, 1971: 29, 69–70, 73, 84; Stanton, 1960: 194; Curtin, 1964: 239).

France

Though there has been a distinct strain of anti-semitism in French writing and politics, relatively few French authors have advanced theories of racial differences. Some might say that one man, Arthur de Gobineau (1816–82) has made up for this, for he has been called the father of racist ideology. Gobineau's influence has often been exaggerated and his outlook misrepresented. He came to the topic of racial differences from a wide reading in German literature, so it should not be surprising to find in his work traces of a similar kind of romanticism. Working on a novel of the kind made popular by Scott's *Ivanhoe*, he had carefully studied the work of Thierry and some of the French authors who interpreted French history as a matter of race. Though he did not stand squarely in that line of debate, being anti-nationalist and pro-European, one strand of the Frankish, anti-Roman, genealogy can be traced through Montesquieu, Boulainvilliers and Montlosier to Gobineau. The novel entitled *L'Abbaye de Typhaines*, dealt with a twelfth-century revolt. Characteristically, Gobineau did not take sides between the peasants, bourgeoisie and clergy. He showed a concern for local liberties but implied that mere love of liberty was insufficient to ensure that people would be able to exercise it.

Gobineau's first significant use of 'race' to account for human nobility appeared in an epic poem and in the *Essay* he made relatively little reference to anthropological authorities for his assumptions. His arguments were less original than he claimed; many of them were expounded by Victor Courtet de l'Isle (1813–67), the Saint-Simonian author of *La*

Science politique fondée sur la science de l'homme published in 1837. Courtet was elected Secretary of the Société Ethnographique de Paris in 1846 and re-elected in 1848; the following year he published his *Tableau ethnographique* and, as many of his associates were well known to Gobineau, it seems certain that the latter borrowed heavily from him without acknowledgement (Boissel, 1972: 83, 178–80). Courtet identified the Germans as a superior race which had formerly been spread over Europe 'like the oil of the nations'. Where Thierry had stressed the conflict of races, Courtet saw the mingling of blood as having 'chemical' consequences which he thought must ultimately be beneficial. Gobineau disparaged Prichard ('a mediocre historian and even more mediocre theologian') and brought into prominence the table of cranial capacity in different races that Carus had taken from Morton. Though he had not had Klemm's book in his hands, Gobineau had heard of his distinction between active and passive races. When he claimed that human activities had their origin in the 'male' and 'female' currents within humanity and that civilisations were born from the mixing of races, the resemblance was close, but Gobineau believed that if the two of them were travelling along the same paths it would not be surprising if they came upon the same truths.

The *Essay* began with a statement that everything great, noble, and fruitful in the works of man on this earth springs from the Aryan family. It expounded his principles for explaining the rise and fall of civilisations and then showed their operation in a lengthy review of the ten most notable (for a summary, see Biddiss, 1970: 112–31). History began after one of the cosmic catastrophes envisaged by Cuvier: the Aryans were living in small independent communities, unable to see as their equals those other creatures which, with their evil hostility, their hideous ugliness, brutal intelligence and their claim to be the offspring of monkeys, seemed to be falling back into the ranks of animals (1853: 442). From this base the Aryans spread out to create first the Hindu civilisation, then the Egyptian, Assyrian, Greek, Chinese, Roman, German,[1] Alleghenian, Mexican and Peruvian civilisations (how Aryans came to create the last two is never explained). Gobineau considered possible causes for the rise and decline of these civilisations: climate, irreligion, corruption of morals, and bad government. He found none satisfactory, and settled for racial mixture as an explanation of both rise and decline. Societies which were averse from all mixture remained small and stagnant. A little mixture might enable one race, like the Aryans, to grow in power so that its members met members of other races in the relations of masters to

---

[1] Gobineau wrote of 'les races germaniques' but this should have been translated as 'the Teutonic races' (cf. Chadwick, 1945: 142–9); Gobineau's Teutons were a larger unit than the people who called themselves Deutsch.

servants. Such a relationship led to increased mixture and thus to the decline of the former. Thus Gobineau celebrated the vigour of the Aryans and asserted that 'the irreconcilable antagonism between different races and cultures is clearly established by history' (1853: 181); nevertheless, in order to avoid disappearing into the masses over whom it ruled, 'the white family needed to add to the power of its genius and courage a certain guarantee of numbers' (1853: 393) and consequently lost some of its potency unless reinforced by further migrations from other Aryan populations. The book's most quoted assertion is:

Such is the lesson of history. It shows us that all civilizations derive from the white race, that none can exist without its help, and that a society is great and brilliant only so far as it preserves the blood of the noble group that created it, provided that this group itself belongs to the most illustrious branch of our species. (1853: 209)

It appears that Gobineau wished to make use of a version of the typological theory without committing himself to all its constituent parts. There is a chapter entitled 'Racial Differences are Permanent' in which the influence of Cuvier is very apparent. In it Gobineau observes, 'the reader will not fail to see that the question on which the argument here turns is that of the permanence of types'. He used the concept of type in two senses. The first is one that relates to the declaration in his dedication of the book in which he said that he was constructing a moral geology that dealt only in series of centuries, occupying himself rarely with individuals, but always with ethnic units. The geology spans four periods. The type of man first created was the Adamite but it must be left out of the argument since we could know nothing of its specific character. In his earliest stages, man might have assumed unstable forms and change would then have been easier, producing races which differed from their original ancestor as much as they differed from each other. In the second stage three races were present: white, black and yellow, though 'it is probable that none of the three original types was ever found in absolute simplicity'. Intermixture is the origin, he says, of what we may call tertiary types, though 'our knowledge of the life of these tertiary races is very slight. Only in the misty beginnings of human history can we catch a glimpse, in certain places, of the white race when it was still in this stage – a stage which seems to have been everywhere short-lived . . . to the tertiary races succeed others, which I will call "quaternary"' (1853: 155–7). A quaternary race could be further modified by the intervention of a new type. Gobineau wrote of the existing races as being descended from the secondary races, as if present-day populations might represent the second, third, fourth, or even a subsequent stage in the process.

The second use of type is that which became important in anthropological theorising; the assumption that there was, or had been, a pure physical form behind the appearances of diversity. Gobineau never defined race and made it clear that he regarded all the contemporary groups to which that label was applied as having in varying degrees lost their true character through miscegenation. For example, he wrote,

as for the Persian race, it no longer exists in the scientific sense of the word, any more than does the French race, and of all the peoples of Europe we are surely that in which the type has been most obliterated. It is even this obliteration which we accept, in physique and in culture, as being our own type. It is the same with the Persians. (Buenzod, 1967: 558 n.38)

It seems as if Gobineau was trying to defend a belief in permanent differences of racial type independent of association with zoological provinces and therefore unaffected by environmental relativism. This is the theme of Aryan superiority. But in other parts of his *Essay* a subsidiary theme can be discerned, as Janine Buenzod has demonstrated. This dealt with the contribution that other races can make to the creation of civilisations, the emergence of elites and the inability of the white race to progress in confined environments (like that of Newfoundland). To the 'moral geology' can be added another evocative expression (which also appears in the Dedication), that of 'historical chemistry'. Gobineau did not think of racial crossing in terms of blending inheritance, as if the progeny inherited equally from both parents. Rather, he regarded the superior race, especially the Aryan, as a catalytic agent, bringing out latent powers in others (as yeast makes dough rise), or, if it was too strong, destroying them (Buenzod, 1967: 328, 384). The principles of this mixing were not understood, a conclusion which recalls the author's earlier remark that 'the science of social anatomy is in its infancy' (1853: 58).

The elements that went into the historical chemistry were no longer pure and all the races contained their own differences of quality. 'When it is a question of individual merit', Gobineau writes:

I refuse completely to make use of that mode of argument which runs 'every negro is stupid', and my chief objection is that, to complete the comparison, I would then be obliged to concede that every European is intelligent; and heaven preserve me from such a paradox . . . I have no doubt that many negro chiefs are superior, in the wealth of their ideas, the synthetic power of their minds, and the strength of their capacity for action, to the level usually reached by our peasants, or even by average specimens of our half-educated bourgeoisie . . . Let us leave these puerilities, and compare, not men, but groups. (1853: 182)

It is from the comparison of groups that Gobineau concluded that the Aryans had overstretched themselves and that the chemistry had gone wrong. It is not difficult to accept the conclusion that 'the chief element in the *Essay* is the idea of the decadence of civilizations and not that of the inequality of races . . . The explanation in terms of race is a key; but the door which has to be opened – that of understanding history in its broadest dimensions – comes before the key.' It demands much more to assent to the same writer's statement 'the central idea, the truly fertile idea in the *Essay*, is that of the complementarity of races' (Buenzod, 1967: 328–9, 471). If there were evidence that Gobineau saw the chemistry as Carus saw the phases of day and night, as a whole, as part of a meaningful design for the universe, it would be easier to agree.

If Gobineau derived such ideas from Carus and other writers he gave them little emphasis. The principal passage came towards the end of the first book when he wrote about the advantages that had followed from the mixture of blood:

Artistic genius, which is equally foreign to each of the three great types, arose only after the inter-marriage of white and black. Again, in the Malayan variety, a human family was produced from the yellow and black races that had more intelligence than either of its ancestors . . . to racial mixtures is due the refinement of manners and beliefs, and especially the tempering of passion and desire. (1853: 208)

Elsewhere Gobineau maintained that for the world-wide movement of cultural fusion to stretch out it was not sufficient just that a civilising milieu should deploy all its energy; it was necessary that in the different regions ethnic workshops should establish themselves to work on their own localities (1853: 867–8). How this fitted with other parts of his vision is problematic. It is also difficult to be sure what he meant when in a discussion of Hindu caste he declared:

a light admixture from the black species develops intelligence in the white race, in that it turns it towards imagination, makes it more artistic, lends it larger wings; at the same time it weakens the reasoning power of the white race, diminishes the intensity of its practical faculties, delivers an irremediable blow to its activity and physical power, and almost always removes from the group deriving from this mixture, if not the right of shining much brighter than the whites and thinking more profoundly, at least that of contending against it with patience, tenacity, and wisdom. (1853: 346)

At times Gobineau poured the new wine of racial typology into the old bottles of romanticism, but he did not always pour it very straight, and the idea of complementarity was, in a crucial passage, clearly subordinated to that of natural aristocracy:

If mixtures of blood are, to a certain extent, beneficial to the mass of mankind, if they raise and ennoble it, this is merely at the expense of mankind itself, which is stunted, abased, enervated, and humiliated in the persons of its noblest sons. Even if we were to admit that it is better to turn a myriad of degraded beings into mediocre men than to preserve the race of princes whose blood is adulterated and impoverished by being made to suffer this dishonourable change, yet there is still the unfortunate fact that the change does not stop here. (1853: 209)

He then went on to sketch the way in which the unions of the degraded lead societies into the abyss of nothingness.

It is remarked time and again that those who write the history of distant periods regularly do so from the standpoint of their own generation. They interpret ancient disputes in the terms that are alive as they write. This observation is particularly relevant to Gobineau and his *Essay*. Joseph Arthur de Gobineau (1816–82) was born into a bourgeois family with aristocratic pretensions that had been devoted to the Bourbon dynasty and completely opposed to the aspirations of the French Revolution. His experiences of family life, with both his mother and his wife, included much that was unhappy. Gobineau earned a living mainly from journalism until the revolutions of 1848, after which he obtained a succession of diplomatic appointments up to 1877. In 1855, when he first came into contact with a black people, the Somalis, he wrote home saying that never before had he seen 'creatures so beautiful and perfect', so personal experiences did not have the influence upon him that they did on Agassiz. Gobineau's short stories about the Middle East reveal an impressive ability to interpret everyday life as it might have appeared to people brought up in the local cultures. A major theme in them and the novels is the existence of an aristocracy of spirit to be found in men and women of different nations, and which is not necessarily displayed by people of great wealth or gentle parentage.

The *Essay* began with a reference to the revolutions of 1848 which Gobineau saw as symptomatic of the decay of European civilisation and he continued to write from the perspective of a man out of harmony with his time. He thought it unnecessary to provide evidence to support his views that the Aryans were degenerating and that there could be no new civilisation (had he known that in 1944 German troops would dynamite a museum created in his honour he might have thought it evidence in favour of the former proposition). As Michael Biddiss explains, his hypothesis was founded in the contemporary world; it was social and political rather than properly biological (1970: 132). Unlike most of those with whom he can be compared, Gobineau did not expound a theory to press a particular solution on his readers. He had no solution, and in his thought the theory worked towards the annihilation of political will and purpose. Though his belief in natural aristocracy, and race as one of its forms, ran through other writings, not one of the seventeen books he wrote after the *Essay* developed his comparison of the major races. It is the history of one race that concerned him and his books about it were a very personal declaration.

That Gobineau's use of the conception of type was in accordance with contemporary French scientific usage is suggested by an essay published in 1859–60. In it Paul Broca, founder of the Paris Anthropological Society, criticised the view 'that the crossing of races constantly produces disastrous effects'. This was far too general, for under certain circumstances it had favourable results. Broca insisted on the importance of distinguishing between race and type. The popular view that people with hair of different colour did not belong to the same race seized the true meaning of the term race, whereas only the scientist, studying the ensemble of characters common to a natural group, could constitute the type of that group (1864: 8). Human types were abstractions and were not to be confused with actual groups of men. The use of 'race' as if this denoted a pure category was to be avoided. 'Every confusion in words', Broca sternly warned, 'exposes us to errors in the interpretation of facts.'

Britain

The pioneer of racial typology in Britain was Charles Hamilton Smith (1776–1859), a disciple and friend of Cuvier who saw military service with British troops in West Africa, the West Indies, and 'on both portions of the American continent' between 1797 and 1807, later translating the works of the master while on manoeuvres. In 1848 he published *The Natural History of the Human Species* which built on Cuvier's foundations a speculative superstructure about man's origin in three aboriginal normal types springing from a common centre near the Gobi desert 'for this was, approximately, either the seat of Man's first development . . . or the space where a portion of human beings found safety, when convulsions and changes of surface, which may have swept away a more ancient zoology, had passed over the earth and were introductory to a new order of things' (1848: 169). Smith maintained that zoology limited the possibilities of colonisation. A race could have only provisional tenure of a region until the indestructible typical form appeared to take over the territory assigned to it by nature. Conquest entailed extermination unless it was one of the great typical stocks effecting an incorporation of its own affiliates. Mulatto strains were eventually infertile. For Smith the three types were the woolly-haired or Negro; beardless or Mongolian; and bearded or Caucasian.

This argument was a development of the views expounded by Cuvier. On the question of whether man was one species Smith equivocated. He wrote that this 'is assumed to be answered in the affirmative', but his whole text was built round the view that man was one genus with three species, and that the variety of types of humans resulted from different mixtures between the original three kinds (see figure 3.3).

Environmental relativism was weaker in Smith's scheme than in Nott's. He allowed more scope for the superior Caucasians to settle outside Europe, while claiming that in extremes of temperature they could maintain their numbers only by further immigration. The Caucasian was described as a veritable paragon, able

to endure the greatest vicissitudes of temperature in all climates; to emigrate, colonize, and multiply in them, with the sole exception of the positive extremes . . . he alone of the races of mankind has produced examples of free and popular institutions . . . he has ascended to the skies, descended into the deep, and mastered the powers of lightning . . . He has instituted all the great religious systems in the world, and to his stock has been vouchsafed the glory and the conditions of revelation. (1848: 371–2)

The Negro's lowly place in the human order was a consequence of the small volume of his brain (the author had noticed how even the smallest British army caps issued to black troops in the West Indies proved too big and required padding an inch and a half in thickness to make them fit but, he added, the caps fitted the non-commissioned officers, who were in part of white descent, without any additional aid; he also stated that white infants who had been fed on the milk of Negro wet nurses subsequently suffered in appearance and temperament). Smith accepted the principle that ontogeny recapitulated phylogeny which established, he thought, that cerebral progress was most complete at birth in the Caucasian type:

the human brain successively assumes the form of the Negroes, the Malays, the Americans, and the Mongolians, before it attains the Caucasian . . . One of the earliest points where ossification commences, is the lower jaw. This bone is therefore sooner completed than any other of the head, and acquires a predominance which it never loses in the Negro. (1848: 125–7, 159–60)

As in other versions of typology, Smith's formulation contained the beginnings of a theory of racial relations, since he referred to 'the deep rooted hatred of the Caucasian races towards the typical Negro'. As in Gobineau, though several years earlier, there was also a subsidiary and undeveloped theme which found in the mixing of races something important to the creation of civilisations. Thus he wrote of the 'amalgamation of the typical stocks, without which no permanent progress in the path of true civilization is made'. The black stock had nothing to contribute since 'the good qualities given to the Negro by the bounty of Nature, have served only to make him a slave'. Thus, 'No people of the typical

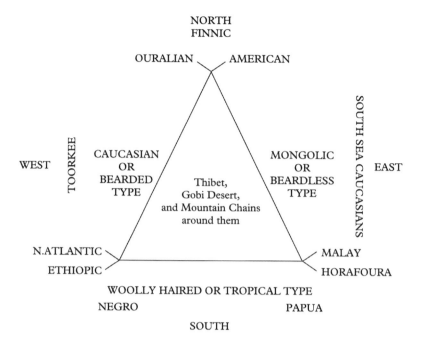

Figure 3.3 Charles Hamilton Smith's view of the primeval location of mankind and the three typical stocks

stocks could arrive at a progressive social existence, without intermixture of one or more branches of the homogeneous nations of the bearded and beardless forms; and through these, such rudiments of advancement as can be traced among the woolly haired, were likewise engendered' (1848: 334, 120, 197, 179). Here, then, in lectures originally given to the Plymouth Institution between 1832 and 1837, was most of the theory that occasioned the controversies of the 1850s.

A more pugnacious propagandist for typology was Robert Knox (1791–1862), the son of an Edinburgh school teacher who graduated in medicine in 1814, and served as an army surgeon in Belgium and for three years in South Africa. He studied in Paris and then went on to establish himself as a very successful lecturer in anatomy in his native city. In 1828 misfortune struck him. Medical teachers in Edinburgh, as elsewhere, needed cadavers for teaching purposes and often had to obtain them from disreputable sources. Two men, Burke and Hare, who were convicted of murder, had sold the body of their victim to an agent acting on behalf of Dr Knox. Though Knox was formally cleared of liability for

the actions of Burke and Hare, his position in Edinburgh became untenable. Thereafter he held only occasional medical appointments and maintained himself for some periods by writing and lecturing. The unhappi-
ness he must have experienced may help to explain the disjointed and
dogmatic nature of his pronunciations upon race when they appeared in
1850) as a book of lectures entitled *The Races of Men*. A second edition,
with a new appendix, was brought out in 1862.

W. and R. Chambers, the Edinburgh publishers already mentioned,
arranged for the publication in 1842 of Quetelet's *A Treatise of Man*. Knox
was responsible for its translation from the French and he added an
appendix, partly on the pulse rate and partly on the effects of climate. In it
he explained that the various climates could be classified as two zones
(inter- and extra-tropical, the latter being subdivided into two or three
regions). The tropical regions of the Old World had been inhabited from
the earliest historic period by the Negro and other dark-coloured races;
the temperate region of the extra-tropical zone had been held by the Celtic
and Saxon races. Celts and Saxons when living in the tropics, unless at
great elevation, suffered greatly from fevers and did not live long. Knox
reviewed the evidence suggesting that neither temperature nor humidity
was the cuase. He contributed his own observation that 'when our troops
occupied Walcheren and Flushing, during the deplorable scheme of
invading Europe, the mortality assumed a most alarming character'.
Fevers killed the French and the British but not the Dutch. Since the
English and the Dutch derived from one parent stock he concluded that
acclimatisation must take several generations, during which relatively few
might survive. The Dutch had survived, even prospered, at the Cape,
presumably because they had never laboured. If the Celt and Saxon were
to maintain their populations in other zones they required a slave population of native labourers. Knox concluded that when these matters had
been more fully investigated, and fitting remedies discovered, Europeans
would be able with confidence to emigrate to Canada and certain other
regions. This opinion he subsequently modified.

In *The Races of Men*, Knox elaborated upon what he called 'transcendental anatomy', an expression used by Geoffroy but which Knox said
was coined by his esteemed friend and teacher (and Cuvier's successor)
H. M. D. de Blainville. Knox described it as originating from South
Germany and from a mixture of the Slav and Gothic races. Its object was
'to explain in a connected chain the phenomena of the living material
world'; to show that 'all animals are formed upon one great plan'.
'"There is but one animal, not many" was the remarkable expression of
Geoffroy; it contains the whole question. What was, now is, under other
forms; but the essence is still the same.' As there was only one creation, 'in

time there is probably no such thing as species' but 'for a few centuries organic forms seem not to have changed'. This theory had been popularised in Britain (and, according to Knox, misstated) by the anonymous author of a best-selling work *Vestiges of Creation*. Geoffroy claimed that the unity of animal forms could be proved by the examination of embryonic forms. Knox also started from the recapitulation theory: 'whatever is irregular in man is a regular structure in some lower animal and was in him a regular structure during his embryonic life. This law . . . is the basis of the law productive of irregular form in man – the law of deformation.' Variety was deformity. It was balanced by 'the law of unity of the organization' (Knox, 1862: 167, 175, 477). Knox summarised his argument as follows:

The races of men differ from each other, and have done so from the earliest historic period, as proved –

1. By their external characters, which have never altered during the last six thousand years.
2. By anatomical differences in structure.
3. By the infertility of the hybrid product, originating in the intermingling of two races.
4. By historic evidence, which shows that no distinct hybrid race can ever be shown to exist anywhere.

But his summary is scarcely complete, for elsewhere Knox insisted on including in his typology of races not only their external characters, but their internal ones as well. He believed that men differ more in their intelligence than their physique. By intelligence he meant what is now called culture, for he included religion, literature and morale in the characteristics of a race. One consequence was his readiness to include racial attitudes among the criteria of classification. This can be noticed in his discussion of 'Hottentots or Bosjemen':

Did the Dutch, the Christian Dutch, consider these races to be men and women? I scarcely think so . . . The coloured men the Dutch called boys, and the coloured women they called maids . . . *De facto*, then, the Dutch did not hold these races to be the same as their own. (1862: 503, 233)

Like Smith (and, before them both, Cuvier) Knox did not distinguish clearly between type and race but used the latter synonymously with species. Perhaps he was the more inclined to do so because of the popular character of his lectures. As Michael Biddiss has observed, Knox's chief concern was to awaken his contemporaries to the fundamentally racial nature of the chief political conflicts within Europe at mid-century. Four main races were the parties to these conflicts. The first was that of the Scandinavians who were naturally democratic but refused to extend to subordinated peoples their own principles of freedom and justice. Second came the Celts, who were notable warriors but had less understanding of liberty, being incapable of implementing ideas of freedom in government. Third were the Slavonians who had great intellectual and political potential. Had they a leadership conscious of the racial nature of their problems they might yet liberate themselves from the Habsburg, Brandenburg and Romanov tyrannies. Fourth came the Sarmantians or Russ, who were incapable of real achievement in literature or science. Their blind obedience to despots made them a threat to liberty (Biddiss, 1976: 249). Knox never drew attention to intra-racial differences or attributed to race any variations within countries, though his vocabulary was often lacking in precision. Thus he wrote: 'The really momentous question for England, as a *nation*, is the presence of three sections of the Celtic race still on her soil.' He referred to the Scots, Welsh and, of course, the Irish:

the source of all evil lies in the race, the Celtic race of Ireland . . . *the race* must be forced from the soil; by fair means, if possible; still, they must leave. England's safety requires it. I speak not of the justice of the case; nations must ever act as Machiavelli advised: look to yourself. (1862: 378–9)

Knox did not explain why the soil of Ireland belonged to the English, for though he wrote at times as if each race had its particular province, and though he could assert that a race could not be changed 'so long as they occupy the soil on which nature first placed them', he suggested no principles for mapping the natural zones of races (as Agassiz had done).

Nevertheless, Knox adhered fairly closely to all three distinguishing tenets of the typological school. As to the first, he maintained that 'human character, individual and national, is traceable solely to the nature of that race to which the individual or nation belongs' and went on to explain that while there was a process of biological development 'organic forms seem not to have changed . . . for a few thousand years'. Concerning the second, Knox wrote, 'I feel disposed to think that there must be a physical and, consequently, a psychological inferiority in the dark races generally.' The third proposition of the typological theory is evident in passages such as 'The various species of Men constitute one great natural family. Each species or race has a certain degree of antagonism to the others, some more, some less.' Of the darker races, 'Furthest removed by nature from the Saxon race, the antipathy between these races is greater than between any other: in each other they perceive their direct antagonists.' Knox stated explicitly that 'Climate has no influence in permanently altering the varieties or races of men' and that hybrids were ultimately sterile. He subscribed to the same kind of environmentalism as Agassiz and Nott and was ready to draw the conclusion that racial superiority was limited by natural boundaries; thus, remarking on the inordinate self-esteem of the Saxon, he insisted:

his race cannot domineer over the earth – cannot even exist permanently on any continent to which he is not indigenous – cannot ever become native, true-born Americans – cannot hold in permanency any portion of any continent but the one on which he *first* originated. (Knox, 1862: v–vi, 53, 224, 449; 1863: 254)

When he wrote a textbook for medical students, Knox was much more cautious. He stated that the human species was 'composed of a number of distinct races, which are usually called varieties, the extent and origin of which have not as yet been determined' though 'they are of vast antiquity'. After listing some, he wrote 'these races differ from each other in their intellectual characters and physical structure; but it is probable, and as regards structure, it is certain, that the differences are to a great extent, unimportant'. The most remarkable differences were those to be found among the Bosjeman (or Hottentots). Races 'thrive best in the land on which they were originally found'. In apparent contradiction to his popular lectures Knox testified, 'Man is everywhere the same; actuated by the same feelings, passions and desires.' He thought it 'by no means improbable' that each race could produce its own kind of civilisation, like the Coptic, Phoenician, Persian, Saracenic, Etrurian, Mexican, Peruvian and Chinese. 'The present forms of European civilization, using the term in its most extended sense, are modelled on these, for it does not appear that any form of civilization ever originated with the western European races' (Knox, 1857: 168–71).

Politically, Knox was a radical who sympathised with the French Revolution, a man who dismissed stories of cannibalism as 'a romance invented by Catholic missionaries' and declared that 'as a Saxon I abhor all dynasties, monarchies and bayonet governments'. His radicalism and his belief in racial zones came together in his criticism of imperialism and 'that den of all abuses, the office of the Colonial Secretary'. Writing about racial antagonism in South Africa, he declared that there the Anglo-Saxon and Dutch Saxon:

so debase the coloured races as to deprive them for ever of all chance of recovering that inestimable treasure beyond all price or value, freedom of speech, thought, and action; in a word, the rights of man. How has this antagonism of race arisen? The truth is, it has always existed, but it never appeared in its terrible form until the Saxon race began to migrate over the earth, to establish free colonies as they are called – free to the white man and their own race – dens of horror and cruelty to the coloured. (Knox, 1862: 27, 222, 470, 546)

Knox's influence was considerable. One of his biographers (Lonsdale, 1870: 292–3) testifies, 'Previous to his time, little or nothing was heard about Race in the medical schools, he changed all this by his Saturday's lectures, and Race became as familiar as household words to his students, through whom some of his novel ideas became disseminated far and wide, both at home and abroad.' Knox's influence was the greater because he attracted an energetic disciple, James Hunt (1833–69). Hunt inherited from his father the ownership of an establishment for the cure of stammering, on which he wrote an authoritative textbook. Hunt graduated D.Phil from the University of Giessen (with which he had a family connection) in 1856 and was awarded an honorary MD from the same university in 1867. He was a man of great energy who led a breakaway from the Ethnological Society to found the Anthropological Society of London (Stocking, 1971, 1987: 247–56; for a review of Knox's biology and his influence on the debates of the 1860s see Richards, 1989). In his presidential address to the new society in 1865, Hunt declared that the Negro belongs to a distinct type. The term species, in the present state of science, is not satisfactory.' He ended with six conclusions much like Nott's, but including

4. That the Negro becomes more humanized when in his natural subordination to the European than in any other circumstances.
5. That the Negro race can only be humanized and civilized by Europeans.

Quite how this humanising and civilising was going to take place was by no means clear, for in a paper published just after his death Hunt (1870: 137) asserted that races could not long survive outside their natural zones. In transmitting the lessons of his science Hunt affected the same tones of Olympian disdain as characterised the prose of Knox, Gobineau and Nott:

Anthropological science cannot consent to consult the wishes or prejudices of the subjects with which it has to deal. Whilst, therefore, fully admitting the power of civilised men to struggle for a time against the decrees of nature, we must yet venture to point out even to the boastful Anglo-Saxon, that the world is not for him; and that although his skill in war and chicanery may exterminate native races, it will yet be demonstrated that in the New World the almost exterminated savages will be amply revenged by a slow gradual degeneracy, and perhaps final extinction, of their conquerors.

Hunt was an effective publicist but no original contributor to his chosen field. In his short and fairly spectacular career he seems to have had no experience outside Europe and to have been motivated primarily by his enthusiasm for a theory which he believed of the greatest relevance to the problems of his age.

The typological school

From the time of Richard Colfax onwards there were authors, especially in the United States, who elaborated upon the alleged deficiencies of Negroes by comparison with Caucasians. Such attempts to explain the differences between two groups were less convincing than theories which recognised variations between a larger number of races and claimed to account for them all in terms of general principles. The Typological Theory was of the greater power because, in the eyes of some people at least, it seemed able to do this. The view which sees typology as the development of trends inherent in pre-Darwinian biological thought is strengthened by its independent appearance in the United States, France and Britain. Because of the tradition of *Naturphilosophie*, Germany did not contribute on the same scale, but there was a distinct echo from the ebullient Karl Vogt (1817–95), or 'monkey Vogt' as he was called when he took up Darwinian doctrine. Vogt was a professor of anatomy at Giessen, a radical and militant materialist, who also occupied a parliamentary seat and participated in the revolutionary movements of his time. He was the subject of Marx's diatribe, *Herr Vogt*. Dismissed from his chair at Giessen, he obtained another in geology at Geneva. Vogt was first a follower of Cuvier who translated *The Vestiges of Creation* into German while standing aside from its evolutionary speculations. His materialism was evident in his *Lectures on Man* (1863) which maintained that the cultural development of races corresponded to variations in their cranial capacity. He asserted that 'the differences in the human genus which we may designate either races or species . . . are original'. Negro intellectual development was arrested at puberty. Vogt quoted 'the general rule of the slaveholder' that Negro slaves 'must be treated like neglected and badly brought up children' (1863: 440, 191–3 and on typology, 214–21). Yet in contradiction of his own arguments he drew attention to measurements reporting a lower cranial capacity for Negroes in the United States than in Africa and asked 'is this the effect of that cursed institution which degrades men to the condition of chattel?' His radical spirit rising, he remarked that as slavery exercised an equally injurious influence on the master it would be worth collecting the skulls of the Civil War dead to test the hypothesis that the cranial capacity of white Southerners had been reduced below that of Northerners. By the end of the book he had grasped the significance of Darwin's message about the mutability of types and was speculating about man evolving from multiple origins to interbreed: 'the innumerable mongrel races gradually fill up the spaces between originally so distinct types, and, notwithstanding the constancy of characters, in spite of the tenacity with which the primitive races resist alteration, they are by fusion slowly led towards unity' (1863: 92, 448, 468).

It is also worth noting a passage in which Vogt bade his hearers look westwards:

the Anglo-Saxon race is itself a mongrel race, produced by Celts, Saxons, Normans and Danes, a raceless chaos without any fixed type; and the descendants of this raceless multitude have in America so much intermixed with Frenchmen, Germans, Dutch, and Irish, as to have given rise to another raceless chaos, which is kept up by continued immigration. We can readily believe that from this chaos a new race is gradually forming. (Vogt, 1863: 433)

Yet it would not include the German Saxon race, for that had become a fixed type which had not changed, even in America. The notion of a 'raceless chaos' was later perverted and popularised by his one-time pupil Houston Stewart Chamberlain. But Vogt's book is more interesting as an example of a scientist's inconsistencies as he comes to accept a new theory; the author's combination of political radicalism with the assertion of racial inferiority is also worth some attention as a pointer to the differences in the intellectual scene of his day and our own.

Unlike Darwin, who led a secluded life and avoided political issues, those who expounded the typological doctrine responded wholeheartedly to the movements of their time. They were also less ethnocentric than most of their contemporaries. For most of them it was important to resist the representatives of organised religion who claimed to determine the proper scope of scientific research. After religion, the main external influence upon their work derived from the political struggles within Europe. In explaining how he came to write his *Essay*, Gobineau referred explicitly to 'the great events, the bloody wars, the revolutions', referring to the upheavals of 1848. That year was described by T. H. Hodgkin as remarkable 'for the savage atrocities which have signalized those wars of races which have disgraced it'. He must have supposed that there were racial divisions within national populations or between them and their rulers. The 'great events' began in the February when the French king was forced to abdicate. In March the population of Vienna revolted and drove out Metternich, the famous Austrian state chancellor. A new constitution was promised. Five days later there was a revolution in Berlin. The king surrendered to the people and it was agreed that an assembly of representatives would meet in Frankfurt. Schleswig-Holstein claimed independence from Denmark. The Italians drove the Austrian garrisons out of Milan and Venice, and nationalist secessions were threatened throughout the Austrian empire. The Czechs took the first steps towards home rule. In April there were riots in London and the government had to bring in troops, barricade the bridges, and garrison many public buildings. All Europe was affected. The uprisings were popular movements directed against hereditary wealth and power. Social and economic changes, which some see as the signs of an expanding industrial capitalism, broke the traditional structures in favour of social mobility and parliamentary democracy. In the long run, the greater competition for status probably made people more conscious of status distinctions, such as those linked with racial differences; the typologists, however, thought that the upheavals demonstrated the power of underlying racial forces. Knox and Vogt, the radicals, welcomed these changes; Gobineau thought they justified his pessimism.

Events overseas probably gave the typological theory an extra plausibility when they appeared as conflicts between Europeans and members of coloured races. The China war, the Crimean war, the Indian 'Mutiny', the civil war in the United States, the Jamaican uprising of 1865 could all be seen as matters of race, but the 1860s were not an expansionist age and Gladstone's cabinet of 1868 is sometimes considered as marking the high point of *anti*-imperialist sentiment. Imperialism was in no sense a popular political idea before Disraeli's second premiership of 1874–80 and there is no clear evidence that British imperialism and Victorian ideas of race are linked in any causal way. Certainly the climate of opinion in Britain was changing at this time. The opportunities for schooling were being extended. Literacy was growing rapidly and there was a burgeoning popular literature. More men were being given the vote. The prospects of greater social mobility increased status consciousness. Douglas Lorimer, an author sensitive to the possible influence of external conditions upon racial thought, and one who has looked closely into the Victorian debate on what was sometimes called 'the Negro Question', has concluded that changes in English society were the main influences responsible for an increase in racial sentiment. The doctrines counted for less. He dates the more strident racialism from the 1850s but believes that it did not materialise before the 1870s and 1880s, so it cannot have exerted much influence upon the writers of the 1850s. Lorimer refers to a 'transition in racial attitudes from an earlier ethnocentric response to a more openly racist one' as reflecting not the 'needs of Empire' but 'new attitudes towards social status emerging within English society' (Lorimer, 1978: 15–16, 208).

To notice the respects in which the typological theory grew out of earlier reasoning about differences between species and varieties is to examine it in terms of the internal history of racial thought. That perspective surely shows that however prejudiced the writers may or may not have been, their arguments were constrained by the available evidence and their need to persuade their audience that their explanations were to be preferred to others. Their arguments need to be studied in the context of their external history also, but no one can assess the significance of the external influences unless their bearing upon the intellectual enterprise of trying to discover new knowledge can be ascertained. Discoveries require hard mental labour and are never the simple product of circumstances.

There was a division within the typological school. Charles Hamilton Smith and Gobineau followed Cuvier in favouring the catastrophic view of geological change; they were correspondingly less inclined to associate racial types with zoological provinces or to stress acclimatisation as a constraint upon European expansion. They allowed for hybridisation among humans and found some complementarity between races. Gobineau in particular left room for major differences of ability within racial groups. The first version of typology could more easily be reconciled with the book of Genesis. By contrast, Nott, Gliddon, Knox and Hunt were more committed to the postulate of permanent types adapted to particular zoological provinces, suggesting that a limited number of racial types (perhaps eight, perhaps more) had existed from the beginning of human life. This version went with the beliefs that racial hybrids were eventually sterile and that races could not acclimatise to new environments. It left less room for intra-racial differences, though Morton thought that some cranial variability might be associated with differences between the social rank of the individuals in question. Those who represented this division within typology expressed themselves forcefully on matters of national politics but were more decidedly critical of imperialism.

It also reveals something of the scientific temper of the typologists to consider how they reacted to Darwin's *Origin*. Knox died only three years after its publication but there is no reason to believe that he had any sympathy for the new theory. His disciple Hunt published a paper (1866) on the application of the principle of natural selection to anthropology which did little more than reiterate old and by then irrelevant opinions in favour of polygenesis. Gobineau seems not to have understood that Darwin had changed the nature of the debate. He thought he could select from Darwin's work the elements that suited him and was attracted to his idea that 'some of our present mongrelized races' might be descended from 'certain beings intermediate between man and the monkey' (Biddiss, 1970: 248). Nott, however, told a friend that he would not have published *Types of Mankind* 'if the prehistoric period of men had been so firmly established as it is at the present day'. He knew that his explanation depended upon a shorter time-scale and that once his assumption was changed, the whole structure was undermined. Another friend also testified that Nott 'was broad enough . . . to accept to the full all of Darwin's views and conclusions' (Stanton, 1960: 186, 237).

This connection between racial typology and seventeenth-century chronology helps illustrate the backward-looking nature of this school of thought when seen within the history of science. Addressing the question, 'Why are they not like us?', the typologists answered, 'Because they have always been different', but they could not explain how it was that each generation of 'us' and 'them' looked like its ancestors. They stressed continuity but could not account for it. Like the eighteenth-century naturalists, they assumed that to classify was to explain.

4   Race as subspecies

In the 1850s two views of human diversity were in contention. The first was associated with a conception of race as lineage and with the ethnological approach. It assumed that all humans had descended from a single ancestral pair and had since diversified, so that it offered a theory of change in which a major influence was exercised in some as yet mysterious way that seemed to be tied to environmental circumstances. The second view was associated with a conception of race as type and with the anthropological approach. It assumed that racial differences had existed from some very early period of prehistory when different stocks had been created either by God or by some natural catastrophe. It offered a theory of continuity based upon the evidence of inheritance. The achievement of Charles Darwin (1809–82) was to subsume these two theories within a new synthesis which explained both change and continuity.

Darwin's method

Darwin utilised a concept of race somewhat obliquely in the fourth edition (1866) of his book *On the Origin of Natural Selection or the Preservation of Favoured Races in the Struggle for Life* (1859). He quoted the reference in one of A. R. Wallace's papers about butterflies in Malaysia, to 'geographical races, or subspecies' as 'local forms completely fixed and isolated'. Because they were isolated they did not inter-breed, and so 'there is no possible test but individual opinion to determine which of them shall be considered as species and which as varieties'. He must have meant that there was no independent test of whether the forms were subspecies, since their geographical isolation prevented any observation of whether they were able to inter-breed. As Darwin was attempting to explain the way living things changed, questions of classification at moments of time were not of central importance. If the general changes in biological thought which he introduced are considered first it should be easier to understand what was entailed in this reference to 'geographical races'. Only now that more than a century has passed since the publication of *The Origin* is it possible fully to appreciate the astonishing range and complexity of Darwin's contribution and the inter-relations between the research he undertook in different fields.

As described by Michael T. Ghiselin (1969: 9–12), Darwin's research and publications can be grouped in six major divisions. The first was that of natural history, in which he assembled observations and gathered specimens more or less as opportunities arose. His years as companion to the captain on the voyage of HMS Beagle exploring the coastline of South America (1831–6), provided many occasions for this kind of natural history. The second division was concerned with geology; it overlapped with the first and was exemplified by three books deriving from that voyage. The third represents his zoological work, such as his studies between 1846 and 1854 on the classification of barnacles. The fourth, or strictly evolutionary, division could be dated from 1837 when Darwin opened the first notebook in which he started to record materials relating to the transmutation of species. In the following year, as a result of reading Malthus' essay on population, it struck him that under conditions of 'struggle for existence . . . favourable variations would tend to be preserved and unfavourable ones to be destroyed. The result of this would be the formation of new species. Here, then, I had at last got a theory by which to work.' In 1842 and 1844 he drafted essays in which he analysed evolution as the outcome of variation, heredity and the struggle for life. In 1858 as a result of the news that A. R. Wallace had independently reached very similar conclusions (also after reading Malthus!) Darwin was impelled to return to this work. A paper under the joint names of Darwin and Wallace was presented to the Linnaean Society. Darwin set about preparing a book that would give a simple account of the views to which he had been led, and this was published as *The Origin*. He later wrote two other books on evolution: *The Variation of Plants and Animals under Domestication* (1862) and *The Descent of Man* (1871). The fifth division of Darwin's work included six major botanical studies, written after *The Origin*, while the sixth division was research of a psychological character dealing both with humans and with earthworms.

There has been no greater scientist than Charles Darwin, and yet there was nothing in his formal education that foreshadowed his later eminence. What enabled him to do such outstanding work? Ghiselin (1969: 4) has no doubt about the answer – his method:

Unless one understands this – that Darwin applied rigorously, and consistently, the modern hypothetico-deductive scientific method – his accomplishments cannot be appreciated. His entire scientific accomplishment must be attributed not to the collection of facts, but to the development of theory.

All the time Darwin worked to gather evidence that bore upon critical hypotheses and he seems to have been puzzled that others should not do likewise, for he wrote to a correspondent, 'How odd it is that anyone should not see that all observation must be for or against some view if it is to be of service.' Again, he wrote that:

False facts are highly injurious to the progress of science, for they often endure long; but false views, if supported by some evidence, do little harm, for every one takes a salutary pleasure in proving their falseness; and when this is done, one path towards error is closed and the road to truth is often at the same time opened.

The finding of the bones attributed to Piltdown Man was a false fact that set anthropologists on a barren trail for decades; the misleading evidence suggesting that Lord Morton's arab mare had borne foals with stripes deriving from a previous mating was another that took longer to put right; Samuel George Morton's misleading presentation of his measurements of cranial capacity was accepted by other people as factual. That the error in the second and third cases arose because someone fitted facts to a mistaken hypothesis shows that it is often difficult to disentangle fact and opinion, but this only reinforces the main argument that research workers need to make their hypotheses explicit and to collect evidence which can effectively test them,

In support of his interpretation Ghiselin asks why, when Darwin had formulated his theory of natural selection, he should have put this work aside to devote eight years to a taxonomic revision of the barnacles? Ghiselin's answer (1969: 113–21) is fascinating. Nothing in evolution is more important than sexuality, for the presence of two sexes produces more genetic variation and permits more rapid natural selection. Darwin had worked out his theoretical views on the evolution of sexuality before undertaking his studies on barnacles. Intending simply to write up some of the work deriving from his South American expedition, he discovered that barnacles furnished evidence bearing upon his theories and so he decided to follow the trail. Some barnacles are hermaphrodites; sometimes there are female barnacles accompanied by dwarf males; Darwin found an intermediate condition in which hermaphrodites were accompanied by dwarf males. This interested him because, as he wrote, 'my species theory convinced me that a hermaphrodite species must pass into a bisexual species by insensibly small states; and here we have it for the male organs in the hermaphrodite are beginning to fail'. Darwin had devised a comparative method by which he analysed vestigal structures to test his hypotheses about the route by which species had evolved. The example shows how he worked out the best questions to ask and then set out to obtain evidence pointing surely towards the answers.

Even so, it was difficult to win other biologists round to his way of thinking. When the President of the Linnaean Society reviewed the work of the society during 1858 he declared that, 'The year . . . has not been marked by any of those striking discoveries . . .' Although *The Origin* made an immediate impact, the theory of natural selection did not win quick or widespread approval. Even Darwin's friends had difficulty understanding it. Thus T. H. Huxley, the man who did most to popularise and defend the theory, and who is reported to have said he was very stupid not to have thought of it for himself, had to struggle with the new perspective. Huxley lectured about it in 1860, yet Darwin wrote that, 'He gave no just idea of Natural Selection' and 'as an exposition of the doctrine the lecture seems to me an entire failure'. One of the reasons why it proved so difficult is that Darwin was advancing not one new theory but several related theories. Ernst Mayr (1982: 505–10) distinguishes five.

Darwin's theories

The first theory, which was the least contentious as far as the scientists were concerned, was that the world was not constant but evolving. The second was the theory of evolution by common descent, which stated that all organisms have descended from common ancestors by a continuous process whereby parental species have split into daughter species. The third was the theory that evolution occurred gradually. This was an argument which those who held an essentialist concept of species could not easily accept, for all their work was built upon the analysis of differences between species. Darwin may have been helped to his views on this matter by his experience on the Galapagos Islands where certain kinds of birds and turtles differed slightly from one island to another. Scientists who worked from fossils could often find no intermediate forms so they deduced that there had been sudden changes and were sceptical of the gradualist view. The fourth theory was that of populational speciation, which held that there was sufficient genetic variability for new species to emerge by a purely random process. This is now known as genetic drift. Two identical populations in similar but separate environments could become distinct without being subject to any external influences. For a long time many evolutionists could not accept this and it still gives rise to debate. The fifth theory was that evolution occurred by natural selection; features which did not help an organism survive in an environment were progressively eliminated.

According to Mayr (1982: 487–8), the single most important step that enabled Darwin to revolutionise biology was the change 'from typological to population thinking'. He was led to it by the realisation, stimulated by Malthus, that the struggle for existence due to competition was a struggle between individuals rather than between species. Those who operated with essentialist concepts assumed that all individual members of a species were fundamentally similar, whereas every animal breeder knew well that no two animals were identical and that by controlling the mating of animals in the herd he could gradually change its composition. Darwin seems to have learned a lot from animal breeders. The essentialists concentrated upon what they regarded as the type or typical form; they regarded varying characters as accidental deviations from the type and as being of no intrinsic interest. Darwin, and those who, after a significant interval, followed him, regarded individual variations as more rewarding of study than the similarities between members of the same class. Population thinking, as Mayr has presented it, requires an understanding of a genus, species or variety as consisting of individuals that are similar in some respects and dissimilar in others. The most generally used criterion to distinguish a species is still that of fertile mating. A subspecies – which is the name now given to what used to be called 'variety' – is defined as a subdivision of a sexual species with all the attributes of a species except that reproductive isolation is partial rather than complete. In other words, *Larus fuscus britannicus* and *Larus fuscus antelius* are subdivisions of *Larus fuscus* which maintain their distinctiveness because they do not share any territory in which they might mate (*Larus fuscus antelius* being found in Siberia) though even if they do meet they may fail to mate, apparently from choice. Gulls belonging to a subspecies may imprint upon parental features like bill, eye colour, eye-ring, etc. and mate only with birds possessing the same features. In this way they can transform themselves into a distinctive species. Among humans, West Africans and Norwegians maintain their distinctiveness because mating is overwhelmingly within the group and there are so few matings between these groups. It is possible that if they shared territory, most individual West Africans and Norwegians would for a time prefer to mate with others of the same appearance as themselves, but their choices would be culturally conditioned since there seems to be little or no imprinting in the human species. Moreover, humans differ in many social attributes, like wealth, which can easily outweigh preferences for physical features. These examples make it easier to appreciate the significance of the conception of a geographical race or subspecies as a distinct local form which maintains its special characteristics; it can evolve to a point such that it is no longer able to inter-breed with other forms that have split off from the same stock. *This* is the origin of species.

Thus Darwin worked with a new conception of species as a genealogical entity. He did not believe, as did the essentialists, that the similarity of species members derived from their common inheritance of a distinctive essence. Nor did he believe, with one school of nominalists, that a species was simply a class consisting of specimens which met chosen criteria of similarity. He saw it as a class which was distinctive because its members inherited common characters but inherited them in different combinations which were subject to continual modification. The grouping of specimens into a species was therefore a matter of judgement, and to this extent arbitrary; but in another sense species were also real entities since their common features derived from the real processes of inheritance and set limits to the exercise of judgement. As Ghiselin (1969: 54–7) writes, this new manner of thinking entailed a concept of population as a system of interacting individuals. The pattern of interaction by its influence upon reproduction, influenced the nature of the individuals which constituted it. This relates to the definition above of a subspecies as a subdivision of a sexual species, because the patterns of reproductive interaction are different in sexual and asexual species.

The implications of sexuality for the evolution of species are developed in Darwin's book of 1871 entitled *The Descent of Man, and Selection in Relation to Sex*. Its central theme is sexual selection as a special case of natural selection. As the sociobiologists have recently emphasised, a male has sufficient sperm to inseminate numerous females, so his investment in a single copulation is usually small. Males are therefore ready to mate with any female and quite often do not even discriminate between females of their own and other species. A female, however, often produces relatively few eggs and may make a big investment in developing the embryos and taking care of the brood after hatching. If she mates with an unfit male or one of the wrong species she may produce an inferior or sterile brood. So it is in her interest to be selective. In some species, therefore (and the peacock is the most obvious example), males compete with one another to develop the sort of appearance which will give them an advantage in obtaining a mate. Darwin observed that just as the poultry breeder can develop the features of his birds which he thinks beautiful, so female birds in a state of nature have, by a long selection of the more attractive males, added to their beauty; the beautiful ones have thus been able to reproduce more than the ugly ones. Selection, whether artificial (by a human breeder) or natural, or sexual, is a matter of differential reproductive success and in the short run at least it may have nothing at all to do with adaptation to the environment. When male birds with beautiful tails obtain a better chance of securing a mate, the population to which they belong has become a system of individuals interacting in a manner that influences the population's evolution. This illustrates Ghiselin's argument.

By the time he came to write *The Descent*, Darwin was willing to follow Francis Galton and W. R. Greg in underlining the importance of natural selection as a process affecting the civilised nations and in calling for eugenic measures. He wrote 'the wonderful progress of the United States, as well as the character of the people, are the results of natural selection; for the more energetic, restless, and courageous men from all parts of Europe have emigrated . . . and have there succeeded best'. A few pages later there was an implicit comparison as he wrote about the declining fertility and likely extinction of savage races – with their smaller brains – unable to change their habits when brought into contact with civilised races. At the same time it would be misguided to attribute Darwin's over-emphasis upon the importance of selection in social change to the temper of his times. Darwin's theory does not depend on any analogy with the kind of social struggle supposed to be responsible for nineteenth-century progress. In the study of evolution something corresponding to 'struggle' occurs when one species uses energy to prevent another species feeding on its territory or otherwise competing for resources. This direct competition is contrasted with indirect competition, in which two species feed off the same scarce resource and whichever can feed faster has the advantage. Indirect competition is usually the more important.

The student of evolution is concerned with fitness not in the sense that the medal-winning athlete is fitter than the person who is overweight, but with fitness as an ability to survive and reproduce. The essential element is differential fertility: those populations which are able to reproduce and multiply in successive generations are fitter than those which cannot. Darwin emphasised selection the more heavily in that part of *The Descent* which seems to have a racialist flavour because he subscribed to a blending theory of inheritance according to which an inherited character appears as a compromise between parental attributes (to over-simplify, a black-haired man and a blonde woman will have brown-haired children). He did not know, as Mendel did, that inheritance was particulate. According to a blending theory, if a clever person married someone stupid, the capacities of the former would all be lost in the next generation (a stimulus to eugenic proposals). As the effects (whether beneficent or undesirable) of a new variant would disappear so quickly, selection would have to be drastic to be effective. The cause of variation was not central to Darwin's problem and his mistaken presentation of it has sometimes led to misinterpretations of his argument.

The changes in prevailing modes of thought which Darwin introduced were revolutionary in many respects. Ernst Mayr (1882: 501) lists six in particular:

1 The replacement of a static by an evolving world
2 The demonstration of the implausibility of creationism
3 The refutation of cosmic teleology
4 The application to man of the principle of common descent
5 The explanation of the natural world in terms of natural selection
6 The replacement of essentialism by population thinking.

The readjustments that had to be made were therefore far more extensive than those entailed by the scientific revolutions in the sphere of physics which are most frequently utilised in undergraduate teaching about the philosophy of science. As was only to be expected, they occasioned long and bitter controversies. Darwin himself did not resolve all the difficulties in the new approach or see all its implications. Other scholars, try as they might, often had great difficulty applying the new principles.

Attempted applications

The year 1859 was also notable for the founding of the Société d'Anthropologie de Paris. For the next twenty years or so scholars elsewhere looked to Paris for the most authoritative declarations about racial classifications. The Parisian school was led by the craniologist Paul Broca and its main basis was in anatomy, so it had some difficulty in coming to terms with the new Darwinian interpretation of evolution. A. de Quatrefages, a monogenist, accepted most of Darwin's arguments but objected that Darwin had no clear conception of species: 'he often opposes *species* and *race*, which he also calls *variety*, but without ever stating clearly what he understands by one or the other.' If species were distinct because they could not inter-breed, what explained the emergence of sterility between units that previously had been inter-fertile? Any conception of gradual and progressive evolution was in conflict with 'the isolation of specific groups from the earliest ages of the world, and the maintenance of organic order through all the revolutions of the globe' (1879: 95–102). Darwinian doctrine generated a host of problems. Physical anthropologists were ready to agree that the groups designated races in popular speech were usually political units of mixed origin, but they were reluctant to abandon the polygenetic idea of underlying differences, particularly those associated with the cranium, for they might one day explain much that was puzzling.

For a time, therefore, the idea of race as type persisted alongside that of race as subspecies. The change-over to a Darwinian mode of explanation was neither simple nor straightforward. This may be illustrated by a consideration of the work of someone who occupied only a minor place in the history of science but was much respected in his own generation. John Beddoe (1826–1922) was a president of the Royal Anthropological Institute, Fellow of the Royal Society, Fellow of the Royal College of Physicians and honorary doctor of laws of the University of Edinburgh. He was honoured by anthropological and scientific societies in Belgium, France, Germany, Russia and the United States. Beddoe was an extraordinarily assiduous collector of information about eye and hair colour and of measurements of peoples' heads; yet he did not accept Darwin's view that progress depends upon an investigator's collecting the sort of observation that tells for or against a theory. Beddoe set out to test, not theories, but the reliability of the material with which theories were, one day, to be constructed (1885: 299). His biggest book, *The Races of Britain* (1885), like some of his articles, consists of as many pages of tables as of text.

Beddoe's belief that problems were to be solved by patient labour did not protect him from confusion. He terminated a series of lectures in 1891 by stating three main conclusions. The first was that, 'We have fairly satisfactory proof that under ordinary circumstances the physical characteristics of well-defined races of men, such as form, colour, and even size, are absolutely permanent'. The second, that 'Natural selection may alter the type'; and the third that acquired characters are not inherited. The first two of these conclusions are contradictory. If natural selection alters the type, there can be no permanence of type. Beddoe called himself an evolutionist; he accepted the theory of natural selection; but he had not eliminated from his explanatory scheme a set of typological assumptions that he probably acquired in the years before he became acquainted with Darwin's theories. At one point he declared, 'The rule is that an anthropological type once in possession of the ground is never wholly dispossessed or extirpated.' At another he told his Scottish audience that Sir Walter Scott was 'the product of the Scottish border, and could not have been born anywhere else' (1912: 53, 188), pronouncements which could have come from Knox or Nott. The question to which he led up was, 'To what races or types is the future to belong?' although he had no technique that would enable him to extrapolate from the past to the future. Among humans, he said, natural selection was complemented by conjugal selection. He had checked the hair colour of 524 Bristol women, to find that among those with red or black hair 76.2 per cent were married; among those with fair, brown or dark hair 86 per cent were married (from which it might be inferred, in the phrase of a later generation, that gentlemen prefer blondes). Beddoe also described processes of social selection. He had the greatest respect for Scotsmen and for fair-haired, long-headed, races, but doubted if the future world would belong to them because their birth rate was low. Blond children needed fresh air and abundant food. They did not adapt well to city life and were more likely to die from rheumatism, scarlatina and throat infections. Because of urbanisation England was experiencing a reflux migration: the Gaelic and Iberian races who had earlier been pushed westwards were moving back and tending to swamp the blond Teutons.

Some of Beddoe's statements sound inexcusable to a modern reader (like his observation that Jews are gradually attracting to themselves the whole moveable wealth of the world) but he did not subscribe to the typological thesis that race determined history. His interest was in the way history – especially because of migration and marriage – was changing the old pattern whereby the peoples of different regions each had their distinctive appearance. He wanted to record what remained of the races of Britain before railways and other contemporary changes mixed them up. Beddoe's objection to such mixing was not racialist, but aesthetic, for he feared that if present trends were to continue 'we should have a general prevalence of dull shades of brown to the confusion and despair of artists'. He concluded his lecture:

finally, there are assuredly diversities of gifts pertaining to diverse breeds of men; and unless we are all reduced to the dull dead level of socialism, and perhaps even in that case, for the sake of relief, we shall continue to stand in need of all these gifts. Let us hope, then, that blue eyes, as well as brown eyes, will continue to beam on our descendants, and that heads will never come to be framed all upon one and the same pattern. (1912: 189)

Most physical anthropologists of Beddoe's generation were interested in craniology and there was no reason in principle to suggest that the enormous labour that went into this research would prove of very little long-term value. It was a blind alley in science, but no one could know that at the time. The really difficult question is to decide what an anthropologist of Beddoe's generation should have been studying instead. If Beddoe was biased, what was he biased away from? In retrospect it can be seen that the years from 1859 to 1930 were a dead period for physical anthropology as a generalising science. No progress could be made in solving the central problems until work in other fields – mainly in genetics but also in the study of human development – had reached the point where they could bear effectively on questions about variation in the shape of skulls, and so on. It was a period when physical anthropologists might have been better employed cultivating their links with archaeologists and developing their subject's historical dimension. Had Beddoe and some of his contemporaries appreciated that 'observation must be for or against some view if it is to be of service' they might not have misdirected their energies into such unprofitable channels.

Other anthropologists who tried to apply ideas of natural and social selection to the human species, and particularly to race relations, were less cautious. The three who are often grouped with Beddoe as representatives of an anthropo-sociological school were Otto Ammon in Germany, Georges Vacher de Lapouge in France and G. C. Closson in the United States. The 'laws' postulated by the two first named have been conveniently summarised by Sorokin (1928: 233–51). Vacher de Lapouge was particularly pessimistic, maintaining that natural selection operated to the advantage of the worst elements in the population. In war-time it was the patriots who were killed, not the cowards. In democratic societies the demagogue and trickster triumphed over the honest man. Charity preserved the weak, capitalism destroyed natural aristocracies and the poor had most children:

I am convinced [he wrote in 1887] that in the next century millions will cut each others' throats because of one or two degrees more or less of cephalic index. This is the sign which is replacing the Biblical *shibboleth* and linguistic affinities, and by which people will recognize one another as belonging to the same nationalities and by which the most sentimental will assist in the wholesale slaughter of peoples.

de Lapouge was a socialist who sought to revise Marxist doctrine to accord with what he considered Darwinian principles (Thuillier, 1977: 53–61).

Much of the literature of this period about physical and social differences has been classed by later commentators as social Darwinist, but this is misleading since it is difficult to find among the various authors any group who shared a common set of principles, apart from those who were supporters of the Eugenics Society (Halliday, 1971). There were writers who subscribed to some theses that can reasonably be described as social Darwinist but were fundamentally opposed to other important elements in this same outlook: such was the case of Herbert Spencer (Freeman, 1974). There were other writers, like William Graham Sumner who wrote in a social Darwinist vein at one stage of their careers and then changed their approach (for a critique of the loose use of the term, see Bannister, 1979). In Mayr's view (1982: 883) social Darwinism 'praised struggle for existence, unmerciful competition, and social bias under the excuse that this was what Darwin taught. Unfortunately the historiography of this subject is as biased as was the movement itself.' 'Social Darwinism' is a label applied by its critics to the lines of argument they criticise. If the views of the authors themselves are to be appreciated properly their various arguments need separate examination.

A central figure in the attempt to develop social policies that took account of the discoveries about inheritance was Darwin's gifted cousin Francis Galton. Yet it is notable that such a systematic thinker as Galton should have had no clear conception of race and have used the word in quite different senses (Banton, 1993).This should serve as a caution to anyone who would generalise about the nineteenth-century idea of race. The belief in white racial superiority appears to have reached its highest level in Western Europe in the two decades preceding the First World War, yet in that time there was no publication which set out succinctly a theoretical justification for that belief comparable to the set of propositions featured in Nott and Gliddon's *Types of Mankind*. The most systematic theorist was Vacher de Lapouge, but it is improbable that he and other theorists contributed as much to the belief in white racial superiority as the literary and historical tradition which had equated race with nation. Soon after his appointment, in 1895, as the British Secretary of State for the Colonies, Joseph Chamberlain proclaimed his belief that 'the British race is the greatest governing race that the world has ever seen'. The theorists would have ridiculed the notion of a British race; they saw the British population as forming a political unit composed of peoples of different race. Chamberlain and those who, like him, talked of race in the context of empire, probably regarded race as a synonym for nation. They may have been content that their claims appeared to be supported by biology, but it is doubtful if their use of the word race had the biological connotations a modern reader might assume. Nor did they necessarily believe that hereditary qualities would overcome adverse environmental conditions. The historian J. A. Froude had concluded (1894: 7–8) that 'the experience of all mankind declares that a race of men sound in soul and limb can be bred and reared only in the exercise of plough and spade, in the free air and sunshine, with country enjoyments and amusements, never amidst foul drains and smoke blacks and the eternal clank of machinery'. The anthropo-sociologists were not the only commentators who thought that city life destroyed the distinctive characters of the finer races. Whites might be superior for the time being but their position was precarious. Parents in the higher and more intelligent classes had fewer children; ill educated Irish Catholic parents contributed disproportionately to population growth; eugenic measures were necessary if the national stock was not to decline. Thus in the early years of twentieth-century Britain 'racial hygiene' became a slogan for a campaign to persuade people to wash themselves properly and to lead a healthy life. The confidence about the British race expressed from public platforms by speakers like Chamberlain and Lord Rosebery was therefore only one aspect of a more complex mood.

Popular beliefs in white superiority were probably conditioned by the success of Britain and other European countries in extending their influence over so much of the world. Since the theorists were members of societies in which such beliefs were widespread they were no doubt influenced by them, but the rise in Germany's power and the growing tensions within Europe exerted restraint. Nor was there any close fit between doctrine and practice in countries where whites were in close contact with blacks. A comparison between East Africa and Nigeria in the period 1880–1914 suggests that the stereotype of African inferiority which emerged in Kenya was a European creation deriving from the social and political desires of the white settlers and not from either genuine observations or from European doctrines (Perraton, 1967: 242). In view of the readiness with which some authors have linked social Darwinist ideas with colonial settings it is also notable that a study of the British in Central Africa comments on the absence (at least up to 1890) of any mention of such doctrines in discussions of racial relations or as a justification for imperial control (Cairns, 1965: 237–8).

In the development of sociological explanations a key figure was William Graham Sumner (1840–1910), who became Professor of Political and Social Science at Yale in 1872. He taught there the first college course in the United States to be entitled 'Sociology'. Coming upon Spencer's work and plunging into Darwin, Haeckel, and Huxley as well, Sumner saturated himself with evolutionism (Hofstadter, 1955: 51–66; Bannister, 1979: 97–113). As a social critic, Sumner's sympathies were with 'the forgotten man' – the middle-class citizen who went quietly about his business, providing for himself and his family without making demands upon the state. Society was a super-organism changing at a geological tempo in accordance with natural laws. Socialists and other social meddlers who ignored those laws and engaged in 'the absurd effort to make the world over' were foolish romantics unwilling to learn the lessons of history.

As his teaching became more systematic Sumner regretted the lack of a suitable textbook; he sat down to write one of his own, which became *Folkways* (1906), one of the most influential works of early twentieth-century sociology. Apart from his own ideas, his inspiration came from Herbert Spencer and two Europeans, Julius Lippert and Gustav Ratzenhofer, though he also borrowed the concept of ethnocentrism without acknowledgement from Gumplowicz (1881: 71) and has been credited with its invention by generations of American sociologists who did not read the classics. In *Folkways* Sumner presented a panorama of human customs, interpreting them as instinctive responses to the stimuli of hunger, sex, vanity and fear, selectively guided by pain and pleasure. His emphasis was upon the limited ability of 'stateways' and legislation to change behaviour with its deep physical and emotional roots. This shifted the stress from the efficacy of competition to the stability of social forms. It is evident in the book's most influential innovation, the concept of *mores* (the plural form of the Latin *mos*, meaning custom).

Folkways is subtitled 'A Study of the Sociological Importance of Usages, Manner, Customs, Mores, and Morals'. It brings together reports from different times and different parts of the world concerning such topics as slavery, abortion, infanticide, cannibalism, marriage, incest, kinship, primitive justice, sacral harlotry, and so forth. Sumner begins with the remark that 'the first task of life is to live. Men begin with acts, not with thoughts.' From man's solutions to problems arise customs. From customs and instincts arise folkways, which gradually become arbitrary, and imperative. They are seen as 'right' and 'true'. When they are developed into doctrines of welfare they become mores; this leads to the definition, 'The mores are the folkways, including the philosophical and ethical generalizations as to societal welfare which are suggested by them, and inherent in them, as they grow.' Later comes a chapter entitled 'The Mores Can Make Anything Right and Prevent Condemnation of Anything'. This proposition was demonstrated by examples of modes of punishment and courting customs formerly accepted in Europe which an American of Sumner's generation would have thought contrary to human feeling.

When he came to discuss blacks and whites in Southern society Sumner maintained that prior to the Civil War relations were based on legal rights and the races lived in peace and concord. The war 'was due to a great divergence in the mores of the North and South' and afterwards blacks and whites were left to find a new basis for living together. Because the whites had never been converted from the old mores they and the blacks had not at that time made new mores:

legislation cannot make mores. We see also that mores do not form under social convulsion and discord . . . The two races are separating more than ever before . . . It is evidently impossible for anyone to interfere. We are like spectators at a great natural convulsion. The results will be such as the facts and forces call for. We cannot foresee them. They do not depend on ethical views any more than the volcanic eruption on Martinique contained an ethical element. (1906: 81–2)

There were powerful forces in the United States in favour of a do-nothing policy with respect to Southern race relations. Sumner's presentation of the problem and his use of the concepts of folkways and mores were widely followed by social scientists, particularly to imply that legislation on inter-racial behaviour would be in vain. If he accepted the mores as a homogeneous, unproblematic, and a fairly static social entity, the observer was likely to under-estimate the differences between individuals and groups and the changes in time. In the present connection, however, it is important to note that Sumner's conceptions of the 'struggle for existence' and social selection, though inspired by Spencer and Darwin, were not really Darwinist, and that his concepts of folkways and mores bore little relation to the elements of social Darwinism in his earlier essays.

An important study which cast doubt upon the value of craniological studies was conducted by Franz Boas of Columbia University on behalf of the United States Immigration Commission. Concern had been expressed that the United States was admitting immigrants of inferior stock. Boas examined the hair colour, height and weight, head length and breadth and face breadth, in European-born Americans and their American-born children. In 1911 he reported important differences, particularly in the cephalic index (relation of the breadth of the head to its length, seen from above). The figures suggested that the round-headed East European Jewish children became more long-headed in the United States, whereas the long-headed South Italians became more short-headed. Both were approaching a uniform type. Moreover, the influence of the American environment made itself felt with increasing intensity the longer the time elapsed between the arrival of the mother and the birth of her child. The significance of this finding was negative. 'I find myself unable to give an explanation of the phenomena' wrote the author. Though the changes were small, the findings were in conflict with prevailing expectations and, because they arose within barely a single generation, it did not appear that they could be explained as an outcome of natural selection. Boas concluded 'as long as we do not know the causes of the observed changes, we must speak of a plasticity (as opposed to a permanence) of types' (see 1940: 71). Subsequent research has shown that there was nothing unusual about the changes reported and that, being small, they could be attributed to environmental influences like that of diet (see also Stocking, 1968: 161–94).

Darwin's work destroyed the notion of racial types without replacing it with a concept that could easily be grasped, even by those specialists who were interested in racial variation among humans. Only in the 1930s did the various new lines of research start to come together again in a synthesis which has enabled the student to appreicate why the replacement for the concept of racial type was that of population. The foundation of this synthesis was population genetics, the branch of genetics which investigates the changes in gene frequencies. According to Mayr (1982: 553–6), it consisted of two largely independent research programmes: mathematical population genetics and ecological genetics. The former was a development of the Hardy-Weinberg equilibrium principle established in 1908. Sir Ronald Fisher and other mathematical geneticists extended the statistical analysis by treating the gene as the unit of selection and attributing to each gene a definite fitness value. Fitness was defined as the contribution a given gene makes to the gene pool of the next generation. Mayr (1982: 588–9) remarks that some, if not most, of the current criticism of the theory of selection consists of attacks on what he considers to be an un-Darwinian assumption that genes instead of phenotypes are the units of selection. Ecological genetics, by contrast, deals with the actual populations of living organisms studied in the field and in the laboratory. Selection favours certain qualities but it cannot simultaneously improve all of them to the same degree. A bottom limit is set by the principle that can be traced to Cuvier, that at all stages of evolution an animal must remain able to feed itself, reproduce and evade predators.

Between 1936 and 1947 biologists from several specialised fields and various countries achieved a consensus which Sir Julian Huxley named the evolutionary synthesis. According to Mayr (1982: 567) they accepted two major conclusions:

(1) that evolution is gradual, being explicatory in terms of small genetic changes and recombination and in terms of ordering of this genetic variation by natural selection; and (2) that by introducing the population concept, by considering species as reproductively isolated aggregates of population, and by analyzing the effects of ecological factors (niche occupation, competition, adaptive radiation) on diversity and on the origin of the higher taxa, one can explain all evolutionary phenomena in a manner that is consistent both with the known genetic mechanism and with the observational evidence of the naturalists.

Many of the objections that have been raised against the Darwinian view of evolution turn upon gaps in the fossil record. For example, it has not been easy to show how reptiles could have evolved into mammals. To take a detailed point, the former have a single earbone and at least four bones in the lower jaw, whereas mammals have two further earbones but only one jawbone. Yet fossil finds in England now constitute an almost perfect transition, enabling the palaeontologist to explain how the forces on the jaw joint changed and how the auditory perception was improved. Other finds have pointed the way to more satisfactory explanations of the evolution of the eye, of flight, and comparable problems. Viruses and bacteria can be traced back to pre-Cambrian times, while laboratory experiments can provide accounts of what must have been the earliest self-replicating systems that must have been close to the origin of life itself.

Huxley also joined with the Cambridge anthropologist A. C. Haddon to publicise the wider political significance of the developments in evolutionary biology. Together they published *We Europeans. A Survey of 'Racial' Problems* to explain 'the relative unimportance, from the immediate point of view, of purely biological factors as opposed to social problems in the broadest sense' (1935: 8). They went on to contend that 'it is very desirable that the term *race* as applied to human groups should be dropped from the vocabulary of science . . . the term *sub-species* has been substituted for "race" . . . in what follows the word *race* will be deliberately avoided, and the term *(ethnic) group* or *people* employed' (1935: 91–2). It should be noted, however, that in writing of ethnic groups they were referring to relatively large groups, at the level of nations, and not to the smaller-scale differences at the level suggested by the expression 'ethnic minorities'. This usage will be taken up for discussion in chapters 5 and 7.

Reductionist explanations

The debate about whether human races were distinctive species or subspecies was a dispute about classification. Darwin upset the debate by advancing a convincing theory which showed that species and subspecies were evolving. It might be convenient for some purposes to have snapshots of what they were like at particular moments in time, but that only distracted attention from the invisible influences which were determining the ways in which they changed. These influences were numerous, and their inter-relations complex: on the one hand was the genetic material of inheritance which, though divisible into an extraordinary number of elements, was, in a sense, of a general or standardised character; on the other hand was the innumerable collection of particular circumstances affecting the ways in which different populations in different environments were organised and interacted with their genetic inheritance. Darwin himself gave an illustration of the way different species could be dependent upon one another when he explained how a particular kind of clover could be fertilised only by a bumble bee because honey bees were not heavy enough to make an entrance to the flower. One of the circumstances determining the availability of bumble bees was the vulnerability of their nests to field mice. There were fewer field mice where there were many cats, and many cats where there were human habitations. So the clover could survive more easily near villages.

To account for the various species and subspecies of clover, bees, mice and cats, and the directions in which they were evolving, was hard enough. To do the same for humans was immensely more difficult for a variety of reasons including the special character of the human species, sometimes called its plasticity or adaptability, and its possession of the special attribute of consciousness. Humans can be aware of themselves as individuals belonging to groups, having a place in the natural world, and utilising particular means to attain their goals, in ways that other animals cannot. They have the power to discover the natural influences that bear upon their evolution and to modify these influences, striving for ends that otherwise would not be achieved. To account for the evolution of a species which possesses this kind of consciousness is more difficult than accounting for one without it (Crook, 1980).

This problem may be seen as a special case of the more important problem of differing levels of complexity which has occasioned arguments about reductionist explanations.

They often start from the probability that the world has evolved from inorganic to organic material, and from forms of life without consciousness to those distinctive of humans. For this reason it is appropriate to count the level of human culture as uppermost. It is then maintained that the objects of study at each level are composed of elements found at the level beneath and that they can, in part, be explained by reference to the same principles as are used when accounting for observations on the lower level. The disputes centre upon what is called the 'remainder', those observations which are not accounted for by an explanation in terms of the next level down. Sometimes the issue is put the other way round. It is said that as life evolves, whenever it reaches a new level, new and previously unpredictable characteristics of organising emerge. To discuss levels in terms of reduction is to look at them from a standpoint often used in the philosophy of science. To discuss them in terms of emergence is to follow the course of evolution. By way of illustration it may be helpful to consider courtship. In many human societies certain kinds of behaviour can be identified as courtship, but they vary from one society to another and change over time. The patterns of behaviour are socially or culturally conditioned by the expectations each generation learns from its predecessors and, in industrial societies, by the advertising of goods as likely to impress the people who are the objects of courtship. Seen from a distance, courtship reveals features which may not be in the minds of the people who engage in it. People tend to court others of similar socio-economic status and people who live close enough for frequent contact. Patterns of expected behaviour differ for males and females, and vary according to their ages. It can nevertheless be argued that under these differences lie biological influences, like sexual drives, and personality compatibilities, so that human courtship can be explained in the same terms as the courtship of other species and be the better understood for being located in human evolutionary history. It might be claimed that no explanation of why, among humans, males take the more active part in courtship, can be satisfactory unless it forms part of such a wider account. Yet the process of reduction does not stop with such an explanation. Courtship behaviour is built up out of locomotion, energy utilisation, metabolic processes, and so on, which can be seen as questions of physiology, and these in turn as the expression of molecular genetics and then, perhaps ultimately, as chemistry or physics. The organisation of scientific activity reflects, if only for convenience, such a series of levels in the complexity of phenomena, though the theories of the basic subjects like physics are no simpler than those of the subjects at the other end of the scale.

The reductionist approach draws attention to certain inter-relations between scientific disciplines but some research problems are not usefully formulated in this way. It may be better to regard courtship behaviour as suggesting different questions to the sociologist, geographer, psychologist, ethologist, evolutionist and physiologist. Each kind of specialist seeks to answer his or her own special questions and these sometimes include questions about the relations between the modes of explanation characteristic of different disciplines.

Discussions of the philosophy of social science have been dominated for a whole generation by the work of two men, Sir Karl Popper and Thomas S. Kuhn, who have been concerned with the growth of knowledge about the natural world and have taken nearly all their examples from the history of physics. This has had the unfortunate effect that many sociologists have defined their subject in terms of what differentiates its methods and approach from that of physics. They have overlooked the important differences between the biological and physical sciences and the argument (set out by Mayr, 1982: 77) that evolutionary biology can be a bridge between the physical sciences on the one side and the social sciences and humanities on the other. According to Mayr's argument there have for thousands of years been two biologies. One, which used to be practised under the name of medicine or physiology, has been an attempt to discover proximate causes or to answer 'how?' questions. The other, which has been known as natural history, has studied ultimate or evolutionary causes by addressing 'why?' questions. For example, at certain times of the year particular bird species migrate. The first kind of biologist, whom Mayr calls a functional biologist, explains the migration as a response to photo-periodicity: the bird is ready to migrate once the number of hours of daylight falls to a particular level and it leaves as soon

thereafter as weather conditions are favourable. The evolutionary biologist explains why birds of this species but not other species migrate, by
referring to a genotype acquired through selection over millions of years of
evolution. In evolutionary biology almost all phenomena and processes
are explained through inferences from comparative studies. These depend upon careful and detailed descriptive studies which often have to be
carried out in difficult conditions. Scientific research of this kind is unable
to manipulate the variables, but depends upon good field work. It is not
much concerned with formulating laws, and such laws as have been
advanced are mostly probabilistic statements which are not falsified by a
single contrary instance. The growth of knowledge in this field, as in much
sociology, consists in the development of new concepts and the repeated
refinement of definitions by which these concepts are articulated.

In the latter part of the twentieth century it is taken for granted that the
processes of socio-cultural evolution occur on a higher level than those of
biological evolution. In biological evolution, information is transmitted
from one generation to the next through people's genes. In socio-cultural
evolution, information is transmitted by teaching of either an explicit or
an implicit character. In modern society people learn a great deal from
attending school, reading, watching films and so on. A library represents a
storehouse of information available to people when they want to use it. As
a process for transmitting the results of learning, this is infinitely more
powerful than the passing on of information by inheritance. Of course,
some authors argued this a hundred years ago too, but the differences
were not always clearly expressed and others were inclined to insist that
though there might be a remainder when social phenomena were explained in biological terms, that remainder was neither very large nor very
important. It was therefore a significant achievement when social scientists first described the emergent phenomena and showed how they
necessitated new socio-cultural processes of evolution. One influential
statement of this kind was the paper by the United States anthropologist
A. L. Kroeber (1917) in which he distinguished between organic evolution and what he called superorganic evolution. A parallel declaration
was that of the sociologist Robert E. Park when he wrote:

The individual man is the bearer of a double inheritance. As a member of a race,
he transmits by interbreeding a biological inheritance. As a member of society or a
social group, on the other hand, he transmits by communication a social inheritance. The particular complex of inheritable characters which characterizes the
individuals of a racial group constitutes the racial temperament. The particular
group of habits, accommodations, sentiments, attitudes and ideals transmitted by
communication and education constitutes a social tradition. (Park and Burgess,
1921: 140–1)

The levels of complexity are distinguished by the mode of inheritance, either biological or biological plus social.

It is not always so easy to distinguish one level from another. Questions arise as to how many levels can usefully be identified, and about the relations between them. Lower levels may set limits to what can be done on higher levels, but do they exercise a continuing influence or an occasional one? Do not the higher levels sometimes influence what happens on the lower levels? One use of the notion of levels that has been much discussed in social science, is that of Karl Marx. In the preface to his *A Contribution to the Critique of Political Economy* (1859) Marx stated that the foundation of social life consisted in the material productive forces (the ways in which humans win a living from nature) and in the relations of production necessary to the harnessing of these forces (e.g. the social organisation used to herd the cattle, till the fields or fish the waters). Upon this infrastructure arose a legal and political superstructure conditioned by the mode of production. The technology for utilising the material productive forces developed; every now and then it reached a point at which its further development was restricted by the superstructure which conditioned the ways in which humans thought about their societies. At that point the productive forces broke the restraining bonds and forced through a revolution in which the superstructure was brought into line with the form that the process of production had assumed. In this vision, the lower levels dictated to the higher ones though in between periods of revolution the superstructure might develop in independent ways. It was a scheme for interpreting history.

The element of reduction in this kind of argument differs from that mentioned earlier. Marx did not maintain that the activity of people engaged in the productive process was to be explained in terms of their physiology and then as a product of their genes. Nor did he claim that the legal and political superstructure differed from the relations of production in the sort of way that human social organisation differed from that of apes, or animal society from plant society.

The notion of levels can be used in varying ways for varying purposes and as many levels can be distinguished as is useful to an argument. For example, it could be argued that with the growth of cities men have competed more fiercely for ownership of the land in the centre than for land on the outskirts because possession of the former confers greater advantages. Such competition occurs on the ecological level and can be compared with the competition of animals for territory within which to forage or nest. Among humans it gives rise to differential land prices. Since land in the centre is expensive it is used more intensively. The buildings in the city centre become multi-storey office blocks. Only very rich people can afford houses in this zone. Thus economic and social patterns are determined by ecological ones. These patterns have their own dysfunctions in the form of congestion and pollution. With technological advance and higher living standards, more people have their own means of transport. Shopping centres and new businesses are then located away from the centre and relative land prices change because new economic and social relations have affected ecological ones. In such an argument it is unwise to push the claim that changes on the lower level determine changes on the upper one because many variables are involved and technological innovation is usually an extraneous factor. Yet the notion of levels is useful because it can be used in a way that, by drawing attention to new parallels, suggests novel questions to ask. In this manner it can open fresh and illuminating perspectives.

Social ecology

The pioneer of ecological analysis in sociology was Robert E. Park (1863–1944). Other writers have discussed his contribution to symbolic interactionism (Lal, 1990; Lyman, 1992) but his contributions to the study of inter-group relations were inspired by the ecological perspective. One of his pupils, Everett C. Hughes, wrote in 1973:

Park was interested in human ecology as early as 1913 and '14 and tried to persuade his son to become a human ecologist starting with the study of biology of the new ecological sort. When he came to Chicago [in 1913] there was such an interest in the city and the things that were happening to the immigrants there, that he fell in with the project and devoted himself to it rather fully for quite a long time. In 1925 or so, he first gave a course in 'Human Ecology'. I was in it. The emphasis was on large scale human geography; the development of navigation, of world-wide insurance, and news-gathering, and all those devices which made it possible to colonize and to establish economic enterprises at a great distance . . . Park was interested in smaller scale problems but that was only a phase, and not the major one of his thought and career. After he left Chicago at the end of the 1920s, he began his more serious writing on human ecology, considering it as the competition and accommodations made by human beings in their occupancy of the whole of the earth's surface. In his later papers he is interested in the division of labor between the races and the nations. He sees migration as the great process; that and competition are very important in bringing about whatever kinds of communities there are in the world.

Park's conviction that something new was to be learned about human society by noting the features it shared with animal and plant society can be seen in the very influential textbook written by him and his colleague Ernest W. Burgess. Entitled *An Introduction to the Science of Sociology*, this appeared in 1921 and contained 174 passages extracted from the works of a variety of authors but bound together in a distinctive synthesis. A prominent place was given to ecological concepts, for Park sought to utilise accounts of the lives of plants, ants, pigs and so on, both to bring out that which was distinctively human and to uncover patterns of unconscious relations. Modern sociologists may recognise concepts of adaptation, colonisation, commensalism, dominance, invasion, isolation, migration, parasitism, segregation, succession and symbiosis, even if they do not use these themselves. They may forget that all of them are ecological concepts that can be applied to plants as well as humans. Plant life, wrote Park, offered the simplest examples of communities that were not societies. Anyone who has tended a rock garden has seen how some species spread at the expense of others, acquiring a monopoly over a territory. Some plants live together in peace. Others migrate or invade and establish their dominance. Sometimes one species gives way to a series of others, establishing a natural succession. Such concepts the Chicago school of sociology afterwards used in their studies of the natural areas of the city.

When using ecological concepts it is often helpful to distinguish different levels of organisation. In 1921 Park and Burgess described competition as the most fundamental of four such levels, relating them to different types of interaction: the most fundamental type of interaction was competition, which gave rise to ecological organisation. This represented human individuals and groups as competing for territory and resources in a manner comparable to animals and plants. On the second level was economic organisation, manifested in the division of labour produced by competition. This was the level on which racial and other forms of group consciousness appeared. The third level, that of political organisation, was a means of dealing with the crises generated by economic organisation. At this level three new types of interaction, conflict, accommodation and assimilation, appeared. Then came the fourth level of social organisation (to give it the name proposed by Frazier, 1957: 34). In 1921 Park did not separate this from the third level, though in 1939 he called it the level of the personal and cultural, maintaining that 'one may think of these different levels as constituting a hierarchy of relations of such a nature that change upon any one level will invariably have repercussions, not immediately, but finally, upon every other' (1950: 107).

The ecological perspective explains why the Park and Burgess *Introduction* gives space to many matters foreign to modern textbooks and neglects some topics that now feature prominently. The chapter on competition includes a famous passage from Adam Smith on the natural harmony of individual interests, explaining how by pursuing his own interest a man is led as by an invisible hand to promote the common good in the most effectual manner. Park did not regard this proposition as necessarily applying outside the economic sphere, yet it is striking that the chapter on conflict includes no discussion of conflicts of interest (indeed the notion of interest appears chiefly in a psychological sense, 'an unsatisfied capacity, corresponding to an unrealized condition'). Conflict is presented only as a feature of collective behaviour without mention of the way conflicts are structured or individuals coerced. It is said that 'the psychological bond of the class is community of interests' but there is no discussion or proper definition of class. The unity of the social group among humans in described in terms of shared social tradition without mention of external oppositions. 'All social problems turn out finally to be problems of social control' (1921: 785), yet there seems to be no place for a conception of power in the elucidation of these problems! Nowhere in the book is there reference to such matters as the inheritance of social inequality. Valuable as was Park's use of the ecological metaphor it may have contributed to some blind spots in his analysis of types of interaction as forming the superstructure of social patterns. The study of collective behaviour needs to be complemented by the study of social structure.

The direction of Park's personal interests may explain his description of Sumner's *Folkways* as 'the most subtle analysis and suggestive statement about human nature and social relations that has yet been written in English'. Park not only included selections concerning folkways, mores, and the in-group/out-group distinction, but adopted in his commentary some of Sumner's basic assumptions. 'As members of society, men act as they do elsewhere from motives that they do not fully comprehend, in order to fulfil aims of which they are dimly or not at all conscious . . . Under the influence of the mores men act typically, and so representatively, not as individuals but as members of a group.' Park distinguished the political from the cultural process. Politics were concerned with matters in regard to which there was division and difference, but 'the political process, by which a society or social group formulates its wishes and enforces them, goes on within the limits of the mores' (1921: 30, 52–3). This meant that every time a Negro appeared in an unaccustomed situation it provoked comment as something contrary to the mores. Though Park might himself have acknowledged that this was a facet of the relations of power between black and white he did not say so and his writing, like that of most of his contemporaries, neglects this dimension in a fashion that must astonish a later generation.

The chapters in the *Introduction* dealing with race relations, like those reflecting the ecological approach, were mostly Park's works. Ecology was rarely absent from Park's view of race relations; it underlay his conception of prejudice which he defined as 'a spontaneous, more or less instinctive, defence-reaction, the practical effect of which is to restrict free

competition between races'. Prejudice was an attempt to restrain competition, to establish a monopolistic hold over a particular social territory
(1921: 623). On another, later, occasion, Park asked why anyone should
expect racial peace before there was racial justice, but the difficulty with
his early formulation was that it left no place for such considerations. Park
observed that caste, by relegating the subject race to an inferior status
gave it a monopoly over the unattractive roles at the same time as it gave
the other category its monopoly. He went on 'when this status is accepted
by the subject people, as is the case where the caste or slavery systems
become fully established, racial competition ceases and racial animosity
tends to disappear. This is the explanation of the intimate and friendly
relations which so often existed in slavery between master and servant.'
Slavery was discussed in the chapter on accommodation, not in that on
conflict. There was no mention, for example, of slave revolts, suicides or
escapes. If conflict, accommodation, and assimilation were types of interaction which were acted out on a basis of the more fundamental phenomenon of competition some means had to be found for analysing monopoly
power and the processes by which part of the population was reduced to
inferior statuses. This Park did not achieve. He saw the process of
competition as resulting in an economic equilibrium on which a political
order was built, and did not consider the ways in which political considerations dictated the terms on which individuals could compete (1921:
510). Racial conflicts sprang from the unwillingness of those of superior
status to compete on equal terms with those of inferior status (1921:
578). The aggressive aspects of prejudice were not mentioned; nor were
ways in which unwillingness to compete was translated into political
action and that action then intensified the original unwillingness.

In 1921 it was not generally appreciated, even among social scientists,
that racial prejudice was a disposition towards other groups that children
learned as they grew up. Perhaps only a minority claimed explicitly that
prejudices were biologically inherited characteristics of a group, but many
more took racial prejudice for granted as something scarcely requiring
investigation. This was the background to the discovery of stereotyping.
In the early 1920s an American educational research worker gave some
classes of school children the following silent reading test:

Aladdin was the son of a poor tailor. He lived in Peking, the capital city of China.
He was always lazy and liked to play better than to work. What kind of boy was he:
Indian, Negro, Chinese, French or Dutch?

To his amazement, he found that many children in the border states were
so impressed by the statement that the boy was lazy that they answered
that he must be a Negro (Lasker, 1929: 237). From his, and others'

observations grew a series of enquiries into the promotion and function of set ideas, followed later by psycho-analytic studies of prejudice. They were intellectually exciting developments that transformed the understanding of race relations. Park is not to be criticised for a failure to utilise perspectives that had not been opened up, though, in retrospect, it does appear as if he failed to appreciate to the full all that W. I. Thomas had written about the social factors influencing the expression of racial prejudice as early as 1904. Park's tendency to see prejudice from the standpoint of the more powerful group was also evident in his description of it as a 'phenomenon of the group mind', presenting prejudice against the Japanese as a reaction to their having the wrong skin colour and not as a consequence of white prejudgements which themselves require analysis (1921: 623–5, 760–1). It is important not to pillory an author by picking out passages that convey an untruthful impression. Park's statements about prejudice are all of them defensible and many of them draw attention to aspects of these phenomena previously neglected. Most of the criticism must be about the inadequacies of his presentation arising from what he failed to say. His pioneering interest in collective behaviour proved valuable for the development of American sociology but a critic must insist that collective behaviour cannot be understood in any depth if it is isolated from the structures that can mould it just as much as the instincts and other qualities of human nature to which Park and Burgess devoted so many pages.

After the publication of the textbook some signs appeared of Park's broadening his approach to these questions. Offering suggestions as to the material needed for a survey of race relations on America's Pacific coast, Park in 1923 opened his remarks with the statement, 'Race conflicts have their biological and economic aspects but it is the attitudes they express and provoke which are of first importance.' He went on to develop an alternative to the earlier view of attitudes as biologically determined, taking from W. I. Thomas and F. Znaniecki the notion that 'personality is the subjective aspect of culture' and that cultures develop their own patterns. The book which these two authors wrote on *The Polish Peasant* was the first, or almost the first, to call attention to the way the situation of the European immigrant in the United States could be defined in terms that implied its logical relation to that of the Negro, although the Negro had been settled in the New World for three centuries (Park, 1950: 159, 358, 198–9). The recognition of this 'logical relation', obvious though it may now seem, was of fundamental significance for establishing a sociology of race relations.

The most mature statement of Park's views in this field was the essay 'The Nature of Race Relations' published in 1939 (reprinted in Park,

1950). This put forward a more complex scheme for examining interaction. In one sense, said Park, race relations were not so much the relations that existed between individuals of different races as between individuals conscious of these differences. From such a standpoint it would appear that there were no race relations in Brazil because race consciousness was absent from there. From another standpoint, however, race relations included relations that were not at that time conscious or personal though they had been in the past. Race problems, he believed, had invariably arisen in response to the expansion of European peoples; this could be seen as a historical extension of European domination accompanied by an increasing integration of, and intimacy with, the races and peoples affected. But he preferred to regard it as a succession of changes connected with, and incidental to, the expansion and integration of a vast and new social organism. The succession ran from trade to political domination, missionary activity, and then, 'the final stage' when 'Europe begins to export not goods but capital' to finance mines, rubber plantations, and eventually factories 'to employ native laborers in the manufacture of commodities which are then sold not only in the colonies, but, as in the case of Japan, in Europe and in competition with European products'. Other features of the succession were the appearance of hybrid peoples, port cities to service world trade, and then the growth of nationalism among both majorities and minorities. This last development was evidence that 'we are at the end of one epoch in human and racial relations and at the beginning of another'. Contradicting some previous writers, he predicted that race conflicts 'will be more and more in the future confused with, and eventually superseded by, the conflicts of classes'. Returning to his opening problem of what precisely distinguished race relations from other fundamental forms of human relations, he offered a further formulation:

it is the essence of race relations that they are the relations of strangers; of peoples who are associated primarily for secular and practical purposes; for the exchange of goods and services. They are otherwise the relations of people of diverse races and cultures who have been thrown together by the fortunes of war, and who, for any reason, have not been sufficiently knit together by inter-marriage and inter-breeding, to constitute a single ethnic community, with all that it implies. (1950: 100, 107–16)

Any assessment of Park's contribution to race relations studies must give a high place to his leadership in formulating an alternative to prevailing conceptions of racial relations as biological relations. For example, the lengthy review *Contemporary Sociological Theories* published by the Harvard professor Pitirim Sorokin included a substantial chapter on the

'Anthropo-Racial, Selectionist, and Hereditarist School' which concluded with the judgement that it 'has been one of the most important and valuable schools in sociology' (1928: 308). Park rejected the theories which defined culture as a racial trait; he saw the backwardness of human populations as a result of their geographical and cultural isolation. Equally, he dismissed the psychological mode of explanation favoured by F. H. Giddings at Columbia, maintaining that 'the thing that distinguishes a mere collection of individuals from a society is not like-mindedness, but corporate action . . . sociology . . . may be described as the science of collective behavior' (1921: 42). By developing his ecological perspective Park was able to break away from a folk conception of race to a degree that Durkheim could never attain (Fenton, 1980). He explained the various aspects of the relations between people belonging to different races in terms of processes influencing all forms of life, human, animal and plant. It was of particular importance that he moved the emphasis in the expression 'race relations' from the first word to the second. He questioned the assumption that race relations and ethnic relations were fundamentally different. The effect of his teaching was to situate race relations in a context of urban sociology and the power relations stemming from the expansion of the capitalist economy.

An assessment of Park's contribution is also an opportunity to call attention to the importance of analogy in the development of new explanations. This runs through the history of racial thought as through much of the history of science. Buffon devised a definition of species based on analogy with human lineage; Prichard interpreted variety in the human species by analogy with change in other species; he also investigated 'the phenomena of resemblance or analogy' in language as a way of interpreting human physical history (Augstein, 1996: xvi, 84, 231). The *Naturphilosophen* used analogy extravagantly but less successfully. Park drew on plant and animal ecology to introduce a way of conceptualising social relations that opened up new theoretical possibilities. One of the sharpest criticisms of Park's approach was that of the black Trinidad-born sociologist Oliver Cromwell Cox (1901–74) who considered the analysis of political organisation seriously inadequate. Stanford H. Lyman has also objected to what he sees as an assumption that the place of the black man in United States society will be determined by processes within the white sector of that society. In his view Park 'systematically presented the stages through which the black would pass on the way to his eventual assimilation in a racially homogeneous world' (1972: 121). Park was surely a white liberal critic of prevailing assumptions about race, and yet, equally certainly, he accepted other assumptions of his generation which are evident only in the light of hindsight. As Cox charged, Park did not identify with sufficient clarity the special characteristics of racial conflicts. Nor did he work out all the implications of the approach he pioneered. When he moved to the view that race relations are defined by present or past consciousness of racial differences, what did this imply for his theoretical framework? When men were conscious of such differences, what form did that consciousness take? Many of the beliefs white Southerners held in 1921 about racial differences are now known to have been false. If what distinguished these relations was a false consciousness and the falsity was eliminated, then unless there was some intervening variable, nothing substantial would remain to divide blacks from whites. Assimilation was the implicit outcome. An author who, like Lyman, criticises this in 1972, has the advantage of more hindsight than one writing in 1948 or in 1939. It is easy now to observe that there was an intervening variable of a kind having something to do with nationalism. Park worked in an intuitive manner and did not reason in terms of independent and dependent variables. If he had done so, he would have been no more likely to predict this. It is striking how many of his contemporaries and even most later critics failed to foresee the kinds of change that occurred in American race relations around 1960. When he criticised Park, Cox was no more prescient, for he testified that the solidarity of Negro Americans was not nationalistic (1948: 545). It is fairly clear that Park did not regard racial conflicts as a special kind of conflict, but tended to emphasise what they had in common with other sorts of conflict. He wrote that the growth of nationalism was changing the consciousness of peoples in the colonial world and therefore changing the character of the conflicts. Race conflicts were giving way to class conflicts, and though Park would not have accepted Cox's conception of class, his view that racial conflicts do not have any special characteristic that distinguishes them in the historical dimension was of great importance to his generation and can easily be defended against criticism today.

Genetic explanations

The course of human evolution has entailed changes both in physical structure and behaviour. The structure of the human body evolved from that of some ape-like ancestor because of the way human ancestors used their arms and legs. Particular kinds of behaviour, among humans, as among animals, could have increased fertility and thus conferred greater fitness in the struggle for survival. If some animals or humans were more successful in competition on the ecological level, this may have been because their genetic inheritance enabled them to behave in particular ways; relative success would then have influenced the size of populations in the next generation. So an approach which sees race in terms of population has to consider the ways in which behaviour on the ecological level can be explained in terms of processes on the genetic level.

A pioneer of this line of argument was Sir Arthur Keith (1866–1955) who started to publish about the time when it was discovered that glands in the body produce hormones which regulate the normal growth of the various parts of the body. He inferred that the division of mankind into races had been brought about by the action of hormones, for if a group were isolated from others for a long period they would be unable to develop new characters. Groups could acquire a culture that encouraged self-isolation and thus reinforce physical difference. Among the kinds of behaviour that kept populations distinct one of the most salient was warfare. This led him to the view that human evolution was controlled by two processes, one operating on the physiological level and the other on the cultural, but nature had organised the physiological one 'to serve her ulterior object – the production of higher and better races of Mankind'. Racial prejudices served her purpose by keeping populations separate so that they could control their own breeding and develop their genetic potential. The spirit of unrest which afflicted the modern world arose because humans were struggling to adapt their biological inheritance to the requirements of international economic organisation. To attain world peace it would be necessary to control that inheritance more strictly: 'peoples of all countries and continents must pool not only their national interests, but they must also pool their bloods'. He told his Scottish audience that the price of such a peace 'is the racial birthright that Nature has bestowed upon you'. Yet even if, recognising the arguments on the cultural level, people were willing to pay that price, Keith believed that Nature would prevent their doing so, because 'without competition Mankind can never progress'. 'This antipathy or race prejudice Nature has implanted within you for her own ends – the improvement of Mankind through racial differentiation' (Keith, 1931: 20, 47–8). Three points should be noted about this theory. Firstly, as an explanation of the patterns of racial prejudice in the modern world it is very weak. The variations in the intensity of prejudice from one set of circumstances to another, and from one individual to another, can be accounted for more satisfactorily by sociological and psychological theories. If any component is explicable in genetic terms it seems relatively small. (For a contemporary criticism of Keith's argument see the lecture reprinted in Boas, 1940): 8, 16–17.) Secondly, to establish that something has an evolutionary function is neither to justify it nor to account for it. War and prejudice may have functions but they also have dysfunctions. If prejudice keeps populations separate the separation is a consequence of the prejudice and

therefore cannot be a cause of it. Thirdly, it is not necessarily the case that
the biological improvement of mankind depends upon racial differentiation. Much depends upon preventive medicine and the improvement of
the environment. In so far as humans have evolved beyond their ape-like
ancestors it has been by the development of plasticity, or the ability to
prosper in varying circumstances and environments.

Most physical anthropologists were unwilling to speculate in the way
that Keith did. The direction in which their subject developed is illustrated by the introductory textbook *Genetics and the Races of Man* published by William C. Boyd in 1950. After summarising Keith's views, it
pointed to the difficulty in extrapolating from the breeding of domesticated animals. A cattle breeder might believe that when he had obtained
cattle that produced more milk he had improved his stock; but by what
criterion was the improvement of humans to be determined? (After all,
cows with a higher milk yield might be less fit in a wild environment.) In
more recent years it has also become apparent that there is a risk in plant
and animal breeding unanticipated by Keith. It is best illustrated in
cereals. A high-yielding cereal may be adopted by almost all the farmers in
a region with excellent results for a time. It may then become subject to a
particular disease so that a new variety has to be bred. The ability of the
breeders to produce a new, disease-resistant, strain may depend upon the
availability of wild strains with different properties that can be bred into
the previous strain. Strains that appeared unproductive may turn out to
be very valuable. This surely reinforces the conclusion that it is difficult to
draw, from animal and plant breeding, any lessons for human breeding.
No one can tell what the future holds.

Boyd set out to show that racial differentiation could result from causes
which definitely did not improve the stock. He started from an exposition
of the principles of genetics and made hardly any mention of craniology.
Indeed, he summarised Sir Ronald Fisher's criticisms that even if precise
and reliable measurements were available of skulls for different places and
times, craniologists could still not determine which were the important
measures or the causes of variation. Boyd went on to observe that, 'The
difficulty which we experience in trying to classify man, or any other
species, into races is quite different from the problem of classifying
organisms into species.' Races were more or less genetically open systems
whereas species, which did not regularly exchange genes, were genetically
closed systems. A race could become a species. It was 'a population which
differs significantly from other human populations in regard to the frequency of one or more of the genes it possesses' (Boyd, 1950: 198, 207).
Any research worker analysing, say, the incidence of a genetically based
disorder, had to refer only to a population. The word 'race' became

redundant. Populations were defined by the procedures of the research workers themselves in drawing samples. Those readers who believe that Prichard was right in 1836 when he warned of the confusions that could result from using the word race as a classification, might say that if a word was needed to identify a set of individuals among whom there was a given frequency of a particular gene, the word 'set' would have been sufficient. Old habits of thought were not so easily shaken off, and some anthropologists who well understood the principles Boyd expounded, nevertheless used the word 'raciation' to identify the process by which sets of individuals became genetically distinctive.

Three senses of the word 'race' have now been distinguished. To start with it was used to identify a lineage, a set of individuals of common descent who, because of out-marriage, could well be of varied appearance. When race was used in the sense of type, this was to identify a set defined by their phenotype, or appearance. Human characteristics change in the course of evolution. Once this was understood, a set of individuals of similar phenotype were better called a subspecies, a class created by shared descent. The boundaries of such a class had to be defined by the classifier. Increasingly, however, research moved away from problems of classification. Research workers drew their own samples without having to consider whether their populations were representative of the sets that other people regarded as races, nations or social groups. Physical appearance was a preliminary indicator of how an individual might stand in relation to what was known about the frequencies of particular genes. Were it not that so many members of the general public still thought in terms of race, it would by this time have been possible to dispense with the word.

Population genetics shifted the level of interest from that of the species to that of the genes which made the species what it was. Yet when they produced organic change the genetic determinants always influenced existing organisms and did not start from the beginning again. Since a species had to be able to survive in its environment while changing, it could evolve in only a limited number of directions. There is a model here for arguments about reductionism in the study of human society. Social continuity and change result from the actions of individuals just as organic continuity and change result from the combination of genes. Social changes are brought about by changes in individual behaviour but the likelihood that any particular individual change will lead to a social change depends upon the organisation of the society in relation to its historical environment.

Research in human genetics has transformed the intellectual landscape described by Huxley and Boyd. To take a British example, genetic investigations have shown that immigrant groups from the Indian sub-continent experience a higher incidence of diabetes, cirrhosis of the liver, cerebrovascular and heart disorders than the indigenous population, and that genetic differences are partly responsible. At the same time there are differences within these groups in the leucocyte antigens and other factors which predispose towards such disorders (Papiha, 1987). This kind of research not only shows that racial classifications are of negligible value but is part of a trend which threatens to supersede both the subspecies and the species concepts. The one area where racial classification is still employed is in the morphometric research which enables forensic anthro-pologists to assign fossil finds to present-day ethnic groups (Sauer, 1992). This has been important to indigenous peoples who want the remains of their ancestors to be treated with the same dignity as other human skeletons. In forensic anthropology racial classifications are still used because of the assumptions of contemporary humans that they belong in 'races', not because these classifications are needed to account for vari-ations in the fossil material.

The contention that human inter-group behaviour could usefully be seen as, in part, an expression of genetic determinants, was revived in the 1970s in connection with the study of what came to be called socio-biology. Early formulations of the theory of natural selection presented biological fitness as dependent not upon the physical and mental powers of an individual but upon the number of offspring he or she left. Fitness was a matter of differential reproduction. But, since a person's brothers and sisters have many of the same genes, these can be passed on as well through one sibling as another. Fitness had to be measured inclusively to estimate the ability of a small population to propagate its genetic charac-teristics. The inclusive fitness of an individual was increased by kin selection and reciprocal altruism. He or she was more able to transmit his or her genes if members of the kin group (who shared those genes) assisted one another; that assistance might be expected to vary in accord-ance with the degree of their genetic closeness, though the individuals were unlikely to be conscious that their behaviour was so motivated. Altruistic behaviour could then be explained as the product of natural selection favouring cooperation between individuals of common descent.

This theory was applied to racial relations by Pierre L. van den Berghe (1981) who proposed that such relations be seen as the product of influences upon three levels: cultural, ecological and genetic. He ac-knowledged that much behaviour could not be explained in terms of the next level down, but contended that group behaviour was powerfully affected by an unconscious tendency to favour people with whom the actor shared a common genetic inheritance. A different physical appearance was a sign that identified a competing population whose members would try to spread their genes to the disadvantage of members of the first population.

That the three levels were not separate, but inter-linked, he demonstrated by analysing the available evidence on variations in pigmentation (van den Berghe and Frost, 1986). A previous study had reported a sex and a class difference in pigmentation among Japanese of high school age. The girls were lighter-skinned than the boys, and the upper class was lighter than the lower class. Pigmentation had been measured by placing a spectrophotometer on a site minimally exposed to sunlight, often the inner side of the upper arm. The ecological factor of environmentally-induced tanning could not account for the difference. Similar findings had been reported by other studies. The *explanandum* was therefore two-fold: (1) why should there be a widespread preference for lighter skin? and (2) why should there be a sex bias in this preference? His *explanans* was the selective mating of lighter-skinned women with higher-status men. Genetic inheritance had determined the amount of melanin produced, affecting the phenotype, and the resulting difference had been evoked by selective mating on the cultural level which had then increased the phenotypical difference. Men and women had different priorities in mate selection, with the men being more influenced by physical attractiveness and the women being more influenced by the resources a man could command.

A search of the Human Relations Area Files flagged 51 societies for which evidence of skin colour preferences had been reported; for 47 a preference for a lighter colour was unambiguous while the remaining 4 were not clearly contradictory. This demonstrated that the sexual asymmetry of the preference for a lighter complexion could not be simply the result of chance. While a dark complexion might have a selective advantage in certain environments, a cultural influence was pulling in the other direction. Genetic and cultural influences were interacting in the course of evolution.

In a more recent statement, van den Berghe (1995) has contended that the formation of a 'social race' has a biological underpinning, and that this contributes to an explanation of the etiology (or causation) of social race and racism in contemporary societies. The underpinning arises because humans, like other organisms, are biologically programmed to be nepotistic. In deciding how they will behave towards someone else they 'use all possible clues of relatedness, with a preference for the ones that are reliable, quick and cheap' whether these are biological or cultural. Racism, defined as discriminatory behaviour based on inherited physical appearance, can then be expected to arise whenever variance in inherited physical appearance is greater *between* groups than *within* groups. This is a relatively rare event and cannot long be sustained if there is inter-breeding. 'The reason why racism became the great pandemic of the nineteenth and twentieth centuries was simply the sudden acceleration of large-scale, long-distance migration across wide genetic clines.' It is said to be 'conceivably a case of culture "highjacking" genes which were selected for different ends (e.g. skin pigmentation regulating exposure to sun radiation in different latitudes) and making them serve a totally different social agenda'. That then 'had an enormous feed-back effect on the life-chances of different groups' (van den Berghe, 1995).

The ecological approach was of great importance in the history of sociology because it enabled sociologists to break away from the assumption that racial relations had to be explained in biological terms. By conducting field research and actually observing inter-group relations instead of staying in their studies, sociologists developed new concepts and refined their definitions in the way that, according to Mayr, underlay the advances in evolutionary biology. They found the ecological perspective stimulating as an analogy but inadequate as a total theoretical scheme.

Immigrant groups come to new societies bringing with them the products of their previous social evolution, which may well include skills that are of particular value in the new environment. How their social life develops in that environment may depend upon whether they are able to establish themselves in an ecological niche and turn a monopoly of some resource to their shared advantage. It is possible to compare the relative success of immigrants from the same part of China, Japan or the Indian subcontinent in various countries of settlement. The immigrants took with them the same skills but the use they could make of them depended upon the socio-economic ecology of the receiving societies. For example, Chinese were recruited as indentured workers for plantation labour in the Caribbean. In Jamaica, once they had escaped from the plantations, they moved into retail trade. They reinforced their economic position by consolidating as an ethnic group, often sending their children back to Asia to receive a Chinese upbringing. After China became Communist in 1949 and Jamaica moved towards independence, the younger generation of Jamaican Chinese determined instead to be Chinese Jamaicans, and pulled their elders with them; they became an integral section of the island's bourgeoisie. Since they sought to conserve their wealth they were ready to marry their daughters only to members of their own group, so a Chinese ancestry, plus Chinese physical traits, distinguished an ethnic subdivision of a class. Orlando Patterson (1975) contrasted this with events in Guyana where the Portuguese had captured the retail trade sector before the Chinese were in any position to challenge them for it. Since no avenue of opportunity was open to them as a group, the Chinese there entered a variety of occupations and identified themselves as individuals with the developing Guyanese Creole culture.

Other immigrant groups in industrial societies have found their own niches: Jews in Britain became tailors and later taxi-drivers; one Native American group in the United States became specialists in steel erecting work at great heights, and a host of groups started restaurants offering an ethnic cuisine. The ecological analyses of the Chicago school inspired a comparable study by John Rex and Robert Moore (1967) of the patterns of immigrant housing in Birmingham. These studies attest to the continuing value of an ecological perspective.

With the recognition that plant and animal (including human) populations were distinguished by the gene frequencies they had acquired in the course of evolution (including their adaptation to their environment) a new foundation was laid for biological science. This advance suggested many analogies for social science but the ecological perspective is best complemented by those deriving from two more comprehensive intellectual traditions, discussed in chapters 5 and 6.

5   Race as status

Popular ideas that individuals belong in racial groups have frequently been used to mark them out as being of different social status. This chapter carries forward discussion of the theories mentioned in chapter 4 in order to assess progress in developing conceptual frameworks that supersede the idiom of race.

In its application to human society, evolutionary theory drew attention to the way in which physical differences served as signs of membership in competing groups and called forth reactions at the level of unconscious behaviour. It also had two particular weaknesses. Firstly, it was unable to do justice to the complexities of behaviour on the conscious level. Secondly, it could not account for the importance of power relations in human society, and especially for those associated with social stratification as a form of inequality persisting from one generation to another. These weaknesses started to be remedied once social scientists undertook empirical studies of the behaviour of people involved in inter-racial relations. An entirely new phase opened in the 1930s when two of them conducted research in Indianola, a Mississippi town with a population of about 3,000, that served as a centre for a rural county in which about 70 per cent of the population was black. The first research worker was an anthropologist, Hortense Powdermaker, who aimed to present a portrait of the town as a functioning community with particular reference to the Negro population. She was followed by John Dollard, a psychologist who had undergone psychoanalysis in Berlin.

Dollard's most striking contribution to knowledge about racial relations was his exposition of a Freudian theory of racial relations. Whereas most whites took their prejudices for granted as the expression of human nature, Dollard showed how these were fashioned to meet emotional needs. At much the same time the first psychological research (using Princeton undergraduates as subjects) was being conducted on the racial stereotypes prevalent in the United States. It did not explore whether the conceptions of other groups reported by the students influenced their actual behaviour, or whether they were simply reflections of the media and popular discourse. Later psychological research moved on to examine more systematically the personality dimensions of prejudice, to assess the effects of contact upon inter-group attitudes and behaviour, to study how subjects account for the kinds of difference they observe; to measure the inter-relations between racial attitudes on the one hand, and opinions about what, on the other, should be the role of government in providing assistance to members of disadvantaged groups, and other political issues. Not only is psychological research now much more sophisticated, but its concepts seek explanations of most group differences in social variables; the possible influence of genetic inheritance is not denied, but it is used only, and then cautiously, in answering highly specific questions.

In presenting his portrait of Indianola, Dollard utilised the colour-caste analysis then being developed by an anthropologist, W. Lloyd Warner. Introducing his use of it, Dollard (1937: 61) asserted that what he had seen in the Deep South was not the white racial soul or genius defending its heritage, but 'a moral and status order . . . whose operators safeguard and perpetuate their position in it'. Rather than following Dollard's psychological interpretation, the present discussion will concentrate upon this conception of a status order and describe the gradual construction, over a period of some forty years, of a distinctive theory which has one of its starting points in Dollard's analysis. The field studies and the conceptual work which made these advances possible were nearly all carried out in the United States and were motivated by the whites' concern with what many called 'the Negro problem'. That there was a problem few could contest. The main arguments were about what kind of problem it was, and the priority given to this question meant that theoretical development occurred within a framework constructed by what people in the United States considered democratic ideals, rather than within abstract categories of scientific reasoning.

Lloyd Warner's conceptions of caste and class were two such categories. Both have been vigorously criticised. To call black–white relations caste relations has suggested to some writers a parallel with the Hindu caste system which they believe quite inappropriate since the latter has religious justifications of an anti-democratic character. Warner's view of class corresponded to what many sociologists would now identify as social status: it was a more systematic formulation of the US folk concept of class as a rank order based upon wealth and style of life. Debate about the best definition of class continues. One way of reducing some of the confusion is to distinguish between a weak sense of class (e.g. as a set of individuals standing in a common relationship to the labour market) and a strong sense (e.g. as a set of individuals standing in a common relationship to the means of production who will in due course be brought to a consciousness of their position in the process by which capitalism develops). When a weak conception is employed class is one among several dimensions along which individuals are differentiated, and it corresponds to the use of the word in much everyday language where it designates socio-economic status. When a strong conception of class is employed, differentiation by class is a long-term determinant underlying other kinds of social differentiation. This chapter discusses theories which use weak concepts of class; chapter 6 considers what theories using strong concepts of class add to the sociological understanding of racial relations.

Structure and function

In the 1930s it was quite common to regard the social system as a machine with its members interacting with one another in historically defined ways. 'This machine has inertia and goes on working according to its traditionally prescribed pattern. The societal unit continues to function until it is in some manner disorganized; it then goes through a cycle from disorganization to reorganization, and orderly life continues.' Such a view of the social system did not satisfy Dollard who thought it plain that powerful pressure was constantly exerted on Negro people to make them display submissive attitudes. The system was maintained not by inertia but by active pressures, social and physical. To identify these pressures it was necessary to discover the differential advantages of membership in particular classes and colour-castes and find out how these advantages were translated into personal and ultimately organic gratifications (1937: 97, 178).

Dollard's answer to this problem was to describe three types of gain which middle-class whites derived from their social position at the expense of blacks, and to some extent at the expense of lower-class whites. There were economic, sexual and prestige gains. The first of them he documented by reference to occupational rewards. The back-breaking and ill rewarded nature of some jobs was epitomised in cotton-picking; middle-class whites picked very little cotton. Relatively, middle-class whites got much higher returns for their work than did the lower-class groups who performed the more laborious tasks. This might well have been the case, but it is not easy to prove that the higher returns were unjustified. In effect, Dollard asserted that whites used their political power to get greater rewards than they would have secured in a free market. Whites were immigrating into the area, which suggests that it offered them economic opportunities. Dollard also contended that the social position of middle-class whites entailed certain costs and that they were imprisoned within an inhospitable socio-economic situation as

much as any other category, but he asserted that they gained more than
they lost by it, and that they therefore had a vested interest in maintaining
that system (1937: 98–115). He described the poverty of of Negroes and
the incidence of pellagra, a disease caused by dietary deficiency. He also
provided plenty of examples of the way white power was used to prevent
black workers getting their just reward, or forming labour organisations,
and to control the allocation of jobs (on the exploitation of tenant
farmers, see Dollard, 1937: 120–4; Powdermaker, 1939: 86–94). The
distribution of rewards in the labour market was clearly determined by
the mobilisation of white power as well as by the market value of individuals' skills. To this extent at least it may be agreed that one factor in the
maintenance of the social system was the economic gain the whites
derived from it.

The second kind of gain was sexual, and in its simplest terms consisted
in the way white men had access to Negro women as well as to white
women. It will not escape notice that, among whites, this was a gain for
men only. Dollard remarked that Negro women also had an advantage in
that they might receive the attentions of men from both racial categories.
In so far as this was a gain for Negro women, it was balanced by a loss, in
that this situation meant the degradation of the Negro male and that in
turn reduced in many ways the satisfactions that Negro women could
obtain from married life. The same situation reduced the satisfactions of
white women. Dollard conjectured that they were idealised in such a way
that white men felt it unbecoming to regard them as sexual objects,
feeling guilty and restrained in sexual relations with them and finding
black women better sexual partners. White women unconsciously envied
the greater sexual freedom of black women (1937: 135–68). In such
circumstances the calculation of sexual gain seems a dubious exercise,
but the reader can go along with Dollard in accepting that the pattern of
sexual attitudes was a factor important to the motivations which maintained the social system.

The third kind of gain was what Dollard called prestige, but would now
be called deference. He had in mind the features of Negro behaviour
which in interpersonal relations tended to increase the white man's
self-esteem. It was illuminating for the traveller to have the experience of
having his bag carried at the Grand Central Terminal in New York and at
a railway station in the Deep South. In the former, 'the Negro is a
mechanism for moving weight from one point to another . . . In the South
he is this, and something more. The Southern porter is extremely nice
about it to boot and does various things that are flattering and exhilarat-
ing.' Dollard was clear that, first, deference behaviour was something
used by Negroes to manipulate whites and, second, that it had functions

in respect of social control. Deference was demanded by whites and any Negro who would not accord it was defined as 'uppity', threatening and in need of correction. But nevertheless deference was psychologically rewarding to the recipient; it seemed to prove that the Negro was not hostile and to allay the anxiety among white people provoked by the fear that the racial antagonism engendered in them. The crucial feature for the white man was that he was receiving deference in advance of demand; it appeared as a submissive affection freely yielded, suggesting that his aggressive demands were being passively received and giving him a gratifying sense of mastery over others (1937: 173–87). In non-Western cultures it often appears from the studies of anthropologists that the highest category of economic values is that which brings command over people, while the disparagement of the role of personal servant in industrial societies suggests that deference is a service commanding a high price in the eyes of both the one who pays and the one who receives the service. The very substantial white deference gain in the South was therefore an index of how much white power affected the bargaining relations of the two racial categories.

The gains were not exclusively on the white side of the colour line. There were many ways in which blacks were able to gratify their impulses though, as Dollard points out, this was often at an appreciable long-term cost. Negroes had greater sexual freedom among their own number; greater freedom of aggression; and the psychological luxury of a dependent relationship in respect of whites. Whites had the satisfaction that went with mastery, superiority, control, maturity, and duty well fulfilled. They had the pleasure of despising blacks. Negroes were permitted slack work habits, irresponsibility and, within limits, more personal freedom than is possible in a competitive, economically progressive society. This helped explain why they did not try harder to change the system. The 'tolerant' attitude of whites towards crime in the Negro quarter and their acceptance of slack work habits further weakened Negro resources for mobilising pressure against white demands (1937: 393, 431–3, 282).

Implicit in Dollard's concept of gain as an instrument for clarifying what was entailed in caste and class relations was the idea of exchange between two partners to a trading relationship. The Negro traded deference for reward. Thus, 'the "Sambo" or "Rastus" type of Negro takes his hat off, grins, strikes the boss for half a dollar, and often gets it in exchange for his submissiveness'. Sometimes the Negro traded his labour power in return for his employer's protection. Thus a particular Negro had been known to threaten to kill some other man, saying that he knew he would not be punished for it; 'he will "farm another acre" that is, do extra work for his boss in exchange for the protection'. Not all blacks were willing to trade on these terms. Some 'local Negroes who had been away to school' were offish, cool, and kept to themselves; they would hardly speak to whites in public and were reluctant to speak first. Their experience of life elsewhere had caused them to set a higher price on their pride. The positions occupied by black people varied in the extent to which they made it desirable for them to have a white protector or patron. A black school teacher, for example, had concluded that the only way to get along was to have a white patron because improvements to school buildings could not be obtained in any other way (Dollard, 1937: 179, 282, 185, 263).

The central feature of Lloyd Warner's analysis was the presumption that two systems, one of caste and the other of class, existed side by side. The caste system ranked whites above blacks, prohibited inter-marriage and placed the offspring of inter-caste sexual relations in the lower category. The class system ranked everyone, blacks and whites, in terms of their entitlement to deference deriving from wealth, education, social origin, style of life, etc. This meant that while all blacks were socially inferior and categorically subordinate to all whites in colour-caste, some were superior and superordinate to many whites in respect of social class. The two systems would have come into conflict more often had there not been a clear understanding that some kinds of social relationships belonged in the first system and other kinds in the second one. Anything relating to sexual relations between blacks and whites, and particularly anything involving black men and white women, was to be regulated by caste norms. Anything of a commercial character was regulated by class norms. It was the whites who decided into which category any incident fell, and often it was the lower-class whites who were the first on the scene. They had the greatest interest in enforcing caste norms since these norms were so important to them in reducing the effects of competition from blacks.

The process by which a situation was defined as being of a particular character entailed many risks for the blacks. Dollard described the situation of a Negro land-owner who had five white people picking cotton for him. Three of them were women. If one of them had alleged that he had 'shined up' to her it might have cost him his life, though in the book *Deep South* an incident is described in which a lower-class white woman alleged that a black professional man had struck her, but she failed to get her definition of the event accepted. Nor did the norm concerning inter-racial sex always protect white men. In Indianola a black man beat a white man for pestering his girl friend; the black man had tried to leave town after a white posse went after him, but the pursuit may have been abandoned after a while. A black tenant who shot a white plantation manager who consorted with the tenant's sister was allowed to return to the plantation by the landlord. A black shopkeeper obtained a court order against a white customer requiring him to pay for the goods he had taken. The customer regarded this as an intolerable affront and came to beat the shopkeeper, but he lost the fight and other whites refused to aid him. A black man, gun in hand, angrily threatened his white neighbour for repeatedly letting horses loose in his corn. A lynching party assembled at the white man's house later the same day but the owner of the horses stopped it 'on the grounds that the Negro did not really know what he was doing'. Automobile accidents in which a black driver killed or injured a white person could also be tricky. A young black driver had his car sideswiped by another so that he was thrown against a white worker in the road, causing him slight injury. The black driver was convicted of an offence and sentenced to serve thirty days at the county farm, where he was badly whipped. A middle-class black driver who had white patrons once hit a car driven by a white woman who happened to be pregnant, an especially unfavourable detail; the police officer abused him, and was about to jail him, when the chief of police declared the matter to have been an accident and ordered his release. In another case a black professional man when driving his car killed a drunken lower-class white man. He was not arrested. Local white bankers offered to lend him money for his defence, while a group of upper-class white women called upon him at his place of business to assure him that they considered him "a great influence for good in the community" and that they intended to see that 'no harm came to him' (Dollard, 1937: 165, 292–3, 288, 92; Davis *et al.*, 1941: 477, 337).

Dollard presented Indianola society as constructed round the interlocking characters of caste and class: 'they organize local life securely and make social co-operation possible . . . Caste has replaced slavery as a means of maintaining the essence of the old status order in the South. By means of it racial animosity is held at a minimum' (1937: 61–2). This statement is worth notice for its demonstration of the weakness of functionalist explanations. Caste and class were equally responsible for the *in*security of local life and for lack of cooperation. By means of caste racial animosity was evoked and heightened. Any community has a degree of integration, the component parts being to some extent interdependent. Every relation between them is therefore to some degree functional and to some degree dysfunctional. To point to a connection between colour-caste and animosity says nothing about whether animosity would be higher or lower if relations between blacks and whites were regulated in some other way.

The structural interpretations Dollard borrowed from Warner's scheme were much more valuable. He argued that in relations with middle-class blacks, middle-class white people combined class loyalty and caste hostility. Situations of economic position and advantage called forth class-based patterns of behaviour whereas situations of social, and ultimately sexual, contact evoked caste-based patterns. The former was not difficult to account for since the middle-class Negro bought more gasoline, better groceries, more insurance, more medical services, engaged a lawyer more frequently, and was in general a good customer. Whites would bid for the custom of such Negroes and found it worthwhile to persuade Negro land-owners to offer workers the same conditions of service as those offered by white employers. One such land-owner said that the whites put pressure on him to treat his tenants as they treated theirs. Another used his influence to dissuade some of the local Negroes from bringing a potentially costly suit for damages and had been given special favours in return. Educated Negroes often found themselves the objects of a more respectful attention, provided nothing happened to evoke caste differences. These signs of inter-racial class sympathy were to be set alongside the striking evidence of hostility between middle-class whites and lower-class whites. A landlord, for example, deplored the meanness and spitefulness of his white tenant farmers, saying that next year he would replace them with Negroes. Poor whites were intractable and undeferential but there were Negroes who 'knew their place'.

Caste and Class in a Southern Town was complemented by *Deep South: A social anthropological study of caste and class* (Davis *et al.*, 1941). This was a study, directed by Lloyd Warner, of Natchez, a town of over 10,000 persons located on the Mississippi river not far away. Both books describe a social system that had continually to adjust to changing circumstances. In 1936 cotton yields increased and there was a shortage of agricultural workers such that 10–15,000 cotton-pickers had to be imported into the region. Law officers dragged tramps from railway box cars and hobo colonies, and rounded up vagrants for work in the fields. Landlords had earlier competed with one another for good tenants and had much preferred black tenants to white, but with better yields competition in areas around Natchez became acute. In such circumstances it might have been expected that dissatisfied Negroes would emigrate and that competition between whites would result in a diminution in discrimination. How, then, was the system maintained? Davis and his colleagues concluded that by far the most important element was the face-to-face relationship between landlord and tenant. Intimidation and legal subordination had bred in the black man a habit of dependence on the landowner. He had become so accustomed to a low standard of living that he left the system only in periods of destitution or at times, such as during the war, when conditions were generally disturbed. Standards were kept uniformly low by upper-class white pressure on industrial concerns able to pay blacks wages higher than those conventional in other kinds of employment (Davis *et al.*, 1941: 401, 378, 261). To examine properly the hypothesis of black dependence it would have been necessary to study perceptions of emigration opportunities; this was neglected, while there is sufficient evidence in the book itself to evoke the reader's doubts about the adequacy of this explanation. Other doubts arise with respect to political relations. The authors describe the antagonism between upper- and lower-class whites. They state that political power was exercised by a 'ring' which was dependent upon the support of rank-and-file middle- and lower-class voters, nearly all of whom were white. Independent organisation by lower-class whites was frustrated. Instead of the system's being maintained by inertia and psychological relations like dependence and habituation to low standards, it seems to have rested on the con- tinued use of governmental power to balance lower-class whites and blacks. *Deep South* very properly emphasised the importance of white power to the maintenance of the system and its authors recognised that 'since political control is vested in the upper middle class of the white caste, it is not surprising that there is a close connection between political power and control of the economic system, which is also in the hands of this class' (1941: 491), but did not relate this as well as they might have done to the political history of the state or to the explanation of the distinctive features of the social system.

The research of Dollard, Warner, and their associates, provided a basic understanding of a two-category system in which membership of either category was defined in what the participants called racial terms. Their analysis can be strengthened by considering the position in such a system of intermediary groups like Native Americans and Chinese who could possibly be regarded as constituting a third category (Banton, 1977: 169–71). Warner taught that community studies should be conducted within the general framework of comparative sociology, placing the study of the Deep South alongside reports from inner Tibet or the Andaman Islands in the Bay of Bengal. This was a commendable aspiration, but it was swamped by one of the dominant characteristics of the culture in which the research workers had themselves been brought up. Citizens of the United States have believed, since their country's independence in 1776, that what most distinguished it was the national commitment to democratic values. The belief that their sharing of values was the most important attribute of a society influenced the form taken by sociology in the United States. It can be seen in the theories of Talcott Parsons which dominated the discipline from the late 1940s until the mid-1960s and which are often designated structural-functionalism. Parsons' approach was introduced to a wider readership through Kingsley Davis' textbook *Human Society* (1947) in which he presented human behaviour as chiefly governed by the efforts of individuals to gain their objectives. This might involve the rational utilisation of means which could help them towards their goal (the means–end relation) but it did not exclude considerations which could not be rationally justified (such as the value placed in Europe on gold, pearls and diamonds). Each individual pursued his or her own ends but society came about because these ends were fitted into a common pattern (the cooperation associated with the division of labour) and because individuals shared common values (the beliefs that murder should be punished and that pearls are more valuable than cowrie shells). The conception of societies as founded upon the sharing of common ultimate ends introduced an element of relativism: social activities had to be interpreted in terms of the value structure of the society in which they occurred. Thus questions of racial discrimination, of assimilation, and of the legitimacy of a minority identity had to be viewed against the background of US political principles. As a means of educating readers about the injustices of discrimination, this had its merits, but it erected obstacles to the comparative study of racial relations. It implied that what distinguished racial relations from other kinds of intergroup relations were the values of the dominant group alone, and it failed to follow up the suggestions of Park and W. I. Thomas for comparing those majority–minority relations which were defined as racial with those defined in ethnic terms.

The use of democratic values as a framework within which to conceptualise racial relations was explicit in Dollard's (1937: 60) discussion of the 'conflict between the dominant American mores, which are expressed formally in the Declaration of Independence and the regional mores of the South . . . Two different and contradictory conceptions of human worth are operating in one social field.' He called it a dilemma, and this formulation provided the main organising principle for Gunnar Myrdal's *An American Dilemma* (1944), a massive collaborative study which owed a great deal to structural-functional theory. Another such principle was what was called 'the white man's rank order of discrimination'. Myrdal said that this was observed by nearly all whites in the South, and he described it as follows:

1. The bar against intermarriage and sexual intercourse involving white women.
2. The several etiquettes and discriminations, which specifically concern behaviour in personal relations (dancing, bathing, eating, drinking together, handshaking, hat lifting, use of titles, house entrance and so forth).
3. Segregations and discriminations in use of public facilities such as schools, churches and means of conveyance.
4. Political disfranchisement.

5. Discriminations in law courts, by the police, and by other public servants.
6. Discriminations in securing land, credit, jobs, or other means of earning a living and discriminations in public relief and other social welfare activities. (Myrdal, 1944: 60–1)

The Negro's own rank order was said to be just about parallel, but inverse, to that of the white man. Being in desperate need of jobs and bread, even more than of justice in the courts or the vote, the Negro was most strongly motivated to resist discrimination on the economic level and least concerned about 'the marriage matter' (Myrdal, 1944: 60–1). A subsequent study of black attitudes in Columbus, Ohio, conformed this conclusion, but one of black and white attitudes in Texas and Oklahoma questioned whether discrimination in public services should not be placed higher in the list. Research in a small industrial town in Connecticut in 1950–2 found that the separation of blacks was most marked in housing, and then, in decreasing order, in social and religious activities, in the more desirable jobs, in public facilities, politics, and education (Lee, 1961: 74). Research at much the same time covering a sample of 248 cities showed considerable variation. In eight cities out of ten it could be taken for granted that Negroes might use the same public rest rooms as whites; but in only four cities out of ten could the same be said for Negro customers in white restaurants, while in less than one in ten could a black man reckon on service in a white barbershop (Williams, 1964: 124–9). Nevertheless, there was a 'strikingly clear unidimensional order' determining the situations in which whites accepted blacks, which did not rest on any single set of economic, political or social interests. It appeared to be the product of 'functionally arbitrary historical circumstances'.

Any analysis that started from values needed to be complemented by one that started from structures. The first sociologist to provide an example of how this might be done in a small-scale study was Everett Hughes in his 1946 article on 'The Knitting of Racial Groups in Industry'. Hughes set out to demonstrate that 'a fruitful way of analysing race relations in industry is to look at them against whatever grid of informal social groupings and of relations within and between such groups [as] exists in the industries, departments and jobs in which Negroes or other new kinds of employees are put to work'. He showed how in the canteen, the fixing room and the polishing room of a particular factory, patterns had been established of labour–management relations, informal seniority among employees, and group control of individual productivity. New employees had to conform to the existing practices or be subjected to heavy informal pressure. Black female workers were accorded a limited degree of acceptance by white female workers but were not admitted to the friendship cliques of the white women. Since the black women were only partly accepted they were not subject to the full pressure to conform to the established output norms, and some of them had high production rates. Management insisted that workers would be hired, retained and promoted strictly according to their individual merits. This had the effect of making all the workers, but particularly the blacks, feel very much on trial, so that 'the Negro worker apparently feels and is made to feel in some situations that he [or she] has to dissociate himself from others and be a "solitary" in order merely to keep his job' (Hughes and Hughes, 1952: 157). This essay discussed circumstances in which an industrial 'colour line' was being breached; some black workers disliked the pressure and left; others stayed, but did not behave in the same way as most of their white peers. To understand this, wrote Hughes, the sociologist had first to understand the factory and then discover in what ways customary attitudes were changed by the introduction of black workers. It examined one kind of cooperation and looked towards the possibility that racial distinctions might some day lose their significance in the factory setting.

Sociologists were slow to follow Hughes' lead. The 'race problem' was perceived as a problem of group conflict. When, in 1958, Herbert Blumer reviewed the research on racial relations in the United States carried out since the Second World War, he concluded that it had been shaped by an underlying interest in bringing these relations abreast of democratic ideals. Had it been under the influence of a different ideology, such as one directed to the maintenance of the *status quo*, other topics would have been studied. The issues on which it had concentrated, the theoretical leads it had followed, and the analytical schemes which it had employed, had not grown out of progressive scientific study of a distinct field of human behaviour. The need for a clear definition of what was meant by racial relations had been disregarded. Most of the research had been devoted to problems which lay along what he termed the 'prejudice–discrimination axis'. It rested on a belief that the nature of the relations between racial groups resulted from the feelings and attitudes which these groups had towards each other. Feelings and attitudes were therefore the chief objects to be studied. They might be the easiest ones to examine, but in Blumer's view they were not the most important ones. Racial relations in his view consisted of the actual behaviour towards one another of members of different racial groups. Because this had not been appreciated, research had been chaotic and lacking in scientific rationale.

Kinds of system

The inter-war period was one of great intellectual progress in the study of racial relations. By its end the nature of one variety of such relations, that which had been established in the Deep South, and had spread in diluted form to other parts of the United States, was much better understood. The next step was to discover how far that variety was representative. What other varieties were there, and how did they differ?

In this connection, a particularly influential study was Donald Pierson's *Negroes in Brazil* (1942), an account of 'race contact at Bahia' as it was in 1935–9. Of all the regions in Brazil, the province of Bahia and its capital city Salvador was one of the best suited to provide a contrast with the United States. It was not representative of Brazil (no city could be), but it was a good locale for the study of a social system in which physical appearance had a quite different significance from that in Mississippi. In the United States any outward sign of African descent served to assign an individual to the category black or Negro. It was the basis for a categorical distinction. In Bahia an appearance suggesting more or less African appearance had an effect similar to the difference in Mississippi between an expensive house and a poor one, an elegant costume or a shabby one, a cultured mode of speaking or bad grammar. It was a basis for a difference of degree, like the calculation of social status. It applied when comparing people whom North Americans would assign to different races, as well as when comparing people assigned to the same race. Pierson mentioned his intellectual obligations to Robert Park, who read the manuscript and then the proofs of the book. As Park did this, so he came to the conclusion that 'Brazil has no race problem'. The realisation that people of different origin could relate to one another unaffected by race prejudice in the sense in which that expression was used in the United States, was of fundamental importance. It proved that 'racial problems' could be solved. Pierson (1942: 331) explained that 'such prejudice as does exist is *class* rather than *caste* prejudice. It is the kind of prejudice which exists *inside* the ranks of the Negroes in the United States, the amount and intensity of which is actually very great.' Class prejudice existed in the ranks of the white people in the United States, too, but because of that country's definition of 'white', Pierson had to look to the black population for a continuous pattern of variation comparable to Bahia's. He thought that Brazilian whites did not express racial prejudice because they had never experienced a categorical opposition in which blacks or mixed-bloods offered a threat to their own status.

Subsequent research in Brazil during the 1950s – much of it initiated by UNESCO – was discussed in the 1967 edition of Pierson's book. It confirmed the claim that physical differences had a quite different social significance in Bahia from that in most parts of the United States – up to the 1950s at least. There was a Brazilian pattern in which signs of African ancestry constituted one element in a continuous scale of social status.

Their effects could be counterbalanced by the effects of other bases for attributing status such as wealth and education. Though there was a profusion of terms for describing differences of complexion, hair, etc. there were no racial categories in the social structure. The darker-skinned people tended to be low down the status scale and the lighter-skinned people to be high up, and inequality was transmitted from one generation to the next, but the association between colour and status was statistical and not categorical. How different this pattern was from the United States was still not appreciated by some writers. As Pierson (1967: xxvi) wrote, to call Brazilians of African descent Negroes, blacks or mulattoes was quite misleading.

Another example suggesting that racial contact need not necessarily give rise to a 'race problem' was furnished by the islands of Hawaii. By the early 1960s their population comprised five major groups: Caucasians, 32 per cent; Chinese, 6 per cent; Filipinos, 11 per cent; Hawaiians, 17 per cent; and Japanese, 32 per cent. Processes of assimilation or integration had been delayed by the entry of new groups of workers who still retained some of the distinctive characteristics of their homelands. Nevertheless the tendency to assign individuals to distinctive racial categories was diminishing. Over 46 per cent of all marriages were either unions crossing ethnic lines or involved persons who were already of mixed racial ancestry (Lind, 1966). Hawaii seemed to be setting a pattern for changes in other parts of the Pacific too.

Hawaii was therefore an appropriate location in 1954 for an international conference designed to lay the groundwork of social knowledge that could inform political and social policies. No one claimed that this knowledge had reached the point at which it could be synthesised. Indeed Blumer, in his introductory essay to the proceedings (Lind, 1955), maintained that there was little likelihood that any body of theory about race relations could be assembled that would comprehend the diversity of the subject matter. Racial experts might contribute to the devising of social policies, but explanations of inter-racial behaviour had to be sought in social and historical circumstances; these were too diverse to permit the formulation of universal propositions. Blumer went on in subsequent essays to argue that the sense of social position emerging from the way in which people characterised their own and others' groups provided the basis of race prejudice (see Killian, 1970). This was an application of what became known as the perspective of symbolic interactionism (see Lyman and Vidich, 1988). In a later publication he and Troy Duster (Blumer and Duster, 1980: 222) outlined a 'theoretical scheme' in order to try and grasp the phenomena of 'collective definition' which they considered central. It entailed a focus upon the ways in which people came to see members of their own and other racial groups, how they defined and interpreted their experiences of one another, and how racial categorisation affected their disposition to behave towards members of their own and other groups. Equally important to their conception of racial relations was the assumption that they entailed the superordination of one group and the subordination of another. Around this division four major forces were said to interact. Within the subordinate group there were the assimilationist and separatist orientations: the former was displayed in the intention and effort to gain adjustment inside established institutions; the latter in the intention and effort to develop a separate institutional world. Within the superordinate group there were the exclusionary and gate-opening orientations; the former was manifested in the intention and effort to hold onto – and sometimes increase – social advantages; the latter in the intention and effort to extend them to members of the other group. The pattern of relations between the groups took different turns as one or the other of the orientations became dominant. This happened as a result of changes elsewhere in society which needed to be explained in terms appropriate to those changes (e.g. economic theories to explain changes in economic conditions). Useful as a study of the processes of collective definition may be, this was a very limited perspective that has not yet been formulated in properly theoretical terms.

Group relations in places like Hawaii could develop towards the Brazilian pattern rather than towards that of the Deep South, and in places where more than two groups were involved the simple superordination–subordination model was inadequate. Another possible variety of race relations was that denoted by the concept of the plural society as this had recently been employed to analyse relations in Burma and Java between Europeans, Chinese, Indians and various native groups. J. S. Furnivall had distinguished between a plural society and a society with plural features. The plural society was associated with the modern tropical economy and arose 'where economic forces are exempt from control by social will' (1948: 306). In its political aspect it had 'three characteristic features; the society as a whole comprises separate racial sections; each section is an aggregate of individuals rather than a corporate or organic whole; and as individuals their social life is incomplete'. (By 'incomplete' he meant that the life of the sections was self-centred or oriented to its homeland rather than to the plural society.) The modern tropical economy was an imperial creation that drew upon both the western principle of freedom and the tropical system of compulsion.

Imperial rule was extended over regions that were already subject to disruptive changes. Thus proposals for the Uganda Railway were approved by the British Parliament on the argument that activities against the East African slave trade must be extended to the interior. Slaves were used as carriers or porters, but porterage was costly both in money and human life so that railway transport could be seen as an immense benefit to the peoples freed from the scourge of porterage. Furnivall cited this as an example of the argument in favour of compulsion. At times people must be obliged, in their long-term interest, to work for ends they do not understand. The western principle of freedom was subject to qualifications which liberal economists in Europe had no reason to explore since they took for granted a sharing of common objectives and values. The most disruptive changes were those which arose from contacts between peoples with different values. Far from regulating these equitably, colonial governments often exacerbated them. Thus in all sections of the nineteenth-century Burmese timber trade Burmans found employment. But Indian convict labour, hired from the government, was cheaper and more docile so it was used to displace free Burmese labour. As Furnivall (1948: 46) noted, 'if convicts had not been available, Europeans and Burmese would have learned to work together . . . and the people of the country would have been developed at the same time as its natural resources. The importation of convicts . . . erected a barrier between Burmans and the modern world that has never been broken down.' The entry of the Chinese and Indian free workers erected further barriers. The inability of the native peoples to control immigration, and the short-term view of policy taken by the imperial powers, has been in many regions a major cause of racial tension. As Furnivall remarks with gentle irony 'the Fiji chieftains invited British protection, and one result has been that half the inhabitants are immigrants from India'. Substantial numbers of 'coolies' were brought from Madras to Burmese towns where they were housed in the worst conceivable conditions, no one counted how many of them died, but the death rate was very high. Burmans were thereby driven out of the towns into the country districts. The one urban occupation open to Burmans for a time was in the printing trade since, thanks to the monastic schools, almost every Burman had learned to read and write. Yet eventually they were driven even from this trade by cheaper Indian labour. Burmese hostility towards the Indian presence grew steadily; marriage between Indian men and Burmese women came in for particular criticism. The Indian minority, hard-working and increasingly prosperous, did not support the Burmese nationalist movement but tried to preserve a distinct identity. They paid a terrible price. Hundreds were slaughtered in the riots of 1930 and 1938. With the Japanese invasion of

1941, all 900,000 took to flight and very many died on the roads to India (Chakravati, 1971).

One of Furnivall's central concerns was with the economics of welfare, and therefore with the analysis of what would now be called public goods. He stressed the distinction between economic progress and welfare. The former consisted in raising production and reducing costs; it was measurable. The latter was largely subjective. 'Order and security are good things, but under foreign rule their value as elements of welfare is debatable; after all, they could be achieved under slavery.' The Burman had his own goals and his own ideas of how much leisure he would forgo in order to attain them. Production was a social function and welfare a social attribute. Burmese society inculcated in its members norms which enabled everyone to increase their welfare, but these norms were neither recognised nor observed by the immigrant groups. The economic aspects of the plural society were therefore revealed in the social regulation of demand and supply. Taking a very basic example, Furnivall observed that 'sometimes a patch of scrub jungle round a village is reserved as a public convenience and it is closed to fuel cutting'. The social demand for a public good prevailed over any temptation to individuals to fell the trees in this area for firewood. But when they came to Rangoon, Indian immigrants saw in these patches of woodland a way to make easy money and cleared them to sell as fuel in the market. A public good was virtually destroyed. The European, Chinese, Indian and native groups all had their own norms of right conduct in business affairs, based upon relations in their own group, but these norms varied. One employer might be unwilling to employ sweated labour but find that he was competing against another producer whose norms allowed him to employ men on terms the first one would consider unfair. The first employer might then reduce his standards. In this way the social controls upon the supply of commodities were reduced to the lowest common factor amongst the various sections.

Other societies might be divided into a variety of groups with distinctive cultures, like South Africa, Canada and the United States (and, indeed, Burma prior to British rule) but Furnivall did not count them as plural societies because their populations shared norms which allowed them to control the economic forces. He considered them societies with plural features. Sociologists declined to follow this sort of distinction. Furnivall had stated a case which they found persuasive for regarding Burma and Java in the first half of the twentieth century as examples of a special kind of society, though doubt has since been cast on his evidence (Coppel, 1997: 566–72). They could be differentiated from other kinds of society on several dimensions: control of the economy, separate racial sections, a coercive social framework, relation to the means of production and so on. For Furnivall's purposes the first of these was the most important. Sociologists of inter-group relations recognised the Burma–Java instance as a form of 'race contact' quite different from the two-category system of the Deep South and the continuous gradation of colour and status reported from Bahia. They were more interested in the parallels with other societies in Africa and the West Indies which had been influenced by European imperialism; some of them generalised Furnivall's insight by writing of 'pluralism'. Thus M. G. Smith stressed the second and third dimensions, defining pluralism as 'a condition in which members of a common society are internally distinguished by fundamental differences in the institutional practice'. Leo Kuper kept closer to the initial assumption that plural societies were a special kind of society, one in which it was 'the political relations which appreciably determine the relationship to the means of production, rather than the reverse, and the catalyst of revolutionary change is to be found in the structure of power, rather than in economic changes which exhaust the possibilities of a particular mode of production' (Kuper, 1974: 226). He saw the social will in political terms and related it to generalisations about how societies change.

The claim that plural societies are a distinct kind of society brings up the philosophical problem discussed earlier as an opposition between realism and nominalism. Those who considered plural societies distinct presumed that there was a significant difference in the objects of study which should be reflected in the student's conceptual armoury. Critics of this position maintained that Burma and Java differed from one another and from all the other possible examples in many ways – and, indeed, that each society was different at one point in time from all other points in time. The complexity could be mastered only if the student developed his or her own set of categories and used them to organise observations about a large range of societies. The analysis of plural societies was the more attractive in the late 1950s because more scholars were then questioning the proposition that societies were founded upon the sharing of common ultimate ends. Burma, Java and South Africa were manifestly not socie-ties whose members shared such ends. But was the United States either? Many sociologists moved to the view that societies were held together by the coercive power of state institutions. From such a standpoint, Burma, Indonesia, South Africa and the other African societies discussed had to be understood less as societies than as states created by European imperi-alism which would be transformed when the dominant power was over-come. This favoured the use of a more general concept of pluralism, one which, for example, made it possible to argue that in the United States

Afro-Americans shared the majority culture but were socially separate, resulting in a substantial degree of social pluralism but only minimal cultural pluralism. Pierre L. van den Berghe pushed this mode of analysis to its logical conclusion in his conception of pluralism as a set of properties characterising heterogeneous societies. Since most states are heterogeneous, and since the approach he advocated entailed studying the entire society, any sharpness in the contrasts between Burma, Mississippi and Bahia was blunted.

Van den Berghe argued (first in 1958) that manifestations of racial prejudice had historically polarised around two ideal types of society which he called paternalistic and competitive. He compared these in respect of six independent variables (economy, division of labour, mobility, social stratification, numerical ratio, value conflict), nine dependent variables (race relations, roles and statuses, etiquette, forms of aggression, miscegenation, segregation, psychological syndrome, stereotypes of lower caste, intensity of prejudice) and two social control variables (form of government, legal system). To write of polarisation implies that the poles are opposite ends of a continuum or scale on which a series of intermediate points can be located. Van den Berghe denied that this was his intention; the differences between his types were qualitative and not quantitative. Intermediate types were inherently unstable and tended to move towards one of the ideal types, usually the competitive one. The present author found this unpersuasive. Situations of 'race contact' or forms of racial relations varied in too many ways. It seemed better to follow Park in conceiving of a series of orders of which could develop out of initial contact: institutionalised contact, acculturation, domination, paternalism, integration and pluralism (Banton, 1967: 68–75). There were also characteristic modes of change: 'acculturation leads fairly easily to integration'; domination often gave way to pluralism, whereas paternalism was more likely to be replaced by an integrated order. The underlying conceptual procedure had been to survey that academic literature which was conventionally labelled 'race relations', like sorting a set of filing cards into piles based upon the possession of common characteristics. This had produced six categories with conventional names, but the six did not differ from one another in any systematic fashion. Had analytical rather than empirical categories been employed this could have identified dimensions of difference and located empirical cases at different points on them, or have produced a bigger framework in which there might have been a number of empty cells as well as cells in which the better known cases would have been placed. Neither this scheme nor van den Berghe's was well designed for the analysis of relations in industrial cities or the structures governing face-to-face relations about which Hughes had written. The present author's scheme, again like van den Berghe's, could help show how circumstances on the macro-sociological level might influence behaviour on the micro-sociological level, but it neglected ways in which behaviour on the micro level could change the macro structures. Neither author had any adequate explanation of change from one kind of order or type to another. As the present author's critics pointed out, Afro-Americans had been thoroughly acculturated in the United States but the nature of their integration remained problematic.

Micro and macro

How to integrate the micro and macro (or bottom-up and top-down) approaches has been a long-standing problem. It was addressed by Hubert M. Blalock in *Toward a Theory of Minority Group Relations* (1967). He started at the micro level, seeing the individual as a person who utilised scarce means in order to attain goals within a patterned social system. As he acknowledged (1967: 49) this was an 'assumption that individuals will act more or less rationally so as to maximize their chances of attaining all important goals. They are expected to select the most efficient means.' The first proposition he advanced was:

In general, the larger the number of feasible alternative means for achieving a given goal, the less likely it is that this goal will be incompatible with a second goal, in the sense that the achievement of the former will reduce the probability of attaining the latter, or vice versa.

Individuals sought to maximise their status, and to this end they avoided being identified with people of low status. There were many alternative means of increasing status and so it was compatible with many other goals. From this starting point, Blalock went on to formulate propositions about economic and status factors as determinants of discrimination. He recognised that in majority–minority relations the dominant group commanded greater resources, and discussed slavery as a type case, concluding that it was usually easier to control slaves by force if (1) they were not members of indigenous groups; (2) they had been transported from long distances; (3) they had diverse cultural backgrounds. Blalock next examined four empirical situations to see what general propositions could be derived from their analysis. They were (a) competition between white settlers and native peoples; (b) middleman minorities in peasant–feudal societies; (c) the Negro and organised labour in the United States; (d) the Negro and professional sports.

Blalock contended that the exclusion of minority members from an occupation turned upon the costs and benefits to particular parties of such exclusion, the awareness of what was entailed, and the power of groups to make others accept their view of the facts or the priorities. He presented his conclusions in the form of general propositions making no mention of particular groups. Thus propositions 42 and 52 stated:

The easier it is to evaluate accurately an individual's performance level, the lower is the degree of minority discrimination by employers.

The lower the degree of purely social interaction on the job (especially interaction involving both sexes) the lower is the degree of discrimination.

The first of these is a more systematic way of saying that people are less inclined to discriminate when the costs to them of their doing so are evident. The second says that people already employed are less likely to resist the entry to their workplace of people belonging to other groups if their relations with them will be of only an impersonal kind. Blalock then added further propositions (to a total of 97) about, for example, the effect that variations in the relative size of a minority were likely to have upon the motivation of majority members to discriminate. His construction of a set of analytical concepts offered a good example of the nominalist method.

As Blalock's discussion showed, the task of integrating the micro and macro approaches is forbidding. Many, perhaps most, sociologists considered that there was urgent research to be conducted that did not require them to specify all the possible micro-sociological determinants of the data they utilised. One such line of enquiry which prospered in the United States in the 1970s was the study of status attainment – that is, of the factors associated with social mobility. The techniques developed for this purpose have been employed in the study of some other societies. For example, at the start of the 'troubles' in Northern Ireland in 1968 the number of Catholics occupying high status occupations was not proportionate to their numbers in the population. Was this due to discrimination? To approach this question it was necessary to allow for the influence of the family in assisting a child's education, shaping that child's socio-economic expectations and perhaps helping him or her to obtain employment. Since Catholics on average had lower status occupations the sociologist would expect Catholic children to do less well even in the absence of discrimination. In the 1968 data, Catholics had, on average, received 6 months less education and earned almost £3 per week less. The interrelation between family background, occupation, education, district of origin, sex, etc., could be measured by multivariate analysis. This showed that

most of the status differences disappeared once education and family background were held constant, while income differences remained significant . . . Catholic children born into elite families suffered substantial differences in education and status, while those born to average families were only slightly disadvantaged, if at all. By contrast, although Catholics generally have less education, those who nonetheless obtain advanced education then get higher status jobs than comparable Protestants.(Kelley and McAllister, 1984: 183–4)

Factors other than discrimination could account for some of the differences. Catholics may not have the same work motivation as Protestants. Higher status Catholics may be employed within their own community which, for various reasons, pays lower wages. The tendency for each community to 'look after its own' in what are regarded as internal matters is a kind of reciprocal discrimination that promotes disadvantage and should be distinguished from the kind of discrimination that is practised in areas controlled by the state, which ought to be above the two communities.

The analysis of status attainment is a technique which could be built out into a theory which would account for the differential influence of education upon the status attained by individuals from different kinds of families and with different levels of educational qualification. Education would be measured by years of schooling, variations in the quality of the education provided being incorporated in the measure by calculations reflecting expenditure on school buildings and teacher salaries.

The status attainment approach informed a comprehensive study by Stanley Lieberson entitled *A Piece of the Pie* (1980). This addressed the question why the immigrants who entered the United States after 1880 from South, Central and Eastern Europe fared so much better than Afro-Americans. He assessed the influence of differences in conditions of settlement, health, participation in the political process, residential segregation, occupations, etc. He had to explain why it was that the position of blacks in the North in the twentieth century started to deteriorate as their numbers increased. Was it because the blacks coming up from the South were less skilled and observed lower standards in their personal lives? Was it because white hostility increased? Lieberson advanced a third explanation, stressing what he called the latent structure of race relations:

if an automobile changes speed as we vary the pressure on the gas pedal, we do not assume that the engine changes in character with more or less gas. Rather we assume that the potential range of speeds was always there and is simply altered by the amount of gas received. In similar fashion, it is fruitful to assume that the reason for race relations changing with shifts in composition is not due to radical alteration in the disposition of whites, but rather that changes in the composition affect the dispositions that existed all along. (1980: 375)

In other words there was an increase in white hostility, but not because of a simple shift in attitudes. Whites were hostile towards anyone or anything which interfered with their progress towards their goals. When blacks became a greater threat, the task of fighting off black competition moved higher up the whites' scale of priorities. Lieberson also criticised what he called 'the great non sequitur': the view that the failure of blacks to advance as fast as whites reflected ethnic deficiencies. His evidence showed that they were at a greater disadvantage in many ways: the life expectancy at birth of blacks in three United States cities on the eastern seaboard was 22 years for males and a little over 26 years for females. Life expectancy at birth in the countries from which the European immigrants came was usually much higher; for example in Italy it was 34 years for males and nearly 35 years for females. Low average expectancies would reflect high infant mortality, but the differential rates suggested how much more difficult it would have been for black families to build up capital and help their children. Other differences had similar consequences. Blacks were barred from membership in craft unions; residential segregation made them pay more for their housing and so on.

A more general synthesis was later offered by Milton Yinger (1994: 171–3) in what he called a field theory of ethnic discrimination. This started with a model of a closed system made up of six interacting factors: (1) economic and political competition and conflict; (2) individual needs and anxieties; (3) traditions of prejudice, stereotypes; (4) discrimination; (5) structured inequalities in occupational, educational, political and religious institutions; (6) low motivation and skill among minority members; extra-legal protests; isolating subcultures. As with Myrdal's 'principle of cumulation', each of these was said to interact with all the others, (3) and (4) appearing to be central. Yinger (1994: 187) observed that

it is almost useless, for example, to try to reduce the ethnocentrism and prejudices of individual members of dominant ethnic groups if institutional discrimination and minority group demoralization are strong. Or, the most powerful attack on the system of discrimination will be insufficient in a context in which we disregard major ecological and demographic problems.

This last remark is his reminder of the need to allow for other factors extraneous to those in the closed model. Like Lieberson's study, it leaves many questions for other research workers to answer. Why have relations in the United States followed a course different from the courses followed in other American countries in which white immigrants have settled? Why has the colour line remained so distinct when the divisions between white ethnic groups have eroded? Is racial status simply one 'factor' that can be measured against others when assessing attainment?

To isolate a set of relations and analyse them as a social system was an important advance. Dollard brought out the bottom-up influences whereby individual sentiment contributed to the maintenance of the social order. Nor was it difficult to describe the top-down influences in the study of a fairly small and relatively self-contained Southern community in which the white elite controlled the community's relations with the outside world, e.g. by excluding blacks from voting in state and federal elections. The expression 'colour-caste' was an advance upon 'race' because it neutralised the biological implications of that word and facilitated comparison with other situations in which there was minimal mobility across a group boundary, but it was not generally adopted. The new studies introduced a form of equilibrium analysis (as can be seen from Dollard's observations on how the system was maintained by active pressures), but this had little value for the study of big cities or whole countries. Once a research worker lifted his or her sights from the small community to larger social units, the greater was the likelihood that he or she would adopt a more historical approach in the attempt to allow for all the many relevant variables.

Discrimination

To treat individuals differently because they are thought to belong in different racial groups is to discriminate. The development of concepts to explain the incidence of discrimination was therefore a major step in superseding the idiom of race. An indication of what was involved can be drawn from a British example. Most students coming to London University during the years following the Second World War had to find lodgings in private houses. Black- and brown-skinned students discovered that if they were to secure accommodation of the same quality as that secured by white students, they had to pay more – either because they were charged a higher rent or because, to find comparable accommodation, they had to travel further afield and incur higher travel costs. This extra premium they had to pay was a 'colour tax' (Carey, 1956: 69–71; Little, 1948: 271–81). The darker-skinned a student was, the higher the tax was likely to be. Such differentials are characteristic of many situations of racial discrimination. One person, A, is disposed to discriminate against another person, B, because B is assigned to a particular racial category. But A is less likely to do so if he or she can be rewarded or compensated in some way for not exercising this racial preference. Thus discrimination may occur at one price level but not at another.

Students came from Africa and India to study at London University rather than at a New York university because of their countries' historical relation with Britain. Their countries were part of the British empire, and they themselves had British citizenship. Why there was a particular relation between Britain and its colonies is a much bigger question than why there was a colour tax. Answers to it depend upon subjective judgements about which out of many influences are the most important; and are not therefore answers of a kind that can be proven. There are more certain answers to questions about the imposition and magnitude of a colour tax thanks to the way economists have developed the theory of discrimination.

The students seeking lodging were consumers within a particular sector of the housing market. The students expressed a demand for a service, whereas the managers of the property controlled the supply. Discrimination could be practised by either party. A male would-be lodger could decide that he did not want to stay in a house controlled by someone of a different race (but he would have difficulty finding someone from his own country able to give him accommodation). Or the manager – often a landlady – could decide that she did not want lodgers of a different race. When demand was weak relative to supply, the student was in a better bargaining position; when demand was relatively strong it worked to the advantage of the landlady. Price also reflected location, students being able to get better terms by travelling further out from the centre. Because one landlady did not know enough about what other landladies were charging or what their rooms were like, prices did not change very rapidly to reflect changes in relative demand and supply; so, by hunting around, students were sometimes able to get a better deal.

In this case, the landladies were white women who preferred to take white students as lodgers, but the sociological problem posed would have been the same had they been black women who preferred to take in black lodgers. It would have been the same had they been house-owners who hesitated about selling their properties to would-be purchasers of a different race or employers who did not wish to engage employees of a different race. Discrimination in all these circumstances may spring from similar motivations which can be classified as factors of taste, risk and profit.

The landladies were often middle-aged women who owned and occupied large houses, renting out rooms. The landladies provided breakfast and an evening meal; they frequently arranged for the washing of lodgers' clothing, might require lodgers to be home by a particular hour, and did not permit guests of the opposite sex to visit lodgers' rooms. So the relationship was sometimes of a quasi-familial kind. Many landladies were middle-class women who had inherited their houses on the death of their husbands or parents. Taking in lodgers enabled them to continue living in the houses to which they were accustomed. Taking in students did not demean their status so much as taking in other kinds of lodger might have done. Their reluctance to accommodate African and Indian students was a compound of fears that interpersonal relations with them might be more difficult (what Krech and Crutchfield, 1947: 222–4, called exposure to the object) and a fear for their own status (identification with the object). If they took in black- or brown-skinned students, the neighbours might think they did so only because they could not get white students, and this would be because the standard of their rooms was not high enough. In such circumstances, the colour tax can be seen as a compensation to the landlady for departing from her preferred course of action. A landlord who did not live on the premises and rented out rooms as a business might not have had the same personal feelings (or tastes) with respect to his property and could have been expected to charge whatever the market would bear; if there were not many such landlords they would have been able to charge the African and Indian students higher rents because of the tastes of other suppliers of accommodation.

A man who wishes to sell his house may prefer to sell it to someone of the same race because of his personal preferences or because he believes his neighbours would otherwise feel let down. He might even fear sanctions against him if he were to depart from an expected pattern of behaviour. He, too, has a taste for discrimination. In all probability, he will sell the house to someone of a different race if, by so doing, he can get a substantially higher price. The variation in price between a same-race sale and a different-race sale represents the strength of his taste or preference for the former transaction. Equally, an employer may prefer to give jobs to men and women of his or her own race, but many people who would not like to have someone of different race working alongside them as an equal do not mind having such a person serve them in a menial capacity. A taste for avoiding contact with persons of a different race – or of a particular race – is specific to particular relationships, especially those entailing social equality and intimacy. This explains why most social distance is displayed when it is a question of a relationship by marriage.

Some landladies who had not previously taken lodgers from Africa or India seem to have thought that doing so might lead to problems they preferred to avoid. They discriminated because of what they saw as a risk. Risk arises when information is lacking about the consequences to be expected from an action, which is a feature of many forms of discriminatory behaviour. Buyers and sellers do not know how a market will respond to future events. They lack information about probable futures, and it would take time or money to collect or purchase the sort of information that would help them decide what to do. If the consequences of mistakes are costly, they will be averse to risky decisions. This general principle leads to what has been named 'The Statistical Theory of Racism and

Sexism' (Phelps, 1972). It can be illustrated from the labour market, starting from what is called search behaviour.

This can be the search of one employer for an employee to perform a certain kind of work in exchange for a given reward, but it can equally well be the search of a would-be worker for a job, a landlord for a tenant, a would-be purchaser for a house, a woman for a husband, or a sports team manager for a player. It assumes that the search carries a cost (because the searcher's time is scarce) and that there is a risk of a further cost if the person or situation selected does not meet the specifications. When deciding whether a particular case falls within the acceptable limits, a searcher will interpret the signs displayed. If he is an employer (and male), he may judge an applicant by interview, references, trial, or some combination of these. How much he invests in researching an applicant's qualifications will depend upon his estimate of the benefits derivable from increased expenditure on selection relative to the costs entailed by taking the first apparently suitable person; this will include a calculation of how long the applicant, if appointed, will stay in the job, and the difficulty of dismissing someone who proves unsatisfactory. The employer will interpret the evidence in the light of beliefs derived from experience and the impression gained from other sources. These beliefs may be without foundation but nevertheless self-perpetuating. If an employer believed that red-haired people were excitable, he might refuse to engage them for jobs requiring coolness; if they got cross about being discriminated against, this could then be taken as proof of their excitability.

Another example derives from a study conducted in England in 1966–7 (Daniel, 1968: 201–3). An Englishman, a Hungarian, and a West Indian applied to different companies for motor insurance, each claiming the same record of previous driving experience. In 6 out of 20 applications, the West Indian was refused insurance cover altogether; on 11 occasions he was quoted a higher premium; and on only 3 occasions was his minority status ignored. The average premiums quoted by the 14 companies that offered coverage to all three applicants were as follows: West Indian £58, Hungarian £49, Englishman £45. So the West Indian encountered a colour tax of nearly 29 per cent, presumably because he was regarded as a greater risk. Because all premium quotations are individual, he might never know he was being charged more and, if the companies never examined their records with respect to ethnicity, they would never find out whether or not such estimates of risk were accurate.

Money is said to have no smell, and one person's money is supposed to buy no more than another person's. If companies are concerned primarily with making a profit, they cannot afford to be distracted by the ethnic characteristics of their employees or their customers. The greater the competition with other companies, the less attention that can be paid to economically irrelevant features such as race; this should increase the cost of any taste for discrimination and any miscalculation of risk. Most markets, however, fall very far short of perfect competitiveness and, in so doing, they open up the possibilities that some individuals will be less than efficient, while others will profit from discrimination.

In many countries laws have been introduced under which any person who denies housing or employment (or other services) to someone on the grounds of race, colour, national or ethnic origin can be fined or obliged to pay compensation to the victim. In the United States, courts have been able to order an employer to follow a recruitment policy designed to increase the proportion of employees of minority origin up to a particular figure. Since the possibility of any such legal action will increase the costs of discrimination, it is likely to reduce its incidence.

Taste, risk, and profit are therefore motivations that are of different importance in different market situations. When the discriminator is motivated by taste, this gives rise to categorical discrimination, the less favourable treatment of all persons assigned to a particular social category. When the discriminator is motivated by considerations of risk, this results in statistical discrimination, the less favourable treatment of persons that arises from beliefs about the likelihood of persons in a particular category having particular attributes. The discriminator may have no personal prejudice or taste for discrimination, and understand full well that some people in the category will have the attributes he seeks, but be disinclined to spend time identifying them. Equally, someone who discriminates for profit may have no such personal attitude. When a discriminator is motivated by profit, he or she takes advantage of a pattern of categorical discrimination in society at large. Thus a landlady could have imposed a colour tax to benefit from the tastes of other landladies.

When discriminators take for granted a prevailing pattern of inequality, it is more difficult to bring about change. From the standpoint of those who wish, for whatever reason, to maintain a divided society (such as that of the US Deep South during the early twentieth century), it is important to prevent members of the dominant group from appreciating that their prejudices have a price. If they were free to decide that price for themselves, some would discriminate less. A white employer might prefer to replace a white worker with a cheaper black worker; by cutting his wage bill he might force other employers to do likewise. The Mississippi studies mentioned earlier in this chapter showed how the maintenance of white supremacy depended on the mobilisation of white power to maintain the colour line and exclude any resort to a colour tax. Blacks had to be disenfranchised. Whites regarded certain kinds of contact with them as polluting. There was an elaborate etiquette that required blacks constantly to acknowledge their subordination. An unsubstantiated report of a breach of the racial code could sometimes result in a lynching. Black subordination could the more easily be maintained because higher-status whites were ready to make exceptions in favour of blacks who conformed to their expectations, and to protect them from lower-status whites. Possibly deviant whites were also kept in line, but the pressure on blacks, especially males, was tremendous. A few were able to emigrate to the cities of the North and a few were able to isolate themselves socially, but for the most part any nonconforming conduct was likely to be interpreted by whites as defiance, and to evoke life-threatening sanctions.

To maintain such a system, every individual member had to be assigned to either the white or the black category. Some individuals with a small amount of black ancestry and who could have passed for white were nevertheless accounted blacks; their presence did not upset the system because most Mississippi towns were relatively small and almost everyone knew or could deduce everyone else's social place. After the Civil War, the competitive pressures in the southern economy had been reducing black–white income differentials, but then the agrarian impoverishment of the 1890s led to the expulsion of the blacks from many of the new jobs they had secured. During the depression of the 1930s there was a similar reaction. Whites had allowed black workers to take certain jobs, but when unemployment rose white workers used violence to take those jobs back.

A greater challenge was posed to the system when there were whole communities which did not fit in, such as the Chinese and the Choctaw Indians in Mississippi. Some Chinese were assigned to the black category but, after a struggle, the community as a whole managed to get itself reclassified. Relatively many Choctaw Indians were recognised as a third category but otherwise were liable to be treated like blacks and, for example, required to use black coaches on the railway, waiting rooms, drinking fountains and so forth. Phenotypical features were used as signs for allocating people to categories with different privileges; because these signs were inherited, everyone in the same household was assigned to the same category. All stratified social systems depend on this principle because if husbands and wives, or parents and children, were assigned to different categories the system would be difficult to operate and doubt would be cast on the legitimacy of the categories themselves.

Discrimination in housing markets

In studying discrimination it is essential to take full account of the special characteristics of different markets. The sector of the London housing market in which colonial students sought accommodation in the post-war period was a small part of a much larger market which was divided, in the first place between the sector in which dwellings were available for renting and that in which they were available for purchase. Either sector could be further divided by governmental controls or informal practices, as the implementation of the 'fair rents' legislation in Britain divided the rental sector and the federal regulation of mortgage lending in the United States was used to channel black access to the purchase of properties. Either sector could also be divided by price.

The divisions within the London rental market were illustrated by a study in 1970 of the rents paid by white and coloured (i.e. black and Asian) tenants in three boroughs (Banton, 1983: 355–6). It found that coloured tenants (a) were underrepresented by 22 per cent among the tenants of unfurnished apartments, (b) were paying rents for unfurnished apartments on average 11.3 per cent higher than those charged to whites (a colour tax), and (c) were paying rents for furnished apartments at rates similar to those which whites were paying. These findings reflected the influence of government controls, imposed during the war because of the special circumstances that then prevailed but which had the effect of preventing landlords from increasing rents to the point at which demand and supply would be in balance. The controls were tighter in the unfurnished than in the furnished sector (it is, after all, difficult to price variations in the quality of furniture). Faced with an excess number of would-be tenants of unfurnished apartments and restricted in their ability to increase rents, landlords allocated tenancies on the basis of personal rather than commercial criteria so that fewer minority people obtained tenancies unless they paid more. The market in furnished accommodation catered to those who were unable to buy their own properties, rent from the local authority, or obtain an unfurnished apartment (as most would have preferred). The whites who sought furnished apartments were in the market of last resort and may not, in the eyes of landlords, have appeared significantly more attractive tenants than the immigrants, but the looser controls might have been expected to result in some differential rent enabling landlords to profit from the weaker market position of the blacks (more Asians may have been lodgers in Asian-owned houses). Any attempt to account for findings such as these after the event is bound to be speculative, but no such attempt is likely to be persuasive unless it takes account of ethnic preferences and the structure of the market in which they are expressed.

The rent controls which structured the renting market were continued for political reasons. The building of houses and apartment blocks for renting by municipalities ('council houses') was part of a political programme. This is a reminder of how housing markets are subject to political control and therefore objects of political struggle. The processes were clarified in a study of a district in Birmingham by John Rex and Robert Moore, *Race, Community and Conflict* (1967). The authors maintained that just as a social class is composed of people with a common position and common interests in the market for labour, so in Birmingham there were seven 'housing classes' composed of people differently placed with respect to the acquisition and use of housing. Members of these classes used their political power to further their interests. Immigrants were at the back of the queue because they were newcomers with little political power.

In its application to the British housing market, the theory of discrimination showed the importance of the racial preferences of suppliers (in the case of the landladies), of distinct market sectors associated with socio-economic status, and of the political dimension to the whole situation. When there is residential segregation of persons assigned to racial categories, this affects the kinds of social contacts they make. Children who grow up in a segregated area are likely to develop different attitudes towards inter-group contact from those who grow up in mixed areas. It is therefore of some importance to note that a comparison of the 1981 and 1991 census results indicates that racial segregation increased slightly during this period (Owen, 1996). Experience in the United States shows how devastating the effects of spatial separation can be.

The present high level of racial segregation in the United States is a twentieth-century phenomenon which cannot be explained as part of the heritage of slavery. Scholars have documented in some detail how in the Northern cities during the years 1900–30 the prevailing pattern of racial integration was broken and ghettos were created. This then affected social norms and influenced racial preferences. In their study *American Apartheid* (1993), Douglas S. Massey and Nancy A. Denton attributed the dramatic increase in residential segregation to industrialisation and migration. Industrialisation meant that production moved from the home or small shop to the factory employing hundreds of labourers. The oversight of industrial methods of production created a new managerial class composed primarily of native white Americans. The retail sector expanded dramatically. Thanks to the new transport systems people who worked together no longer needed to live together in the same neighbourhoods. Whereas many of the blacks living in the Northern cities had been professionals or relatively educated persons, the new demand for labour attracted from the South large numbers of poor blacks whom the whites did not welcome as neighbours (Sowell, 1981: 66–74) and who were repeatedly used as strike-breakers in Northern labour disputes between

1890 and 1930. Denied access to trade unions, the black workers had little to lose from crossing picket-lines, and this added to the cycle of mutual distrust between white and black workers. Black immigration led to what Massey and Denton called a 'new regime in race relations', in which any blacks who lived away from recognised 'black' neighbourhoods had their houses burned or bombed. After 1920, they said, generalised communal violence aimed at the expulsion of blacks from white neighbourhoods gave way to a more systematic and targeted violence along the periphery of an expanding ghetto. This was complemented by the formation of white neighbourhood 'improvement associations' designed to prevent black entry, particularly by devising restrictive covenants under which residents contracted not to sell or rent their property to blacks. Real estate agents quickly found that by 'block-busting' and similar tactics (described in Banton, 1983: 343–6) they could profit from managing the process by which blocks on the edge of ghettos had eventually to change because of the pressure of black demand. The concentration of black settlement in ghettos also brought benefits to black politicians and businessmen. The end result was a pattern in which many in both racial groups had short-term interests in the maintenance of a divided market.

Changes in residential patterns have been measured using indices of dissimilarity which calculate the proportions of minority persons who would have to move house in order to achieve an even spread across the whole city. Calculations based on 'wards' show an increase in segregation over the period 1910–40 of 59.2 to 89.2 for Northern, and from 38.3 to 81.0 for Southern cities. Higher figures are obtained using measures of racial isolation based upon 'blocks' instead of wards. One such study showed an increase in black residential isolation in 17 Northern cities over the period 1890–1930 of 6.7 to 29.9. Five dimensions of segregation have been identified. There is *unevenness* as a result of over- and under-representation in residential areas, *isolation* because of no sharing with members of other groups; *clustering* when the areas are contiguous; *concentration* when they are dense; and *centralisation* when they are within the urban core. As segregation accumulates across the different dimensions, its effects intensify. Not only are blacks more segregated than other groups on any single dimension but they are more segregated on all dimensions simultaneously, leading to what Massey and Denton called 'hypersegregation'.

The increase in black urbanisation in the 1950s, coupled with the availability of federal finance for urban renewal, led to a great expansion in public housing. Apartments in many of the new housing projects were allocated only to blacks, thus creating a 'second ghetto'. The Fair Housing Act of 1968 inspired some hope that the discriminatory practices upon which the whole system was built might at last be modified, but politically motivated opposition had emasculated the law's enforcement provisions and it was not until amendments were agreed in 1988 that these hopes could be revived (see Goering and Wienk, 1996, for information on federal action against racial discrimination in mortgage lending and the use of 'audits' to measure discrimination).

The analysis of discrimination in housing markets shows how micro and macro factors are inter-related and reinforce one another. This had been emphasised earlier when Gunnar Myrdal advanced what he called the 'principle of cumulation', describing how 'White prejudice and discrimination keep the Negro in low standards of living, health, education, manners and morals. This, in its turn, gives support to white prejudice. White prejudice and Negro standards thus mutually "cause" each other' (1944: 75). Myrdal also wrote of an 'American Dilemma' as a conflict between a desire to act in accordance with a belief in human equality and the norms of everyday life which embodied inequality. Housing studies have shown that blacks and whites believe in integration as a general principle but find it well-nigh impossible to live according to such an ideal.

Since Myrdal wrote, understanding of the processes underlying residential segregation has been deepened by the analysis of 'tipping points'. Members of all groups have their preferences as to 'ethnic mix'. Some like to live exclusively with members of their own group; others like varying degrees of diversity. Some will tolerate a certain proportion of others but will sell up and move if their threshold is passed. Thus an 'integrated' neighbourhood can suddenly change as the tipping point is passed; members of both groups want a degree of integration but because their preferences differ neither group gets what it wants (Schelling, 1978: 137–66). This may also explain why it is that there are some localities in the United States which have recently experienced declining segregation. It may be that whites accept a certain proportion of blacks in their neighbourhood but still retain objections to a neighbourhood which is more than, say, one-third black. The areas which are less segregated may be predominantly white with black minorities below the whites' threshold of tolerance. The study of preferences for ethnic mix in residential areas will be increasingly important if any such process continues. This approach reopens the micro–macro problem in a new way because if people's micro preferences are to be realised, ways will have to be found of regulating the market.

Residential segregation affects elections. It means that in constituencies with a majority of black voters, a black legislator can be elected who may feel that his or her prime obligation is to serve black interests. If the proportion of black legislators does not correspond to their proportion in the state, constituency boundaries may be redrawn to achieve that effect. The US Supreme Court has been required to rule on a series of appeals against state actions of this kind. In *Miller* v. *Johnson* (1995), the court held that if a state, in order to meet its obligations under the Voting Rights Act 1965, drew boundaries that were bizarre, this was a violation of citizens' rights under the equal protection clause of the US constitution. The underlying problem is whether the segregation of political districts by race, in order to achieve the short-term objective of racial equality in representation, has so serious a long-term effect of deepening racial divisions that it should be prohibited.

Discrimination in employment markets

Since discrimination is not the only cause of unequal treatment, analyses of employment markets often need to compare its effects with those attributable to other causes. For example, in countries like the United States and Great Britain, the average earnings of whites tend to be higher than those of blacks, and the earnings of males higher than those of females. Since incomes differ in accordance with qualifications, education, age, union power, occupation and region, as well as with race and gender, to weigh one factor against another while allowing for historical variations in economic circumstances is a complex task. Nor is it easy to discover what are the real determinants lying behind what appears to be a racial factor when this is compared with something else. It may that the proportion of blacks with sought-after qualifications is relatively low and that the average quality of the black labour supply is therefore lower than that of the whites. It may be that white employers discriminate between blacks and whites and that there is a difference in the demand for the two categories of labour.

The main factors on the supply and demand sides which have been identified in the debate about the causes of racial inequalities in earnings are set out in figure 5.1. Much of this debate has so far consisted of attempts to demonstrate the importance of particular components and much remains to be done in assessing the extent to which different components interact and complement each other in the explanation of particular inequalities. Some participants in the debate have emphasised the supply side and would discuss this first. However, it is easier to begin with the factors on the demand side by drawing upon analyses developed in the United States; a discussion of inequalities in Britain, where some members of racial minorities are relatively recent immigrants, can then introduce new factors on the supply side.

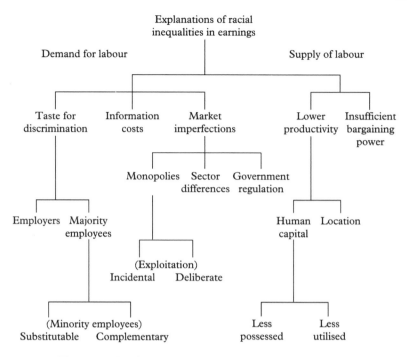

Figure 5.1 Explanations of inequalities in earnings

Economists often define discrimination in a way which suits their purposes and diverges from its legal use. English law – which has followed the law of the United States in this field – defines racial discrimination in the first place as occurring when, on racial grounds, someone treats another 'less favourably than he treats or would treat other persons'. This conception of direct discrimination has then been extended by the addition of penalties for indirect discrimination, defined as the unjustified imposition of a requirement or condition with which members of another racial group can less easily comply (in the United States, this is the distinction between disparate treatment and unjustifiable disparate impact). It is only actions and practices which can be declared unlawful because discriminatory. If members of a minority are on average less well qualified, their earnings will be lower than those of the majority; this will be an inequality, but it will not be proof of discrimination. When economists identify an inequality which cannot be attributed to such variables (or other factors incorporated in figure 5.1), they infer that this residual is the result of discrimination without necessarily identifying who discriminated or where the discrimination occurred. Sometimes they infer that the characteristics of the minority labour force are an outcome of previous discrimination. If no qualified blacks apply for a post because none have been trained, the employer has not discriminated; if none have been trained because none thought it worthwhile acquiring the training, those responsible for the training have not discriminated; but why did no blacks think it worthwhile undergoing training? Was it because their expectations of white discrimination were so strong that they thought that training would be insufficient to get them such a job? Since blacks have lived in the United States for so many more generations than most of the white ethnic groups, at what points in the chain of causes are the inequalities starting? No remedial policy is likely to succeed unless the nature and influence of every relevant factor has been examined.

The demand-side factors represented in figure 5.1 begin with the concept of a 'taste for discrimination' advanced by Gary S. Becker (1957). White employers may, for whatever reason, prefer to have whites working for them rather than blacks, while white workers may sooner have white workmates. An all-white workforce would have for them an amenity value, just as the location of a house in a conveniently situated and high status residential neighbourhood has an amenity value in the eyes of a would-be house-purchaser. White workers who are required to work alongside blacks may leave their employment unless they are compensated for the disamenity, just as they will object to working in unpleasant conditions unless they receive additional reward. An individual is said to have a taste for discrimination if he or she acts as if he or she were willing to pay extra or to forfeit income in order to avoid transactions with people assigned to the category which is the subject of discrimination. In this way a disposition to discriminate is measured by its effect on actual behaviour in a situation of choice.

Becker began by imagining a society consisting of two racial groups, blacks and whites, with similar work preferences. The whites preferred to avoid associating with blacks, so a white employer would, other things being equal, engage blacks only at a lower wage. Whites would be paid rather more and blacks rather less than they would receive in a colour-blind market. Though it started as a model of a single society, Becker's model came to represent a situation in which a white society rich in capital traded with a black society rich in labour. Though whites lost income because black productivity was not fully utilised, both parties benefited from the trade.

The economist who employs Becker's model can assume that white employers have a taste for discrimination while white workers and consumers of the product do not; equally, he can assume that either the white workers or the consumers have such a taste and that the other two parties do not. It is not necessary to follow through such possibilities, but it should be noted that some outcomes depend upon whether black workers are substitutable for white. If black workers are as productive as whites in a particular occupation and will work for lower pay (because they face discrimination in alternative occupations also) it will be in the employer's interest to replace that section of his workforce with black workers, and this will be easier to do if the section is a segregated one. If, however, the black workers are complementary to the white workers instead of being potential substitutes (e.g. because they will work as assistants to more highly skilled workers), the white workers may want extra pay as compensation for having to work with blacks. The outcome of a white taste for discrimination in these circumstances will therefore be an increased racial wage differential.

Hiring workers must always entail some uncertainty about how they will perform. It may not be worthwhile for an employer to investigate the background and previous work history of every candidate for a vacant post. As has already been mentioned, the search costs may be too high. Statistical discrimination may enable the employer to reduce the costs of recruitment but, if other employers behave similarly, they transfer a burden to society as a whole by creating a disadvantaged minority. It gives rise to what an economist would call an 'externality', a public cost that can be compared with that of pollution.

Calling something a 'market imperfection' will, for many people, imply that the thing in question is undesirable. It is easily assumed that all monopolies are bad. Yet some restrictions upon competition are now taken for granted in industrial societies, and none more than those on which the professions are based. In a completely free market citizens would be at liberty to engage anyone they wished to remove their appendixes or to present their cases in court. They are denied this power by rules which, with the backing of the state, enforce a monopoly allowing only qualified people to practise medicine and law.

The simplest example of an imperfectly competitive market is that of monopoly (one seller, many buyers) in which the seller is able to exploit a position of power to charge a higher price or be less efficient. Another example is that of monopsony (one buyer, many sellers). Thus employers in the South African mining industry, seeking black labour, established a common recruiting agency to enlist workers at standard rates, paying them less than they would have done had the companies been bidding against one another. They created a monopsony and benefited from the greater bargaining power it gave them (Banton, 1983: 218–21). The black workers were subject to a kind of colour tax. South Africa under apartheid offered an example of a triangular relationship between the (white) employer, the higher-paid (white) section of the labour force, and the lower-paid (black) section which until a late stage was forbidden to form trade unions and was therefore in a weak bargaining position. The greater bargaining power of the white workers enabled them to get a bigger share of the employer's wage bill and therefore to profit from the exploitation of the black workers' weaker position. How such profit has been – and is – divided between the employers and the higher-paid labour is an empirical issue to be analysed industry by industry. If the higher-paid labour has fully exploited its advantage, an employer might derive no benefit from racial discrimination. Because the state defined which jobs might be performed by black workers, there was an incentive for employers to redefine jobs and create new categories to give more work to the less costly black workers. If a new group of workers appears (as by immigration) offering to supply labour, employers may be interested in engaging them at rates lower than those paid to existing employees. It will be the existing employees, not the employers, who have an interest in discriminating against them.

Market imperfections also result from the way technological change affects the structure of the labour market. One industry may be declining because of changed methods of production, competition from elsewhere, or reduced demand for its product, whereas another industry that is favoured by the pattern of change may be making greater profits and paying its employees higher wages. Two such industries may recruit their workforces in different ways. An industry in what is called the secondary sector, employing mainly unskilled workers and with a relatively stable technology and a high expenditure on labour relative to capital equipment, should have a management anxious to reduce the wage bill. If there is a plentiful supply of labour, workers will compete with one another for employment, which will be offered to those willing to work for the lowest wages. An industry with the opposite characteristics is said to belong to the primary sector. Its management will spend much more on employee selection and training, and an internal labour market will be created with offers of promotion for those who keep abreast of technological change. The management will seek to minimise (relative to the level of output) the costs of both training and of wages. Workers will compete with one another on the basis of their relative positions and the posts will go to those who can be trained most cheaply. Ethnic minorities tend to be concentrated in the secondary sector whereas the primary sector is dominated by ethnic majority persons of high education.

A third set of components in the demand for labour is constituted by government regulation, for this can have a profound effect upon the structure of a labour market. Governments finance occupational training and services for putting potential employees in touch with employers; they provide financial assistance to some industries and subject others to controls. They either combat monopoly power or close their eyes to it. Governments compose and enforce the laws about employment, the conduct of disputes and how much power a trade union can mobilise if it wishes to either attack or defend a discriminatory practice. So markets are always embedded in political processes.

The division between the demand side and the supply side in the explanation of earnings differences is an analytical one which, of itself, has no political intent. That is not how it is always read, for the demand-side factors are interpreted as evidence that the lower earnings are attribu-table to discrimination by others while the supply-side factors attribute lower earnings to the lesser value of the labour supplied under prevailing market conditions. According to Thomas Sowell (1981: 291–2), the prevailing ideology of social science has led most commentators to under-estimate the supply-side factors. In his words: 'not only history but also economics argues against the widespread assumption that group income differences are largely a function of discrimination rather than human capital differences or differences in age, geographical distribution, and other factors. Translating subjective prejudice into overt discrimination is costly for profit-seeking competitive firms.' In a separate book he has assembled a mass of evidence from around the world 'to demonstrate the reality, persistence, and consequences of cultural differences – contrary to many of today's grand theories, based on the supposedly dominant role of "objective conditions", "economic forces", or "social structures"' (Sowell, 1994: xii).

A group's resources include natural resources (like oil fields or a strategic location), physical capital (like systems of roads, railways and harbours constructed by earlier generations) and human capital (notably the education, skills, and motivation of the people). In the Second World War much of Germany's physical capital was destroyed. One school of theorists would argue that the human capital of the nation enabled both the Federal and the Democratic Republics to equal or surpass the national income of countries that in 1945 were more fa-voured in respect of natural resources and physical capital. These theor-ists would also maintain that human capital can be transferred, as when migrants with technical skills or high work motivation have gone to new countries and overtaken native groups in their average earnings. With technological progress human capital tends to grow (e.g. through the knowledge of how to build ever more efficient machines) but some kinds of knowledge become obsolete. Motivations can be damaged by political instability and the fear that a man may not be able to reap where he has sown. Economic aid that is badly planned or administered can leave a poor country worse off. With the introduction of mass production, talents that have counted as human capital can lose their value through a process of de-skilling.

In this way the theory of human capital can be used to explain the relative mobility of ethnic or racial groups, just as the theory of status attainment sets out to explain the mobility of individuals. Sowell (1983: 248) attests:

> Numerous confiscations of the wealth of Jews in Europe or of the Chinese in south east Asia have been followed by their rising again to prosperity and wealth. In the United States, penniless refugees from Cuba, Korea or Viet Nam have begun in the most menial occupations and within one generation have produced a business-owning middle class.

Sowell contends that the effect of enslavement was to destroy much of the human capital that Africans brought to the New World. Irresponsibility and evasion of work were pervasive under slavery and continued after it. Blacks moved out of the South into the Northern cities, in the late nineteenth century, under very unpropitious circumstances. Their prior experience was less valuable than that of European immigrants coming from urban backgrounds. So 'Blacks are unique only in how far they have come and the degree of opposition they have encountered' (Sowell, 1983: 132). This theory states that cultural characteristics determine people's responses to incentives. If the circumstances are such that they are satisfied by the rewards they receive, the original attitudes are reinforced. People develop attention to detail, punctuality, perseverance, willingness to obey orders and a readiness to work as members of a team. These are constituents of human capital in an industrial society, and by drawing attention to them the theory can furnish a plausible explanation of why things happened as they did. Most of what pass as sociological theories can do this. The objection is that without an independent measure of human capital no one can tell how important it is or whether it is genuinely an independent variable.

Lower productivity may stem not from differences in human capital so much as from differences in the utilisation of their work capacities by different groups. Economic analysis deals only with the capital at the time it is utilised, but there is also a sense in which it can be invested. Economically successful parents can give their children a better start in life, as by buying them a more expensive education. The kinds of school attended, for how many years, and the qualifications obtained, can all be measured, but economic success also depends upon motivation, attitude to work, and personal qualities which are difficult to measure and sometimes evident only after the event. An analysis of data obtained from the US census of 1970 concluded that ethnic groups differed in their investment in their children's schooling. Up to their teens children benefited from having a parent who gave them attention time. Once they became teenagers they benefited more from their parents' earning power (Chiswick, 1988). So if a parent who could have been in employment chose instead to give time to a young child the parent's human capital would be used in a way which brought a later return in economic terms.

Sowell's interpretation of the black experience in the United States is strengthened by his comparisons with the economic success of the Chinese and Japanese minorities, but some of their success can be attributed to their having settled on the west coast rather than the east, and of their having been in the right position to take advantage of the new opportunities opening up there. Some of the inequalities in earnings can be attributed to variations in the return upon capital investment in different regions and industries. As a source of inequality, such variations arise from the interaction between the demand for and supply of labour, but they can be regarded as belonging on the supply side since in a perfectly competitive market workers would migrate from the low-paying to the high-paying regions and industries, and the differential would be reduced. If there is a regional difference it is because workers have other reasons for not migrating.

Earnings are affected by differences in the relative bargaining power of employers and employees. In some occupations it is relatively easy to organise a trade union and ensure that everyone who follows that occupation becomes and remains a member. In other occupations, like that of farm worker, unionisation is difficult. A powerful union can increase the earnings of its members relative to those of workers in occupations which cannot mobilise so much bargaining power.

Labour markets also demonstrate the inter-generational transmission of inequality. Those who have been successful in economic terms are able to use their wealth to give their children the advantages of more expensive schooling, neighbourhood services, educational experiences, introductions to better-paid employment and so on. So if, in one generation, members of one group enjoy a higher socio-economic status than members of another, much of that differential will be transmitted to their children's generation. In some circumstances the chances that young people starting at the bottom of a status hierarchy have of overcoming the obstacles that face them are so small that they are said to constitute an underclass. Since the criteria for defining an underclass are not agreed (Martinello, 1996) this is a contested issue, but there can be no doubt that the inter-generational transmission of inequality is of the greatest importance to the maintenance of racial and ethnic inequalities in all societies.

Before leaving this topic, it may be appropriate to note that the market model can be utilised even in circumstances in which participants are not conscious of being influenced by market considerations, such as the selection of partners in marriage. In Hawaii up to 1945 almost every Japanese–Hawaiian bride married a Japanese bridegroom but, by 1980, 59 per cent of Japanese were marrying spouses from other groups. The Japanese girls had stayed on longer in the educational system; they had met boys of other groups and were better informed about the expectations of marriage that prevailed outside the circles in which they had been brought up. Many were not attracted to the prospect of playing the traditionally deferential role of the Japanese wife. As a result, the non-Japanese bridegroom obtained a bride who was more solicitous than the brides in his own group. Thus when the Japanese women married out, both of the partners got a better deal, in that she did not have to be so subservient and he got a more deferential bride. This put pressure on the Japanese men and the non-Japanese women to be less demanding in their expectations of the marital relationship. Similar trends have been noted in Los Angeles. They recall the complaints of women in the United States that so many of the servicemen stationed in Germany after the Second Word War were coming home with German brides because German women conceded men more authority in the home.

Ethnic origin

When Huxley and Haddon contended that it was more accurate to speak of ethnic groups than races, they were writing about the names for relatively large groups that were sometimes called nations. When Lloyd Warner and his associates first referred to ethnicity in the United States they were discussing an attribute of minorities within a state. The word 'ethnicity' has therefore been used as a name for two social forms which are best distinguished. The ethnicity of the Italians and Poles in Europe can be called a primary ethnicity because their ethnic alignment coincides with their national alignment. The ethnicity of the Italian-Americans or the Polish-Americans can then be accounted a secondary ethnicity in which ethnic group members compare themselves within a framework of shared citizenship. Sometimes a national boundary changes, or a new state is created, and in such circumstances a secondary ethnicity can become primary. Ethnicity is not just a question of the kind of self-identity people profess, but also the kind of social identity accorded by others. Sometimes majority groups fail to perceive their ethnic distinctiveness and count only minorities as possessing an ethnicity. This has been called 'minus one' ethnicity because members of the dominant group omit their own when adding up the number of ethnic groups.

International law (and the national laws of many countries) prohibits discrimination on the grounds of a person's ethnic origin, not that person's ethnicity. Ethnic origin is to be determined objectively by reference to persons' ancestry not by reference to any sense of identity. The expression 'ethnic origin' can be used transculturally to compare the significance vested in commonality of ethnic origin in one country compared with another, so it has advantages over looser references to a person's ethnicity which pretend that ethnicity is as clear-cut an attribute as nationality.

This chapter began with an account of Dollard's dissatisfaction with the view of the social system as a machine which simply went on working according to an established pattern. In 1969 a Norwegian anthropologist, Fredrik Barth, expressed a similar dissatisfaction in a path-breaking essay about the way social scientists had been approaching the study of ethnic groups, whether primary or secondary. They had not asked how such groups maintained their boundaries when there were individuals who crossed them in either direction. Then Michael H. Lyon (1972) suggested that ethnic groups could be defined as constituted by inclusive boundaries and distinguished from those that were formed on the basis of race. He opened the possibility that a group might be both racial and ethnic. Others followed. Sandra Wallman (1979) held that:

the value of ethnicity [she might have written 'shared ethnic origin'] varies. It can be regarded as a resource which will, for some purposes and in some situations, be mobilised to the advantage of a social, cultural or racial category of people; will have no meaning or value at all in other situations; and will, in still others, in which other needs and objectives are paramount, be construed as a liability to be escaped or denied as far as possible. Ethnicity is not, therefore, the same as culture or 'race'. It is not simply difference; it is the *sense* of difference which can occur where members of a particular cultural or 'racial' group interact with non-members. *Real* differences between groups of people are no more (and no less) than *potential* identity markers for the members of those groups. This potential is taken up and mobilised only where it suits the purposes of a particular encounter.

This view was generally adopted and became the basis for further studies.

At much the same time new directions for research on ethnic relations were mapped by Nathan Glazer and Daniel P. Moynihan (1975: 19–20). They noted that some writers conceived of ethnicity as a primordial attribute, assuming that everyone has an ethnic identity which may be fundamental to his or her very being. Other writers they called circumstantialists because they regarded the character and intensity of ethnic consciousness as the product of circumstances. Thereafter anyone who wrote of 'ethnicity' was obliged to think more carefully about the sense in which the word was being employed. Members of some minorities have been particularly inclined to a primordial self-conception and unimpressed by any suggestion from an outside observer that this is a reflection of the group's circumstances.

The possible elaboration of the distinction between race and ethnicity was of interest to social scientists outside North America because they have long been hesitant about the way the word 'race' was used in the US Civil Rights Act of 1866 and then accepted by social scientists in that country. The Europeans have doubted whether it would ever be possible to correct the misunderstanding implicit in the idiom of race if the word was used in the US way. They have had to confront in their own countries political problems different from those in the United States. In that country African-Americans were citizens whose ancestors had been in the country for many generations; the prime remedy for the injustices they suffered was to be sought in securing more effectively their constitutional rights as citizens. In European countries the physically distinguishable minorities (which would in Canada have been called the visible minorities) were immigrants. When they were already citizens (as in the United Kingdom) they were still perceived as strangers who had to legitimate their right to residence.

The vocabulary developed for describing inter-group relations in North America was not always acceptable elsewhere. The French rejected what they called the Anglo-Saxon model because they thought it gave official approval to the recognition of differences which were the result only of popular prejudices. They have given the word *racisme* a broad meaning, as including ideology, attitudes and discriminatory behaviour to correspond with what the English have called 'race relations' (e.g. Taguieff, 1988: 228). In Germany the word *Rassismus* had too many associations with the Nazi era to be acceptable, and so hostility towards foreigners was designated *Fremdenfeindlichkeit* or xenophobia. These were folk concepts belonging in the ordinary language, but they pointed to some of the ways in which attitudes differed from those in North America and they help explain why European social scientists had to undertake conceptual analyses of their own.

At the outset they had to consider in what ways the social frameworks in their countries differed from one another and from that in the United States. France provides the clearest starting point because in 1789 the French created a secular republic based on a constitution articulating novel and distinctive values. Over the next one hundred years they built a nation, a *political* community, giving institutional expression to these values (see Weber, 1976, for a remarkable account of the processes of change in the countryside). More recently, in 1991, the Constitutional Council decided that the legislature could not refer to *le peuple corse*, even as part of the French nation, because this would admit a distinction based upon ethnic origin contrary to Article 2 of the constitution. If Corsicans, Bretons and Basques could not be recognised as minorities, nor could immigrants from North Africa. The French will not admit or officially recognise either racial or ethnic differences between French citizens. On the other hand, because they have worried about maintaining the size of their population they have been ready to extend citizenship to anyone born or schooled in France on the assumption that anyone who has experienced this socialisation will accept republican principles. They have not minded if new citizens retained citizenship in some other country, at least until recent times when doubt began to be cast on the loyalties of Muslims of Algerian origin who chose to serve their period of conscription in the Algerian army. Girls who come to school wearing an Islamic scarf challenged the school's mission to train pupils in republicanism.

Germans felt themselves to be a people, a *Volk*, before they were able to come together in 1871 as members of a state. They were an *ethnic* community, and continue to see themselves in this way, starting from a conception of *Volkszugehörigkeit*, or ethnic belonging. They have accepted as fellow-Germans all those descended from people who lived on what counted as German soil in 1913, plus persons of German origin whose ancestors were invited to settle in the Volga river valley in 1762 but who no longer spoke German. The Germans contrast with the French both in their readiness to recognise ethnic origin as a factor in social organisation and in their unwillingness to accept dual nationality. To become German by naturalisation an applicant must renounce any other citizenship because no one can be allowed to identify with a second ethnic community, unless he or she belongs to a legally recognised minority. Only a group of citizens of the same origin and living in the same area can be accounted a minority, so there are just two, the Danish minority near the frontier, and the Sorbs in Dresden and Cottbus. For the German state the key difference is that between citizens and aliens; there is no recognition of racial differences. Representatives of the state maintain that Germany is not a country of immigration, though there are problems when *Gastarbeiter* decide to remain. Most children of Turkish immigrants are and will remain Turkish nationals.

The British, deeply divided on class lines as they are, have seen themselves as a *historical* community. People enjoy the rights of British subjects which Edmund Burke, reacting against the French idea of universal human rights, represented as a patrimony from their forefathers. The sense of a national community has been weakened by three special characteristics. Firstly, by the vagueness of the identity 'British subject'. Whereas in Germany citizenship has been an identity reinforcing an ethnic self-conception, in Britain the category 'citizen' has been multiethnic and multiracial. Immigrants from the New Commonwealth were already British subjects, so any difference in ethnic origin was not confounded with citizenship. The French conception of citizenship was reinforced by the provision whereby persons in the '*départements d'outre mer*' voted for *députés* in the metropolitan legislature, but in Britain comparable proposals for Gibraltar, Malta, etc. never came to anything. Secondly, for many people it is the national identities – English, Welsh, Scottish and Irish in the Province of Northern Ireland – that matter, not the shared identity 'citizen of the United Kingdom'. Contrast this with the French refusal to acknowledge distinctive identities for Corsicans, Basques and Bretons! Thirdly, because of geography, history and the continuity of language, the United Kingdom has in some respects an open frontier *vis-à-vis* the United States of America. Afro-Caribbeans have shared in some of the ideological movements of African-Americans. They have imported into Britain assumptions about the nature of race as a social construct and a black identity which have been fashioned by experience in North America. These complicate the sense of national community in the United Kingdom in ways that differentiate it from comparable conceptions in France and Germany.

The US conception resembles that of Britain with a dash of the French conception of citizenship. It could not resemble that of Germany because the United States has never known a comparable conception of ethnic community at the national level. The United States was founded on a sense of political community in opposition to the British crown, but it was married to a sense of historical community represented in the constitution of 1776 and, recognising the ethnically diverse origins of its settler population, it was ready to acknowledge ethnic divisions within its population. A US citizen is protected from racial discrimination by the rights which that constitution has conferred upon citizens. These rights are unique, the fruits of a struggle such as that venerated by Edmund Burke. The Swedish writer Gunnar Myrdal's book *An American Dilemma* (1944) testified to the impact on a Swedish observer of the explicit use of the constitution, in the classroom and in political dialogue. This is very French, and very un-British. But Americans cannot represent racism as a pathology attacking their society from outside because racial discrimination was built into the society of 1776. It took another seventy years to interpret the constitution as prohibiting racial discrimination. So at the end of the twentieth century official policies in the United States resemble those in Britain in starting, not from ideology, but from a conception of racial discrimination as a normal, if deplorable, form of behaviour.

An audacious attempt to account for variations of this kind has been advanced by a French demographer, Emmanuel Todd (1994). He asks how humans in the first place came to see themselves as unequal and finds his answer in the family, particularly in the rules of inheritance. Where brothers have an equal right of inheritance, people believe in the equality of humans and of peoples. Where brothers have different rights (as when the first-born son succeeds to the family estate) people grow up believing that humanity is diversified and segmented. The law that associates family structure with ideological representations is said to apply both to societies which receive immigrants and to the behaviour of immigrant populations. Each group has an enduring culture, and the status of women is at its core. Todd claims that in this way it is possible to account for the different political attitudes displayed in the Paris basin and those in the more peripheral regions of France. The Parisian tradition is egalitarian and universalist whereas in Germany and the peripheral regions of France a differentialist vision predominates. In Germany the differentialism takes an ethnic form, in Britain a class form. Immigrants to the United States who came from regions of Europe predisposed to inequality were the more able to abandon this outlook because in the United States they could share in the presumption that whites were superior to blacks. Whether differences of such a kind can endure in modern times is doubtful, but cultural variation is not easily analysed and Todd's is a interesting way of approaching it.

Even if this or some other explanation of the origins of ideas about inequality were to be accepted, it would provide no basis for comparisons in the present. It could not furnish a mode of analysis which would cumulate knowledge about how humans react to racial and ethnic differences while allowing for variations in time and space.

Another French writer who has outlined an approach quite different from that prevailing in US sociology is Michel Wieviorka. He has maintained that during the industrial era until the 1960s most European countries had succeeded to some extent in integrating three basic components of their collective life: *an industrial society, an egalitarian state*, and *a national identity*. As industrial societies they were acquainted with conflict between the working class and the middle class, but this provided a structure for a great range of economic and social activity. The state ensured the equal provision of a range of services, while national identity was important to the self-conception of individuals. In the course of *une grande mutation*, these had all been weakened. The working-class movement was breaking up. Trade unions had lost influence. Job security had been diminished for everyone. The welfare state could no longer afford to maintain all its services. European economic integration and greater awareness of the world outside Europe affected conceptions of national identity so that they became loaded with xenophobia and racism (Wieviorka, 1991/5, 1994).

The 'global argument' is indeed one of extraordinary generality, both in its conception of racism and in its time scale:

> Racism, both as a set of ideologies and specious scientific doctrines, and as a set of concrete manifestations of violence, humiliation and discrimination, really gathered momentum in the context of the immense changes of which Europe was the centre after the Renaissance. (Wieviorka, 1994: 174)

It has developed ever since. 'If we want to test the idea of a certain unity of contemporary racism in Europe, we must elaborate sociological and historical hypotheses, and then apply them to the facts we are able to collect.' This postulated unity is said to be more than a similarity between events in different countries and to express the crisis of modernity which all European countries are experiencing.

A source for one such hypothesis might be found in the production process. As described by A. Sivanandan (1976), in the 1960s many employers in western Europe sought cheap unskilled labour. Possibly they could have managed without it had their governments, like the Japanese government of the time, raised the obstacles to the importation of labour and forced employers to invest in automation and labour-saving machinery, but many of the employers did not have access to the capital needed and it might not have been financially justified for them to invest to this extent; they would have been forced to cease production. The cheapest solution was contract labour, in which a worker came alone without dependants and the employer was not responsible for the worker's housing or social services; those costs were incurred by some-one else. Countries like Britain, France and the Netherlands, which had admitted people from their colonies as citizens, were pressed by the exigencies of the capitalist system to move towards tighter controls on the pattern of contract labour. By dividing the working class, immigra-tion control 'took discrimination out of the market place and gave it the sanction of the state. It made racism respectable'. Then came the 'sec-ond generation' of young blacks born in Europe who could not be fitted into the system. The 'public interest' required that they be protected from discrimination, but in practice that interest was going to be the interest of the ruling class which would cultivate racism for its own purposes.

When racism is defined in the broad terms of Wieviorka and Sivanan-dan, it may be inappropriate to speak of the testing of hypotheses. The kind of explanation – or interpretation – sought may place these argu-ments with those considered in chapter 6, but the possibilities of empiri-cal testing have been opened by the distinction between a classical, inegalitarian racism and a new, differentialist one. This was pioneered by Pierre-André Taguieff (1988: 18–20, 31, 38–9), who has sought to separ-ate a heterophile racism (which, as in some imperialist policies, seeks to elevate and eventually assimilate the other-group) from a heterophobe racism (which seeks to keep groups separate and distinct); each of these then evokes as its double, a distinctive anti-racism. He and Wieviorka have drawn a further distinction which echoes what Cox wrote about racism and intolerance. There is a principle of inferiorisation and exploi-tation which allows the victim group a place in society so long as it is at the bottom. There is also a principle of differentiation which represents the other group as so different that it must be segregated, expelled or de-stroyed. Opposition to continued immigration in many European coun-tries has in the last thirty years drawn much more upon ideas of persisting cultural incompatibilities than upon ideas of racial superiority and in-feriority. Is this a new form of racism, or a different phenomenon, one that might perhaps better be called xenophobia? Since Wieviorka (1991: 90–4; 1995: 42–5) seeks to account for a historical trend, he prefers to present racism and xenophobia as two aspects of the same social trend. But it would not be difficult to construct separate scales for measuring these two dimensions of inter-group attitudes. One scale could measure a tendency to keep others at a distance because they are considered inferior and the other a tendency to keep them at a distance because they are thought to be different (though the latter would need a better name than xenophobia because a desire for distance does not necessarily spring from an irrational fear).

One way of measuring trends is by the analysis of discourse. Susan Olzak (1993) examined newspaper reports of ethnic conflicts in the United States between 1876 and 1914, in an attempt to test a hypothesis that the intensity of disputes related to various measures of competition (occupational segregation, economic depression, status of workforce training, immigration rates, etc.). She found that while the incidence of ethnic dispute was not associated with the immigration rate, it was associated with the proportional change in that rate. The suggestion that this constitutes a successful test of the rational choice theory has been criticised by Andreas Wimmer (1997: 20–1), but the original research remains interesting as a technique for measuring changes over time. The analysis of racial discourse has been developed by Teun A. van Dijk (as, for example, in his 1991 study of passages in the British and Dutch press) but covering only a short period of time. David Theo Goldberg (1993) has analysed racial discourse in the United States to demonstrate that 'racial thinking is a function of the transforming categories and conceptions of social subjectivity throughout modernity', but he has not pursued it to the point of formulating hypotheses for empirical testing.

Much of the recent writing which starts from a conception of racism has an ethnocentric character in so far as it concentrates upon the majority group or society in order to uncover the majority's prejudices. Since the only place it leaves for members of the victimised minorities is as people who resist racism, it does not properly allow for them as acting subjects. Some of the writing displays a political inspiration which suggests that it should be classed as social criticism rather than as social science (which is not to disparage the important function of social criticism).

Assessment

Most of the research reviewed in this chapter was conducted by US social scientists working within their own country. Most of the exceptions, such as the first British research, were studies carried out by scholars who followed the trail pioneered by their transatlantic colleagues. So while much was accomplished, it was paradoxical in its effects.

On the one hand, the new knowledge corrected the idiom of race by providing better explanations, particularly with respect to the prejudice–discrimination axis. Research showed that prejudice was not inherited but learned; that whether or not prejudice was translated into discrimination depended upon a variety of situational factors, some of which could be manipulated to influence outcomes, either for better or for worse. The concept of discrimination was itself a new one. Differential behaviour was shown to be a consequence not of some inherent racial disposition but of the social construction placed upon physical characteristics. Social institutions, like those of the housing market, operated on the assumption that the social construction in question was relevant to decision-making. There was a long cycle of cause-and-effect whereby white residential preferences were subject to manipulation, and then estate agents, mortgage lenders, city planners, black and white politicians, all reinforced expectations of residential segregation. A pattern of inequality in one generation was transmitted to the next, and often strengthened in so doing. Research provided the kind of information necessary to any political programme for change.

On the other hand, the very process by which this knowledge was

gained reinforced old assumptions by itself employing the most fundamental feature of the racial idiom: the acceptance that it was proper to
designate blacks, whites and Indians as 'races'. This was particularly
marked in economics where research used statistical sources based on the
folk concept, and which often posited a black–white dichotomy (as in
Becker's, 1957, analysis).

Biologists had been able to take a bottom-up approach in studying how
organisms adapted to changes in their environment. The human species
is unique in its ability to modify its environment, so social science has to
account for relations at additional levels of social life. This points to a
major limitation upon the concept of race as a sign of social status. In a
small town like Indianola in the 1930s the status 'black' or 'white' decided
what opportunities were open to an individual in most social situations,
but the whole social system could be, and was, changed by pressure from
outside. Following an inductivist philosophy of science, research workers
could accumulate a large number of studies of racial differentiation in
local communities but would still not be able to generalise from them
without a theory to explain how those communities differed from one
another and how they were interrelated. Lloyd Warner's approach was
indeed extended to the study of racial differentiation in Chicago (Drake
and Cayton, 1945) to show how racial status remained important in a
more complex social system, but this marked no significant theoretical
advance. Social science could scarcely restrict itself to the analysis of how
racial status was an adaptation to a social environment. It had to comprehend the ways in which status differences contributed to movements to
modify that environment.

Analyses starting from structure and function had a limited view of
conflict and were weak on the political dimension. Moreover, processes
of globalisation were gathering speed. They most obviously affected
employment, as manufacturing was moved to the countries where labour
was cheapest, but globalisation was also significant in the realm of ideas.
At one level there was the international movement for the protection of
human rights which generated pressure upon governments to bring their
laws into line with new standards. At the popular level the media of mass
communication: press, television and cinema, spread particular ways of
looking at life and interpreting experience in the light of new alternatives.
These influences have been addressed in a variety of separate researches
opening up new perspectives. The author will sketch his view of the way
ahead in the final chapter.

6   Race as class

The typologists sought to account for the special features of human races, and of the relations between them, by subsuming these within a general theory of the permanence of types. Social scientists have sought to account for the social aspects of racial differentiation by bringing the same data within the ambit of their own theories of group formation and group relations. To do so, they have extended general theories by adding extra propositions designed to allow for the ways in which racial groups differ from other kinds of groups. However, among the social science theories there is a deep gulf between those discussed here in terms of status and class. The proposition that physical signs can be used in the ascription of social status is not limited to the societies of Europe and North America. It can be applied in China, Japan or India. The severest critics of the approach from status assert that the explanations it produces are academically trivial and politically diversionary. They see the writings of the typologists not as a theory but as a smokescreen which served to distract attention from the injustices generated by the capitalist system, especially in its imperialist stage. It is said that those who try to replace the typological theory by elaborating concepts of status are closing their eyes to the political imperative when they should be using their specialist knowledge in the cause of radical reform.

This is the opposition between orthodox social science and Marxism. Chapters 5 and 6 contrast the two positions in terms of status and class, though the contrast could be almost as well expressed as an opposition between strong and weak concepts of class, because in everyday language the word 'class' is sometimes used in a sense synonymous with the sociological concept of status. The root distinction, however, is not between the two words but between the kinds of explanation sought, and the Marxist claim that class struggle is a key to the understanding of history. The sources of the conflict can be traced to two contrasting epistemologies, the one associated with the name of Kant and the other with Hegel, though the difference is also expressed as an opposition between positivism and realism, and parallels the opposition between nominalism and realism discussed earlier. The difference is illustrated by the way that teachers in the former tradition have asked their students 'what is your problem?', assuming that they should start from an intellectual problem, while those in the latter tradition have contended that social scientists should ask themselves 'what is the problem?' assuming that they should address the most politically important issue.

The classic Marxist proposal for superseding earlier racial theories was that advanced in 1948 by Oliver Cromwell Cox. Other writers have since corrected his use of some Marxist concepts and improved some of his analyses, but none of them has written a treatise of comparable ambition. Cox would have dismissed any idea of a transcultural social science valid for all kinds of society. For him, such a science had to be historical, showing how the use of racial ideas had developed as part of the expansion of capitalism. In this respect, his vision was Eurocentric. Other authors whose work is discussed in this chapter have posed questions requiring the kind of comprehensive answers that only a historical analysis can offer. They may not have attributed the same significance to class struggle, or have referred very often to Marx, but they have sought a kind of understanding of their data that sets them apart from the writers discussed in chapter 5. Some of them replicate ideas of Cox's without being aware that they are doing so. Whether or not they acknowledge any debt to Marx, nearly all work with a conceptual framework that has been based upon the course of European and North American history.

Epistemological assumptions

It is the more difficult to describe the difference between the two epistemologies because there is no neutral ground. Any formulation must be framed from the standpoint of one or other of the two contending parties. A contemporary exponent of the Kantian approach, Sir Karl Popper, contrasted what he called philosophical pluralism and philosophical monism. (The appropriateness of these names is disputable, and it should be noted that Kant did not subscribe to pluralism in the usual philosophical sense.) According to philosophical pluralism in Popper's sense, there are three worlds (1) the world of matter; (2) the mental world of subjective states, and (3) the world of objective knowledge which results from humans' attempts to understand what is around them. This knowledge 'is the product of men just as honey is the product of bees' (Popper, 1972: 154). In this tradition, a definition has to be suited to its purpose, depending upon the theory to be tested and developed. What appears to a (male) research worker as a problem is decided by his training and his interest in following up a line of thought. He uses the theories of his subject to organise and refine his observations. Solving one problem, he discovers more, and from this activity of problem-solving an intellectual tradition emerges.

Those within the Hegelian tradition subscribe to what, by contrast, Popper called philosophical monism. The observer is within the world, but there are laws of its development which he can grasp. The world of knowledge is not separate, and what humans think they know is determined by their position in societies at particular stages in their development. A person who has grasped the principles according to which the world is developing should use that knowledge to hasten its development, serving, in Marx's phrase, as 'a midwife to history'. Definitions must correspond to the nature of the things defined and these can be understood only if they are located in the processes of change. A Marxist would be sceptical of the suggestion that it is possible to select a problem and then compare the power of orthodox and Marxist theories to resolve it. The Marxist insists that the task is not to interpret the world but to change it; therefore the social scientist should identify the politically significant problem and concentrate upon that.

The Kantian stance dominated social science in the United States during the first half of the twentieth century to such an extent that it was taken for granted. Twenty years passed before the seriousness of the challenge presented in Oliver C. Cox's *Caste, Class and Race* was appreciated by more than a small minority. The social movements of the 1960s brought an upsurge of interest in Marxism as an approach which promised to unite history and social science. As an exemplar of Marxism, Cox's work has grave defects (see Miles, 1980), but it is of prime historical significance for any discussion of how racial theories have developed.

What distinguished Cox's philosophy of social science can best be seen in his statements about how the phenomena of racial relations are to be defined. Early in that section of the book devoted to race he set out to eliminate certain concepts which he believed to be commonly confused with that of race relations. One of the concepts to be eliminated was that of racism, because studies of its origin substituted 'the history of a system of rationalization for that of a material social fact' (1948:321). He did not state this explicitly, but it can be deduced that in his view material social facts could be understood only as features of historical constellations. He concluded that 'probably the crucial fallacy in Park's thinking is his belief that the beginnings of modern race prejudice may be traced back to the immemorial periods of human associations' (1948:474). According to Cox, Park failed to appreciate the differences between the social formations of classical antiquity and modern capitalism. Something quite new occurred when Europeans appropriated territory in the New World and created a system of social relations based upon the principles of capitalism. For this system to develop, labour was required. The system could grow more rapidly if that labour, or a large section of it, could be bought and sold just like any other commodity and the labourers treated as chattels rather than as people. A supply of labour was found in Africa which could be marketed in this way since Africans were physically distinctive and could therefore be made subject to special laws. If white workers could be persuaded that black workers were different, then they might not perceive that the true interest of all workers lay in their taking common action against their exploiters. The 'material social fact' was therefore a complex system of relations which would develop in a historically predictable manner.

In 1948 Cox understood 'racism' to 'refer to a philosophy of racial antipathy' though more writers at that time defined it as a doctrine, dogma or ideology according to which race determines culture (i.e. as a component of an explanation). Its use as a concept in that sense was discussed in an address of the author's published in 1970. Cox commented privately on that address that

if racism is not societally based – an emanation of a given society – it is not anchored in time and space. We become concerned with an historical study of intellectual usage . . . racism . . . can be dead only if changes in the society itself demonstrate it.

This suggests that, if not in 1948, then at a later date Cox was willing to regard 'racism' rather than 'race prejudice' as an appropriate name for 'the socio-attitudinal facilitation of a particular type of labour exploitation' (1948: 393). It is not a distortion of Cox's line of thought if, in accordance with a meaning the name has acquired in the last thirty years, it is said that in Cox's view, racism was a new phenomenon that was part and parcel of the growth of capitalism. It had become the *explanandum* instead of being part of an *explanans*.

The sociologist's task was to study social interaction, so 'any group of people that is generally believed to be, and generally accepted as, a race in any given area of ethnic competition' was a race, even if 'the assumed race is not a real *race*. What we are interested in is the social definition'.

Calling it by some other name would make no difference to the nature of the *explanandum*. Therefore

we may think of race relations as that behaviour which develops among people who are aware of each other's actual or imputed physical differences. Moreover, by race relations we do not mean all social contacts between persons of different 'races', but only those contacts the social characteristics of which are determined by a consciousness of 'racial' difference. Two people of different 'race' could have a relation that was not racial. (1948: 319–20)

This reads just like Park's statement quoted on p. 107; it follows the usage adopted by the US Congress in its 1866 law. It is also incompatible with

Cox's arguments in other places where he insists that things are not to be defined by the parties' consciousness but by the functions of the things in the social order: 'race relations . . . are labor–capital profits relationships; therefore race relations are proletarian–bourgeois relations and hence political–class relations' (1948:336). In such circumstances it is to be expected that people will become conscious of actual or imputed physical differences, but the object of study is a complex of relations existing on different levels (productive forces, relations of production and ideological forms) located in a historical sequence.

This same stress upon function was apparent in the way Cox distinguished anti-semitism from racism. Anti-semitism was a form of intolerance, 'an unwillingness on the part of a dominant group to tolerate the beliefs or practices of a subordinate group because it considers these beliefs and practices to be either inimical to group solidarity or a threat to the continuity of the status quo'. Whereas racism facilitated exploitation, intolerance was directed towards the conversion, expulsion or eradication of the minority:

the dominant group or ruling class does not like the Jew at all, but it likes the Negro in his place . . . the condition of its liking the Jew is that he ceases being a Jew and voluntarily become like the generality of society, while the condition of its liking the Negro is that he cease trying to become like the generality of society and remain contentedly a Negro. (1948: 393, 400–1)

The psychology of anti-semitism and the psychology of racism might have much in common, and the same racist doctrines might justify both, but since their political functions were different, they were accounted different phenomena.

For Park, the phenomena of race relations had many facets, and presented many problems to the social scientist. Racial differentiation occurred in an ecological context as different human groups competed for resources. It could also be studied in terms of prejudice, an expression of the consciousness of a group seeking to defend a privileged position; or in terms of social distance, as members of such a group regulated the kinds of relations they would enter into with varying sorts of non-members; in terms of personality, for example, the effect of occupying a socially marginal position, and so on. There were as many problems as there were useful ways of looking at the evidence. For Cox, there was one inclusive problem; the historical fact of racial differentiation; the sociologist's conceptual framework had to be adjusted to grasp the object of study and to reveal the principles which explained its changing character. The opposition between these two views is at root epistemological. For the intellectual tradition in which Park stood, knowledge grows from the ordering of evidence within concepts derived from a theory; for Cox, knowledge was revealed in history to those who could study it unhindered by the biases of class interest.

Discussion of these issues has been hindered by the diversity of ways in which, especially since the late 1960s, the word 'racism' has been employed. For a scholar working within the strictly Hegelian tradition of Marxism, according to which underlying historical forces generate the social forms, what matters is that blacks, browns, reds, whites and yellows have been differentiated so that they occupy different positions within social orders even though there is no biological justification for racial inequality. The influences upon the consciousness of individuals that stimulated them to differentiate themselves are worth investigating provided it is remembered that they lead to no final answer. The real determinants are to be found on a lower level, and they are structured by opposing class interests. Beliefs about race do not have the objective reality of class; they encourage a distorted view of social affairs; by acting as brakes upon the class struggle they delay the challenge from the working class. From this standpoint it is the fact of racial differentiation which matters and which should be the criterion for a definition of racism. To take a contemporary example which may illustrate this point even if for some readers it may seem to neglect the magnitude and pervasiveness of racism, some of the British immigration laws have been labelled racist because they exclude a greater proportion of non-white than white would-be entrants; if they excluded equal proportions they would not be so labelled. What matters is not the intentions of the people who passed the laws but their consequences. If, after a time, the laws no longer excluded a greater proportion of non-whites they would no longer be racist. This, of course, is not the only current sense in which the word racism is used, but it illustrates how, for those who start from a particular reading of history, it is the fact of racial differentiation which should be the focus of interest and should guide the manner in which the building blocks of history are defined. Since scholars in the two traditions have different intellectual objectives, they are bound to work with different definitions of concepts such as 'racism'.

According to Cox, the class struggle was the motive power behind the history of our era:

Racial antagonism is part of this class struggle, *because* it is developed within the capitalist system as one of its fundamental traits. It may be demonstrated that racial antagonism, as we know it today, never existed in the world before about 1492; moreover, racial feeling developed concomitantly with the development of our modern social system.

This reflects the strong concept of class as the key to history; racial division affects the class struggle but, since class is the more important in the long run, racial alignments have to be seen as influences upon class formation rather than the other way round. Cox did not wish to be read as stating that the white race was the only one capable of racial prejudice: 'It is probable that without capitalism, a chance occurrence among whites, the world might never have experienced race prejudice.' A peculiar feature of his book is the way that chapter 16, concerning the history of racial antagonism, suddenly yields place to a chapter describing seven situations of race relations. As the author is chiefly concerned with the qualities of social systems, the reader expects a typology that shows how structures of race relations are associated with particular social systems and phases of their development, but Cox advances his seven situations simply as the major forms in which racial conflicts presented themselves in the modern world. A systematic typology would have stated the criteria of classification and would probably have ended up with a set of boxes, some of which might well have been empty.

Having defined race relations as 'that behaviour which develops among people who are aware of each other's actual or imputed physical differences', Cox had quite a lot to say about the kinds of awareness that characterised the various situations. The most important of these were the ruling-class and bipartite situations and it is under these headings that Cox compared the societies he knew best: Trinidad and the US South. The first three situations were of a different kind: stranger, original contact and slavery. Stranger and original contact situations could develop later into either ruling-class or bipartite situations. Slavery resembled the latter but had a different legal basis. The last two situations were also equivocal. Cox counted Brazil as representing an amalgamation whereas it seems on his criteria to belong in the ruling-class category. It is when describing the amalgamative situation that he chiefly discusses nationalism as 'an exploitative, socio-psychological instrument of actual or potential ruling classes'. The seventh category, the nationalistic situation, was described only briefly and inadequately; to deploy the theory that he stated elsewhere Cox would have needed to describe the material forces in Haiti in 1792 or India in 1857 which were the basis for the uprisings he mentioned. The nationalism of the underdogs appeared as the sort of process by which peoples lifted themselves up, but any suggestion that beliefs could be prime movers was in Cox's view mysticism, and he pushed it out of sight. Relations necessary to the social system had pride of place. 'Haiti might be taken as the classic illustration of an exploited racial group which has achieved nationhood. Negro Americans will probably never become nationalistic; the numerical balance of the races will not allow the development of nationalistic antagonisms on the part of the coloured people' (1948: 403). In this scheme the white ruling class was given the power to rule the minds as well as the bodies of the black citizens to an extent that was never possible even under slavery.

It may also be justified to examine Cox's typology from a different perspective and to ask whether there was not here another chain of reasoning of which the author was not himself fully aware and therefore did not develop as he might have done. Elsewhere, Cox criticised Myrdal for assuming that beliefs about the nature of race were 'primary social forces'. Myrdal failed to acknowledge that the propagators of the ruling ideas in the United States knew that these beliefs were without objective justification but deliberately spread them because they served a purpose (1948: 531). This is a clear statement of the thesis that race is a political idea. If a sociologist adopts this standpoint and defines race relations in terms of an awareness of 'actual or imputed physical differences', he or she should try to identify the kinds of political and economic structures which generate a racial consciousness. Cox did indeed present the bipartite situation as one in which 'definite racial attitudes are developed', but he did not analyse his seven situations in terms of the cultivation of racial beliefs or even in terms of exploitative relations. Some of his situations provided illustrations of neither of these and in this respect his typology was inconsistent with his own theories.

In his concluding chapter Cox handed down his judgement that the race problem of the United States

is primarily the short-run manifestation of oppositions between an abiding urge among Negroes to assimilate and a more or less unmodifiable decision among racially articulate, nationalistic whites that they should not . . . the solidarity of American Negroes is neither nationalistic nor nativistic.

The racial policy of the country was formulated by Southern ruling-class whites and the Negro's political position was one of great weakness. For him to come to full manhood and citizenship the liberation of the Southern poor white would also be necessary: 'A great leader of Negroes will almost certainly be a white man, but he will also be the leader of the white masses of this nation.' Cox seems to have thought that he would need to be someone like Franklin D. Roosevelt (1948: 545, 581–2). Time has not dealt kindly with this diagnosis and it is necessary to ask whether there was anything in Cox's sociology that led him astray. It looks as if he over-estimated the integration of the capitalist system and under-estimated the independence of beliefs in social processes. In this connection, his discussion of religious movements was symptomatic. He wrote, 'In all significant social revolutions, organized religion will necessarily be involved . . . the Church is normally rightist' (1948: 171). There was no recognition of religious belief as an inspiration in slave insurrections or in movements for status change. Religious belief has often been associated with the nationalism of unprivileged groups and it played a crucial part in the process by which African-Americans attained a new consciousness of themselves. Oliver Cox's assumptions prevented him from seeing the significance in his own observation: 'One is amazed at the strength of the simple faith of the older, unlettered, rural Negroes. Powerless in the hands of their white exploiters they go beyond them directly to their omnipotent God, almost happy in the assurance that retribution will come' (1948: 566). Here was something that was not determined by the needs of the social system, and it was out of this kind of psychological strength that a new movement emerged.

It may assist the further argument to make one matter clear at this point. The author accepts that it is perfectly feasible to write an account of the development of racial relations as a world phenomenon, especially over the past four centuries, regarding them as a consequence of the growth of European capitalism, and that this can be a corrective to analyses limited to single countries. Such an account can well employ a philosophy of history which assumes ownership of the means of production in a context of technological innovation to be the predominant factor influencing class formation and, thereby, the course of events. What is at issue is whether this view of history is promulgated as the writer's personal vision of how the past has produced the present or as something objectively demonstrated. Is it a philosophy of history or a possible science of history? Does it operate with a model of society or does it state laws according to which societies are said to change? If someone takes the second of these two positions how does he or she prove the truth of the claims? It is for this reason that the epistemological issue is inescapable (on this, see Banton, 1986). To put the issue in this way is to make difficulties for those who rely on a Hegelian epistemology, because to them their way of looking at things seems so superior to any alternative that they consider that what requires explanation is other people's failure to appreciate what should be obvious to them. (There are obvious parallels with the position of those who see history as the record of God's relations with humanity.) The Hegelians are on stronger ground when they criticise the weaknesses in Kantian philosophy, in particular (from their standpoint) for its failure to allow for the way in which any scholar is himself or herself part of a historical process. Yet if there is no reason to believe in an underlying level of historical determination, no one should be blamed for neglecting it. The main difference today between the orthodox sociologists and the Marxists lies in the questions they think should be asked rather than in the answers they give. The Marxists, because of their use of Hegelian epistemology, believe that it is possible to answer in a social scientific manner questions about the development of whole social systems. Moreover, since they believe that future developments can be anticipated and inform present-day politics, they contend that there is a moral obligation to direct research towards such issues. That is why a student should ask 'What is *the* problem?' The sociologists believe that, while it may be useful to ask such questions, they cannot be answered in a social scientific manner. Answers depend upon subjective assessment of what is significant. The student should start with a theory and choose a problem which will help him or her to improve the explanatory power of that theory. That is why they ask 'What is *your* problem?' (though for a cautionary comment, see Mason, 1986: 3).

The scholars who are accounted Marxists differ significantly among themselves. Those who take the position that Marxism offers a theory of history as the product of class struggle belong in what has been described as the Hegelian tradition. Those who believe that Marxism offers a model of society either belong in the Kantian tradition or are engaged in trying to bridge the gulf between the two. Though that gulf is very deep, bridges can be thrown across it in several places.

Despite their divergencies, Marxists can agree with sociologists about what constitute satisfactory answers to certain kinds of questions. Marxists have posed questions neglected by orthodox sociologists, and many of their contributions can be accepted and welcomed by sociologists who do not share their historical and political perspectives. For example, there need be no dispute about the importance of understanding the position of a group in relation to the processes of production, to the structure of power and to the utilisation of resources controlled by the state. There is therefore an area of overlap in the analysis of particular societies. The possibilities of theoretical overlap have been enhanced by the development of 'rational choice Marxism' associated with authors like Jon Elster, Alan Carling and David Little; this is developing, within Marxism, a bottom-up approach to balance the top-down tendencies of writers like Cox and Miles, and it stimulates the formulation of testable hypotheses. However, this approach has not yet produced a class-based theory of interpersonal relations that can be compared with status-based theories.

Adapting the model

As already mentioned (p. 134 *supra*) Leo Kuper contended that plural societies were distinctive in that their conflicts followed the lines of racial rather than class cleavage. The class model needed substantial modification for the analysis of plural societies. A further revision has been the split labour market theory advanced by Edna Bonacich (1972, 1979, 1981a). It shows up the gaps in status-based theories and raises issues which will have to be addressed if sociological theory is eventually to supersede the idiom of race. Bonacich considered that none of the prevailing interpretations of black–white relations in apartheid South Africa was satisfactory. None of the studies which had been classed as liberal dealt adequately with the connections between position in the labour market and position in the political structure, while those considered Marxist failed to explain the behaviour of the white workers. Against both these interpretations, Bonacich argued that ethnic antagonism was produced by the kind of competition that arose in split labour markets. The better jobs were reserved for a labour aristocracy whose members seized on the physical differences between them and their competitors to develop an ideology justifying their privileges. There was thus a pattern of conflict between three classes: a business class whose members wanted as cheap and docile a labour force as possible; a higher-paid working class and a lower-paid one. The interests of the higher-paid workers were threatened by the third class, because the very weakness of that class ensured that it could easily be controlled by the business class. From the difference in the *initial* price of labour a complex class struggle developed which exacerbated the relations between different groups of workers.

Why, Bonacich asked, was South Africa apparently trying to prevent the full absorption of the African population into the capitalist sector? To find an answer it was necessary to go back to the increased demand for labour generated when first the mining and then the manufacturing industries started to compete with the farming sector. The demand for craftsmen and other skilled workers could be met only from the immigrant white labour force, and this gave them a corresponding leverage in demanding a share of the profits from exploiting the country's valuable natural resources. There was also a demand for unskilled labour which could be met either by whites or blacks. The native Africans were not much attracted to wage labour so the business class had to recruit Africans from outside South Africa's boundaries. Indentured workers were also recruited from India and China. It was in farming that black workers first competed successfully with whites. Their progress offended white farmers and politicians. The Natives Land Act 1913 was introduced apparently to exert greater control over black labour and to block this opening (see Banton, 1983: 220–1, summarising research by Francis Wilson). During the First World War black workers became better established in the gold mining industry; fairly soon they could be used to fill jobs that previously had been reserved for whites. As profitability declined, this became more attractive to the employers; it sharpened their conflict with the white workers and led to the Rand strike of 1922.

Capital, wrote Bonacich, is attracted to cheap labour of any colour and, if permitted, would have made more use of blacks, displacing high-priced white labour. White workers therefore had a choice. They could follow an inclusionist policy, trying to bring Africans into the working-class movement, helping them to raise the price of their labour, and thus ending the split in the labour market. Or they could follow a protectionist policy, attempting to prevent any under-cutting of their own position by limiting capital's access to cheap labour and creating a kind of caste system. The policy options were mutually exclusive. If either were to succeed it had to eliminate the other. The inclusionist alternative was unattractive because the African 'reserve army of labour' seemed so huge; there was so much potentially cheap black labour within the country that frontier control, important as it might be, could not suffice; the South African business class was particularly powerful because the employers controlled the mining compounds and could easily act against attempts to unite white and black labour; Afrikaner workers, with their rural history and frontier ideology, were ill disposed towards inclusionist strategies; finally, after the suppression of the Rand strike, political power was used to create a state apparatus ready to crush the earliest moves in such a direction. It was therefore mistaken to infer that the antagonism of white workers towards blacks resulted from their having been either duped or bribed by capital. The first of these false explanations suggested that capitalists had developed an ideology of racism to deflect white workers' hostility away from their real enemy; the second saw white labour, especially its leadership, as having been bought off. Bonacich rejected the second because she read the evidence of displacement as indicating that capital would sooner dispense with costly white labour than pay the price of bribery. (For further evidence and supporting argument on both of these points, see Lipton, 1985: 183–226.) Bonacich also argued that the black struggle for liberation had been shaped by the white class struggle; the reactionary stance of white labour had pushed the conflict towards a racial rather than a class confrontation. This added to the forces delaying the incorporation of the African population into the capitalist sector.

This attempt to explain why the African population was not being absorbed was sharply criticised by Michael Burawoy (1981). Where other writers had perceived the split labour market as one factor underlying the social order Bonacich, he said, represented it as the factor which above all else determined racial antagonism: 'she inverts the logic of enquiry by constructively appropriating history to illuminate a theory rather than appropriately constructing a theory to illuminate history'. Thus the matter at issue was not just whether Bonacich had answered the question, but whether she had asked the question that Burawoy believed to be crucial. He doubted whether a theory of racial antagonism was possible. He argued that to understand the differential access of races to resources required a theory of the more general allocation of resources, which in turn pre-supposed a theory of capitalism. To understand why the African population was not being absorbed into the capitalist sector it was necessary, according to Burawoy, to look at the part played by the state apparatus, at the difference between individual and class interest, at the specificity of South African development, at the events of different historical periods and so on.

In Bonacich's rejoinder (1981b) she observed that Burawoy's way of posing the problem was remarkably like that of sociological functionalism. When the state supported a colour bar it was said to be acting in the interests of the capitalist class by reproducing a system of exploitation. When the state attacked the colour bar it was said to be acting in the interests of a capitalist class which 'required a more flexible approach to apartheid'. Whatever action it took concerning trade unionism was similarly 'explained'. The underlying assumption was therefore ideological. Bonacich protested, 'It is the racial aspect of the South African social structure I was trying to explain, not every aspect of the social structure.' In that event she should have defined her problem more closely. She did not advance a very satisfactory explanation of why South Africa was apparently trying to prevent the full absorption of the African population into the capitalist sector; what she did was to explain the constraints bearing upon the strategies of the white workers and, in a more limited way, upon those of the major white employers, plus the significance of these constraints for ethnic antagonism (in itself a major contribution!). Though they might be criticised in detail there is nothing of a general kind about these explanations which should make them unacceptable to a sociologist who starts from the perspective of race as status; indeed the question of whether black and white labour is substitutable has long been a central issue for those who study discrimination in labour markets in terms of neo-classical economics.

The debate between these two writers remains interesting for any assessment of the potentialities of the Marxist model despite the subsequent events which have transformed the country's political structure. In 1994 the first election based on a universal suffrage was conducted and the first democratic government installed. Analyses of the class structure have now to start from different premises. However, the split labour market theory can be usefully applied in other countries (Makabe, 1981). In the United States the possible abolition of slavery was a subject of controversy during the decades prior to its abolition in 1863. Some whites who had been against slavery had nevertheless opposed the granting of rights to free blacks. Others seemed to favour slavery, yet fiercely resisted proposals to extend it to new territories as the US frontier moved westwards. Since the whites in both North and South agreed that blacks were inferior, why should they have fought one another so bitterly from 1861 to 1865?

Black workers and white workers were substitutable forms of labour. They could, when permitted, perform the same work. To use black slaves, an employer first needed the capital to purchase them, but thereafter his costs were much lower than if he hired free white labour. Originally it had been possible to purchase white labour also, by buying up the indentures of immigrant workers who had been given a passage because they had entered into such a contract. Buying indentures gave the purchaser the right to a man's labour for only a specified number of years, and it was never politically possible to establish any form of servile labour by whites. Blacks were different because they were more easily segregated and controlled, so that in some states at some periods an employer owned his slaves as he owned his farm animals. Black workers could therefore be made to work longer hours than whites, making their labour cheaper to the employer. The capitalists brought in black slaves to develop Southern agriculture and a split labour market was created as the white owners of small farms were pushed out of the fertile lands most suited for cotton plantations. Thus slavery created a powerful capitalist class based on cheap labour and it weakened the bargaining position of free workers and small farmers (who were nearly all white).

Bonacich (1975) maintained that there was a continuous process whereby white workers were displaced by black. Slaves were used in textile and tobacco manufacturing, in the iron industry, in sugar refining and rice mills, on the docks, canals and railroads, and in mining, construction and lumbering. Some slaves became skilled workers who, when not needed on the plantations, were hired out by their owners. Faced with this kind of competition, many white workers left the South. Others tried to reserve certain jobs for whites only, adopting what Bonacich called the 'caste solution'. Their ability to do so was increased by the extension of the franchise in the 1830s which enabled white workers and small farmers to exercise greater influence. This was also a period in which laws were passed to restrict the right of slave owners to give slaves their freedom. It has frequently been argued that such legislation expressed the slave-owners' fears of slave insurrection, since free blacks were seen as a disruptive influence. Bonacich suggested to the contrary that slave owners had no collective interest in preventing the manumission of individual slaves. Other slave societies with strong slave-owning classes permitted individual manumissions, while the Northern and Western regions of the United States, which had no slaves, produced as many laws directed against free blacks as the South. From this she inferred that the pressure for the Southern legislation against manumission probably came from the white working class.

Outside the South, white workers feared any moves which threatened the introduction of cheap labour. They therefore approved the maintenance of slavery in the South while opposing its extension. Behind their support for slavery in the South lay the fear that abolition might mean the northward migration of former slaves to increase the competition for jobs in their regions; even though this would be free labour, it would be the labour of people willing to work for lower wages and therefore a considerable threat. White workers in the United States were thus faced with a problem comparable to that of white workers in South Africa. Were they to protect their short-run interests by trying to set up a kind of caste system which would reinforce the split in the labour market and acknowledge their right to the better-paid jobs, or were they to adopt the radical inclusionist policy of trying to build up a working-class movement that transcended racial differences? Bonacich's essay deals with the period 1830–63 when this problem had to be addressed by the first trade unions, which were craft unions representing skilled trades. Other evidence which she does not review (see Banton, 1983:378–9) shows that where black craftsmen were already established, the union had to include them. Craft unions formed in later periods were discriminatory from the outset. As in South Africa, the white class struggle influenced the form taken by the black liberation movement.

The split labour market theory is therefore able to throw new light onto inter- and intra-racial tensions in this period. Its exposition is less persuasive when arguing that 'Abolition of slavery occurred, in part, because there were major classes of whites whose interests were at odds with the perpetuation of the "peculiar institution".' Spokesmen for those interests rarely spoke in such terms and Bonacich's own scheme does not provide very much support for the interpretation. Conflicts between North and South had been reduced by negotiation in the past; whether they could have been negotiated in 1861 no one can know. Any assumption that the Civil War was inevitable is purely a supposition and takes it out of the realm of causal explanation to which social scientists' theories are directed.

Passing over several intervening decades, Bonacich took up the story again to contend that a split labour market analysis helped explain the higher level of unemployment among African-Americans in the industrial era. According to the census of 1930 the level of black unemployment was lower than that of whites, but afterwards it started to rise until by 1954 the black rate was twice the white rate. That disparity had persisted. Operating with her three-class model, Bonacich maintained that employer paternalism led black workers to believe that they had more to gain by allying with capital than with white labour. She quoted Marcus Garvey as saying, 'If the Negro takes my advice he will organize by himself and keep his scale of wage a little lower than the whites . . . By doing so he will keep the goodwill of the white employer.' Since white workers would never help blacks to get jobs, it was a good tactic to take jobs offered to them because white workers had gone on strike. By the 1930s the white workers' strategies for preventing competition from black workers were in disarray. Then the New Deal changed the picture; the National Recovery Act introduced protections for trade union activity and empowered the President to prescribe minimum rates of pay. This made it difficult for blacks to be used as cheap labour, though it was only in this way that they had any chance of improving their share of the job market. Bonacich nevertheless maintained that once white fears about cheap labour had been allayed, white unions could become more active in recruiting black support, so that one of the short-term consequences of the 1933 Act was that black and white labour were able to come together in a 'radical coalition'. Protective legislation had shifted the balance of power against the employers and threatened some of these with bankruptcy. The capitalist class could respond in one or more of three ways. Firstly, by relocating part of the industrial process overseas to make use of cheaper foreign labour. Secondly, by relocating in parts of the country – such as the South – where labour was unorganised and relatively cheap. Thirdly, by investing in machinery to reduce their labour force. They followed all three courses; blacks suffered more from their consequences than whites because the black workers were less educated, had less seniority in the lay-off queue, were less easily able to migrate or commute when factories were moved out of the highly taxed central cities, and were less able to protect their interests when decisions about jobs were taken. Capitalists, in this view, did not benefit from black unemployment; they were ready to utilise cheap black labour whenever they could, but government regulations, job requirements, location and other factors, including white prejudice, reduced these opportunities (see Bonacich, 1976).

An alternative explanation of higher black unemployment (Lewis, 1985:62–6) was that especially since the 1950s wage levels for unskilled labour had been rising faster than productivity, so that the demand for this kind of labour had not kept up with the increase in its supply due to mechanisation (especially in agriculture), increased female employment and illegal immigration from Mexico. A higher proportion of black workers were unskilled so that their unemployment rates increased more than those of white workers.

Racism and capitalism

The writer who has done most to re-evaluate and develop Cox's arguments is Robert Miles. Where Cox criticised the expression 'colour-caste' as making inappropriate use of the concept of caste, Miles has criticised other sociologists for inappropriate use of the expressions 'race' and 'race relations'. He contends that both those who use the former expression, and those who believe that the discourse of race has now been changed into an ideological weapon which empowers minorities, use 'race' as if it were an analytical concept. Their choice of words serves to keep alive an assumption that the group differences are ultimately biological and to hamper recognition that the real problem is that of racism. Miles tries to move forward from Cox when he maintains that there is no necessary relation between racism and capitalism and that the former can be defined in general terms without extrapolating from the experience of a particular society or historical period. So he would have no major difficulty incorporating into his framework the evidence of racial discourse in nineteenth- and early twentieth-century China (Dikötter, 1992). In the same spirit, too, he has questioned arguments that the origins of racism are to be found in the attempts of whites to justify colonial rule. Ideas of race were applied to groups within Europe before they were applied to groups outside it. The colonial model cannot account for the origin or persistence of anti-semitism, for differences between European countries, or for the reproduction of colonial imagery (Miles, 1994: 199–203). Like others, he has noted the rhetorical value of the adjective (or epithet) 'racist' because of its implicit moral condemnation. The result of its application in the 1970s to an ever-wider range of circumstances gave rise to what he deplored as 'conceptual inflation'. He and Mason (1994: 853–4) have also criticised the assumption that if something is named as racist it has thereby been explained.

To explain the production and reproduction of the idea of race, four key concepts are offered (Miles, 1989: 73–90). The first of these is *racialisation*, a dialectical process by which meaning is attributed to particular biological features of human beings, as a result of which individuals may be assigned to a general category of persons which reproduces itself biologically; this occurs in both pre-capitalist and capitalist societies. The second is *racism*, which is often associated with exclusionary practices but is to be distinguished by its ideological content. It is defined as a particular form of (evaluative) representation which is a specific instance of a wider (descriptive) process of racialisation. The third key concept is *institutional racism*, used to denote institutional practices which are racist in effect even if they make no explicit use of the idiom of race. The fourth such concept is then *ideological articulation*, which denotes the interrelation of ideologies – for example, racism, sexism and nationalism may reinforce each other.

This scheme is quite limited in its utility to account for particular observations. It would be stretching the evidence too far to conclude that the London landladies mentioned in chapter 5 were motivated by an idea of race. Even if an idea of race is present, that by itself is insufficient to account for a colour tax and the gradations in the degrees of discrimination which have been uncovered in empirical research. Miles' research programme, which may be called that of the racism problematic, assumes that racial discrimination is a kind of social pathology. The race relations problematic, which he assails, assumes the contrary, that discrimination is a normal form of social behaviour – just as Durkheim held crime (or deviance) to be normal. The social vision which underlies the racism problematic leaves only a minor place for members of racial and ethnic minorities and for the communities they build. Their capacity to resist majority racism may be celebrated, but there is no interest in their cultural distinctiveness or their ability to mount a moral critique of the majority society. While those who advance the claims of a class interpretation have made valid and constructive criticisms of the blind spots in the work of those who favour status-based theories, they have little to say about the interactions between groups, while what they propose to put in place of the theories they criticise is more limited in scope than might first appear.

Cox has been criticised for too readily assimilating the racial aspects of social relations to class relations by an author who, like him, is of Caribbean origin. Stuart Hall has sought to establish a new theoretical paradigm which takes its fundamental orientation from Marx without accepting certain of its limitations (listed as economism, reductionism, 'a priorism' and lack of historic specificity). The proposed new paradigm sets out to rectify the lack of an 'adequate theory of racism' capable of dealing with the economic and superstructural features of societies structured in dominance 'while at the same time giving a historically-concrete and sociologically-specific account of distinctive racial aspects' (1980: 336). 'Racism is not dealt with as a general feature of human societies' (as Miles would have it), 'but with historically-specific racisms.' There are different fractions within the working classes which are racially differentiated and which may stand in different relations to capital. Race may be intrinsic to the manner in which the black labouring classes are constituted and enter into their struggles so that class relations function as race relations and

> race is . . . the modality in which class is 'lived', the medium through which class relations are experienced, the form in which it is appropriated and 'fought through' . . . racism is also one of the dominant means of ideological representation through which the white fractions of the class come to 'live' their relations to other fractions, and through them to capital itself.

As this passage should indicate, what is being sought is an interpretation of events on the grandest of scales. From the standpoint of chapter 5, it is an attempt to elaborate a philosophy of history, not to contribute to social science. The questions asked do not permit answers as specific as, to take the same example again, questions about the preferences of landladies. It would also appear that Hall follows Cox in employing the social definition of race embodied in the US Act of 1866. This, of course, is unacceptable to Robert Miles (1993: 40–2) who objects to Hall using 'race' as if it were a reality that could act autonomously: 'Without additional clarification, the claim remains vacuous and each new, approving citation only reinforces the unintelligibility.' Noting Gilroy's (1987: 247) elaboration of Hall's usage, which describes race as an effect of discourse, a political category, and a relational concept, Miles protests that if one represents race 'as a concept which can be employed to explain social processes, it must refer to a real, identifiable phenomenon which can have (autonomous) effects on those processes'.

The tendency to represent race as a reality is marked in much US writing, such as the study of *Racial Formation in the United States: from the 1960s to the 1990s* by Michael Omi and Howard Winant. They criticise attempts to subsume the analysis of racial relations (either inter-racial or intra-racial) under the analysis of ethnic, class or national relations. For them 'race is a concept which signifies and symbolizes social conflicts and interests by referring to different types of human bodies' (1994: 11–12, 55). Their criterion for definition of the concept is the function served in contemporary society by a word which forms part of the practical language. This means that, as they say, the concept is unstable and subject to constant transformation by political struggle. It varies from one time and one place to another and cannot be measured. A Swiss sociologist, (Wimmer, 1997: 18) has this sort of usage in mind when he refers to 'an antiracist concept of race', apparently in acknowledgement of the dubious claim that the appropriate criterion is not the function of the concept in the wider society but the intention of its user. Omi and Winant consider that the concept of race is of no use to social science but believe it must be retained because in the practical language the word structures and represents the social world. The task for theory is to explain this, and, in particular, the socio-historical process of racial formation by which racial categories are created, inhabited, transformed and destroyed. The process is driven by 'racial projects' which make links between the social structure and cultural representation. Racial projects connect what race means in a particular discursive practice to the ways in which both social structures and everyday experiences are racially organised. They can be defined as racist if they create or reproduce structures of domination based on essentialist categories of race. The politically partisan character of Omi and Winant's argument is overt. Its implicit message is that the mobilisation of new social movements, led by the black movement, has expanded the terrain of political contest and set the stage for the general reorganisation of US politics, despite the disappointments of the Clinton era.

The first definitions of 'racism' depended upon on acceptance of the social definition of 'race' given Congressional authority in 1866. When Eric Williams maintained that racism was a consequence of slavery (as mentioned on p. 26) he was using the word to mean what Cox meant by race prejudice in 1948. In the mid-1960s English-language writers accepted that there was a field of study, properly called 'race relations', which had three dimensions: the first of these was the ideological, using 'racism' to designate the doctrine that race determined culture; the second was the attitudinal, using prejudice as its basic concept; while the third was behavioural, starting from social relationships and relying on the concept of discrimination. This formulation was brushed aside by two leaders of the Black Power movement within the United States, Stokeley Carmichael and Charles Hamilton (1967: 19–21) who insisted 'By "racism" we mean the predication of decisions and policies on considerations of race for the purpose of *subordinating* a racial group and maintaining control over that group.' They went on to distinguish between individual and institutional racism, stating that

institutional racism relies on the active and pervasive operation of anti-black attitudes and practices. A sense of superior group position prevails; whites are "better" than blacks, therefore blacks should be subordinated to whites. This is a racist attitude and it permeates the society, on both the individual and institutional level, covertly and overtly.

In Britain, John Rex (1970: 38) spoke for others when he objected to any definition of racism which limited it to the study of ideas. He viewed racism as one example of a deterministic belief system, and conceptualised such systems as justifying particular kinds of social structure. This kept the focus upon social and political function which was appropriate for answering certain kinds of question but neglectful of others.

In the following years the word was used in many new senses and for many new purposes, so that 'racism' took the place of 'race relations' as the designation for a field of study. Instead of its having three dimensions of similar status, attitudinal and behavioural phenomena were presented as the consequences of ideological causes. The effect of this was to prioritise attempts to answer large-scale historical questions and to pass over some of the smaller-scale distinctions (like that between racist attitudes and ethnocentric attitudes) that had previously been found useful. It has also encouraged a simplistic conception of the political issues, such as in the European Year Against Racism (1997) in which 'key decision-makers' were called upon to 'commit themselves to the fight against racism' as if a moral decision was the main requirement. No one would have invited them to commit themselves to fight against crime, but the one task is as complex as the other.

Whether or not the theoretical language of social science needs a concept either of racism in the abstract, or of particular racisms or new racisms, is a separate question, the answer to which must depend upon whether the concept is important for the resolution of intellectual problems. In the 1950s there was a campaign against the misuse of the race concept. One of the most successful popularisers of anthropological writing on this, Ashley Montagu (1964: xli), drew a parallel with 'phlogiston', a substance supposed by a late seventeenth-century chemist to be present in all materials and to be given off by burning. A hundred years later Lavoisier demonstrated experimentally the processes of combustion and proved that there was no such substance as phlogiston, yet nevertheless some quite distinguished scientists were for a long time unwilling to abandon their belief that there was such a substance. The proposition that humanity was divided into a limited number of distinct races was no more valid or useful as an explanatory principle. So Ashley Montagu concluded 'race is the phlogiston of our time'. Some twenty years later, dismayed by the tendency to attribute so many effects to the operation of racism without defining the term adequately or indicating how the truth of these claims could be tested, the present writer (Banton, 1983: 13) complained that 'in some quarters it is not race but racism that is the phlogiston of our time, a supposedly elemental force which is never clearly located in human psychology or social structure and which offers only circular explanations of racial discrimination'. Its value is rhetorical.

Social rhetoric

Since the end of the 1970s there has been a turning away from the attempt to build a social science of racial and ethnic relations. One of the new tendencies is part of the wider movement known as postmodernism. This began with deconstructionism, a sophisticated mode of criticising taken-for-granted concepts in the practical language. It maintained that texts had no fixed meanings; they could be understood only in relation to one another and not in relation to some objective truth. Postmodernism rejects modernity's belief in empiricism, progress and scientific rationality in order to elevate the subjective dimension of human experience. Some versions of postmodernism in its application to racial questions retain the aspiration to understanding embodied in the Hegelian tradition. For example, Ali Rattansi (Rattansi and Westwood, 1994: 2) writes:

In part, modernity and postmodernity have emerged as attempts to replace political and social scientific metanarratives such as Marxism, Weberianism, liberalism, social democracy and varieties of conservatism which have come to be regarded as no longer adequate to the explication and control of events in an era characterized by culturally heterogeneous, rapidly changing social configurations, structured by new forms of globalization and the all but complete collapse of communist blocs.

To assert that previous doctrines are 'no longer adequate to the explication and control of events' is to imply that events can be explained and controlled, and that the new viewpoint is capable of this. Neither proposition can be proved. As was noted at the beginning of this book, ideas about what constitutes a satisfactory explanation can differ. In one locality people may be satisfied to learn that someone has malaria because of a mosquito bite. In another, they may want to know why the mosquito bit that person rather than another. There can come a stage when people of one culture, or one generation, are satisfied, but others are not. In social science the key question is whether proposed explanations which cross a certain threshold advance scientific propositions capable (in principle) of proof, or whether they rest upon personal belief. For example, Marxists and non-Marxists can agree about many of the correlates of labour demand. The relations between this demand and the regulation of immigration on the one hand, and the expected returns to automation, on the other, can be empirically determined. In seeking to fit observations about the demand for labour into an interpretation of the development of capitalism, however, an author can step out of the realm of the demonstrable into a philosophy of history.

The writers whose work is discussed at this point share with Rattansi and Westwood an aspiration towards a comprehensive historical understanding, whether or not they share the tenets of postmodernism. If the truth of the kind of understanding they seek cannot be demonstrated, then the exercise in which they are involved is one of rhetoric (the art and language of persuasive speaking). Their writings become attempts to persuade the reader to accept the author's interpretation, and this is often of an overtly political character. It is certainly impossible in social science to exclude the political biases of authors in their selection of research problems and in the background assumptions which constitute their philosophies of society and of history, but those who seek to develop a social science have to discipline themselves by trying to formulate issues in ways that are acceptable to persons who do not share their assumptions and to find answers that compel the assent of colleagues who approach them with different political presuppositions.

The centrepoint of Rattansi's (1994: 16) own contribution is the description of a postmodern 'frame' which highlights eight features. These say that the student must take account of the present condition of Western society, including the construction of some persons as being 'other', globalisation, the de-essentialising of 'subjects' and the 'social', consideration of how time and space contribute to the formation of identities, the relation between the 'psychic' and the 'social', and 'an engagement with questions of sexuality and sexual difference'. This is then a preliminary to comments on the Holocaust, ethnicities, race and racisms, institutional racism, sexuality and psychoanalysis. These comments could stand independently of the proffered frame and there is no consideration of criteria for determining whether a frame is complete or satisfactory. The whole procedure is rhetorical in being an attempt to persuade the reader to accept the writer's philosophy of society.

A similar rhetoric characterises the work of Floya Anthias and Nina Yuval-Davis (1992: 19) when they write (emphasis added) 'We are arguing for an analysis of racialization and racism that *pays attention* to the relationship between race phenomena and ethnic phenomena . . . an analysis that *looks at* the question of race structuration . . . Racism should also be *looked at* with regard to practices and discourses.' This stress upon ways of seeing things is in part an attempt to escape from misconceptions encouraged by the practical language, but the authors do not limit themselves to specific issues or attempt to establish relationships that are so cogent that colleagues who start from a different political standpoint have nevertheless to accept them. Anthias and Yuval-Davis' procedure is to try to persuade others to see the social world as they see it. The extent of their ambition is evident in the subtitle of their book, 'Race, nation, gender, colour and class and the anti-racist struggle'; everything has to be brought together in a philosophy of history. How they identify 'an effective analysis' is left unclear, but it would appear to be one that advances 'the anti-racist struggle'.

US writers who stress the specificity of race are anxious to maintain that its effects cannot be explained in terms of any other factor, like class or ethnicity. On this point Omi and Winant's argument may be contrasted with the view of Anthias and Yuval-Davis (1992: 8, *i*) who contend that 'ethnicity at its most general level involves belonging to a particular group and sharing its conditions of existence'; this leads them to maintain that 'the concept of race has to be located within the wider category of ethnos'. The contrast is also one between a US and Caribbean perspective on the one hand, and a European perspective on the other. For blacks in the United States the concept of race is important as signalising an experience different from that of European immigrant minorities to their country, and it appeals to blacks in the United Kingdom for similar reasons. When comparing group experiences it should be possible to acknowledge differences without endorsing a tainted concept. When researching particular problems, like, say, the grounds of discrimination, the tasks themselves can decide what are the most helpful concepts, and how they relate to each other.

The value of the ethnicity perspective is more evident when the cultural differences between groups are greater. For example, when from the late 1950s Sikhs from the Punjab settled in Britain, they recreated the social life they had known in their homeland, not just their temples and the cycle of calendar festivals and rites of passage, but the giving of dowries and the whole set of expectations about how men and women, kin and affines, seniors and juniors, should behave towards one another. It was an extension of the sociology of the Punjab. No account of relations between the minorities and the majority can be satisfactory if it ignores the way in which ethnic groups maintain cultural differences, and when 'racism' is the conceptual starting point this is always a danger.

In an introduction to recent writing in this field John Solomos and Les Back (1996: 60) concentrate

on two themes: first, on how the various theoretical paradigms have attempted to account for the phenomenon of racism and its role in shaping social and political relations in contemporary societies; second, on the various historical contexts within which ideas about race were developed.

They present racism as an *explanandum*, not an *explanans*, while their top-down stress upon the historical contexts of ideas is neglectful of the quality of imagination needed to conceive theories and the objective nature of the knowledge that can be won through intellectual work. They mention 'questions which need to be addressed in a fuller manner. For example: how does one account for the emergence and persistence of racialized inequalities in employment, housing, social welfare, education?' but add 'we do not seem to have moved much closer towards resolving them. Rather we have seen deeply politicized public debates.' Since social scientists have made great progress in answering fairly specific questions about the sources of inequality in all the fields mentioned, the reason for the authors' negative assessment must lie in their aspiration for a large-scale interpretation of the kind sketched by Stuart Hall. This hope may lie behind the assertion that 'the processes which structure the relationship between racism and social exclusions have to been seen in the context of specific historical circumstances' (Solomos and Back, 1996: 64). Both the terms 'racism' and 'social exclusion' need to be clearly defined if a research worker is to investigate if there is any relationship between them, and if so, what. As a further step, it might then be possible to discover what difference it made, if any, if this relationship was seen in a historical context. Maybe Solomos and Back would dismiss such comments as failing to understand the kind of knowledge they seek. In their view 'the main question' is 'how do we understand the role that race plays in shaping key facets of social relations in contemporary societies?', which is not a question that can be answered by the methods of social science and leads back only into the politicised debates of which they write.

An emphasis on the historical context of ideas is a two-sided weapon because it can be turned against those who would use it. The turning away from the goal of a social science in recent sociological writing can itself be contextualised. It may be a flight from the more demanding kinds of academic work. It may spring from a personal fascination with the subjective dimension of social life manifested in the concern with identities. Thus Anthias and Yuval-Davis (1992: 196) describe another author associated with Stuart Hall, Rosalind Brunt, as maintaining that the 'return to the subjective' does not imply a withdrawal from politics but opens up possibilities for political action based on 'unity in diversity', founded not on common denominators but 'a whole variety of heterogeneous, possibly antagonistic, maybe magnificently diverse, identities and circumstances'. Anthias and Yuval-Davis conclude that this rests on a naïve assumption that all popular struggles are inherently progressive, which may well be the case, but the passage quoted also demonstrates the preference for political rhetoric which has become so noticeable in British sociological writing about race and ethnicity. In so far as these new trends are simply the products of circumstance they will contribute little to the supersession of the idiom of race. Placed alongside Blumer's criticism of US research in 1958, they demonstrate no progress in explanation.

Assessment

The main advances in developing social science explanations to supersede those of racial typology, summarised in chapter 5, left other questions unanswered. The writers who have followed Oliver Cox have offered an additional explanation of why it was that many people continued to believe in an obsolete kind of explanation, but underlying their claims is a larger challenge. In biological science, a bottom-up theory starting from the gene was the more satisfying because it could be contained within a top-down theory of evolution by natural selection. Marxism claimed to be a social counterpart to the theory of evolution, explaining how all the lower-level processes fitted into a comprehensive account of how the social world had developed. That vision retains a capacity to inspire and challenge social scientists who do not accept its claims to scientific status.

The issues are far from simple. The five theories distinguished by Mayr (and listed on p. 84 above) comprehend much that is testable and scientific, but if they are considered as a whole (and called 'Darwinism') there is still some philosophical doubt as to their status. Popper (1974/76: 168) wrote that: 'I have come to the conclusion that Darwinism is not a testable scientific theory, but a metaphysical research programme – a possible framework for testable scientific theories.' In similar fashion, it can be said that Marxism also offers a metaphysical political programme which includes a set of guidelines for research and a framework for the interpretation of findings. It may be deficient, but orthodox social science has no alternative research programme of comparable power.

The parallel between organic evolution and social or cultural or superorganic evolution is the closer because the former is not necessarily a process of increasing differentiation. When Darwin studied sexuality among barnacles, he could be concerned with the way two sexes appeared where previously there had been one. In some circumstances, though, hermaphroditism could be a better solution to the problem of maximum fertility when there were few sites on which they could reproduce. Equally, some species die out either in spite of the way they have been evolving or because of the way in which they have been evolving. Evolution is not necessarily progressive in the way that humans judge progress. The Darwinian theory predicts that if organisms are classified according to their resemblances and differences, the resulting classes can then be related to one another as parts of a branching tree. If different characteristics demanded different trees, this could demonstrate that something was wrong with the original theory. The same line of descent had to be deducible from all the organs and structure of a particular species. Since differences between such classes can now be quantified in respect of many enzymes and proteins, this greatly increases the explanatory power of the theory, enabling more parts of it to be tested, but it does not permit any more than very limited predictions about the future evolution of any species or subspecies.

Marxists see history as a progressive development in some respects comparable to organic evolution. They do not claim to predict the future of particular societies, but believe that they can identify the components of change so that their understanding of its character has improved in a manner comparable to the results of testing in other branches of social science. They presume that by viewing racial groups in class terms something more can be learned than when they are seen purely in status terms. One reason why this approach has been found attractive is that all the alternatives have glaring weaknesses.

Even the theories of physical science are problematic from some standpoints. In his autobiography Popper (1974/76: 149) explained that when he wrote his postscript to *The Logic of Scientific Discovery* he stressed that he had 'rejected all attempts at the justification of theories, and that I had replaced justification by criticism'. On another occasion (1972: 265) he added:

A scientific result cannot be justified. It can only be criticised, and tested. And no more can be said in its favour than it seems, after all this criticism and testing, better, more interesting, more powerful, more promising, and a better approximation to truth, than its competitors.

One of the problems with this approach (which is often called positivist, although Popper did not accept this label) is its tendency to rely on what Ernest Gellner (1985: 58) called a granular metaphysic, conceiving of the world as consisting of discrete grains which can be separated from each other for the purposes of analysis. 'Things in themselves' cannot be fully comprehended, yet every research worker must be able to locate them in some metaphysical view of the world. Criticism can lead people to modify their metaphysical views but these are usually several steps removed from any process of trying to confront theories with empirical observations.

The limitations of the positivist approach are often manifested in discussions of social policy. When arguing about what should be done to ameliorate racial discrimination people have to make assumptions about the nature of social groups. Are black people so different from white people that any policy should assume that they will continue to be different? If so, what is the nature of the difference? If not, what factors are responsible for the present differences? Such questions rest upon assumptions as to what constitutes the black category. The Marxist believes that in the long run the fundamental differences are those of class, so that the short-run problem is to understand the process of class formation and the ways in which racial identities constitute impediments. It is not beyond the bounds of possibility that there could one day be a social counterpart to the theory of organic evolution (Dennett, 1995: 345–68). There might then be a bottom-up theory starting from race as status which could be contained within a top-down theory of social evolution. For the foreseeable future, however, those who see racial groups as fashioned by circumstance must draw upon their personal philosophies of history and of human nature whenever they envisage likely future developments and the chances that these might be influenced by social policies. Unlike Hegelianism, positivism cannot provide the tools required to legitimate its philosophical position (Gellner, 1985: 67).

Miles' attack on the use of the folk concept of race as a term in social science theory was a necessary part of his attempt to subsume 'race' under the analysis of class. To judge from subsequent writing that attempt has failed, but the attack itself has had a highly constructive effect in forcing a reconsideration of fundamental issues. Later writing in the same epistemological tradition which has cut loose from the Marxist scheme has lost the intellectual (and political) impetus and become less systematic. To take but one example, while the analysis of racial discourse may well prove valuable, it is still several steps removed from the explanation of actual conduct.

Chapter 7 will describe an alternative bottom-up approach in social science that is still rudimentary but, if it can be developed, may remedy some of the deficiencies of the theories discussed so far. It subsumes both the category 'race' and that of 'ethnicity' under the concept of a social group as a social construct, while rejecting some current uses of that metaphor.

7   Race as social construct

Properly to explain how a social category is created by reference to the physical features called 'race', it is necessary to draw comparisons with what is known about the creation of other categories, such as those identified by gender, class, national and ethnic origin and so on. The problem has to be subsumed within a more general theory of how groups of all kinds are constructed. This may be a way to differentiate a theoretical from a practical language and to resolve the dilemma of nomenclature mentioned at the beginning of the book.

This chapter offers a report on progress towards a bottom-up theory which could supersede the use of 'race' in the attempt to explain why it is that the outward differences between persons, and the cultural characteristics associated with differences in national or ethnic origin, appear to cause social and political tension. It pulls together and restates some of the conclusions drawn in earlier chapters.

Socialisation into groups

Human individuals are born with differing talents and personal characteristics. During the course of their socialisation they learn about the society into which they have been born, how its members are categorised and with which groups they should identify themselves. They learn whether they are male or female, and what kinds of conduct are expected because of this distinction. They may learn that they belong to national, regional, class, caste, religious, racial or ethnic categories or groups; that they should align themselves socially with fellow members of such categories, and that in any event others will treat them as category members. At times it is important to recognise a distinction between a category and a group (a conclusion also emphasised in Jenkins, 1994). A category is defined by the categoriser, as when persons earning incomes of more than x and less than y are made a category for the purposes of taxation. They are not necessarily a social group, because a group is constituted by the relations between its members; they are conscious of belonging to it, and identify themselves with it in varying degrees. A category of persons who are treated differently by others may come to identify with one another and transform themselves into a group, while if they fail to maintain any group organisation they may revert to being a category. It is not always necessary to insist on this distinction, so for reasons of convenience and in line with current practice, the word 'group' will sometimes be used to designate categories as well. Nevertheless, there are circumstances in which the distinction can be important.

Social categories and groups are social constructs, constructed from the material in their environment. The different expectations of males and females define the categories of gender which are constructed partly from the biological differences of sex and partly from group culture and social organisation. For example, new technology creates new occupations. If a new occupation comes to be thought of as a male or a female speciality this is more likely to be because of ideas about gender appropriateness than because of physical differences between males and females.

A national category or group is constructed largely from the division of the political world into states. A regional category is constructed from geographical features and the social differences associated with spatial relations. A social class is constructed from shared ideas about people's place in the labour market or in the status structure. A caste group is a special form of class distinction, which in the Indian case is associated with religious beliefs about the world and the place of humans within it. Racial categories are constructed from the evidence of physical differ- ence, more particularly of complexion and physiognomy; that these are social constructs is demonstrated by the way in the United States anyone with any evident sign of African ancestry has been accounted black even if most of their genetic inheritance was European. Ethnic categories and groups are based on their members' belief in their common ancestry, but given meaning by sentiments of shared culture (either a long-standing distinctiveness, such as that of language and religion, or a more recent distinctive experience, like that of discrimination). Just as a passport is evidence of nationality, so may costume and names serve as signs of gender, class, religion or ethnicity; and in like manner skin colour may be a sign of the racial category to which someone is conventionally assigned.

Collective action may transform a category into a group, in which case it may be constructed from several of the forms of difference. When, in the case of *Mandla* v. *Dowell Lee* (1983 1 All ER 106) the judges in the House of Lords had to decide whether Mandla, as a Sikh, was a member 'of a group of persons defined by reference to . . . ethnic or national origins' they held that in order to qualify under the law, an ethnic group must 'regard itself, and be regarded by others, as a distinct community by virtue of certain characteristics'. It must have 'a long shared history, of which the group is conscious as distinguishing it from other groups, and the memory of which it keeps alive'. It must also have 'a cultural tradition of its own, including family and social customs and manners'. Certain other characteristics, of geographical origin or descent, language, literature, religion and size, though not essential, might also be relevant.

The legal interpretation serves to reinforce the conclusion that in everyday life racial or ethnic groups will be known by proper names (like Sikhs or African-Americans) and that they may be distinguishable on several dimensions. The English law against indirect racial and ethnic discrimination requires a concept of a 'racial group'. Strictly speaking it is not a group but a category, because it was not necessary that Mandla should participate in any group activities; his less favourable treatment was related to his being assigned by others to an ethnic category. Differentiation between racial and ethnic categories for the purposes of social science has proven particularly troublesome because of the meanings of these words in the practical language (of which legal language is a refined form). Racial distinctions have conventionally been thought to be physical ones, and ethnic distinctions to be cultural, though the members of a racial category may feel themselves to be members of a group and to share elements of common culture. Racial classifications have been thought to derive from objective assessments made by an outside observer, whereas ethnic ones were thought to derive from the subjective sentiments of voluntary self-identification. Racial distinctions have been used primarily to exclude persons from civil and other rights, whereas ethnic identification has functioned to create inclusive groups. The English language recognises the possibility of racial differences within an ethnic group and the possibility of ethnic differences within a racial group, like the differences in many African societies which are called 'tribal'.

In the United States the word 'ethnicity' is in fairly common use, so that many people think of themselves as belonging in an ethnic minority as well as belonging in a racial category. The words are part of the practical language. Where there are no corresponding categories in popular use the social scientist who wishes to generalise is confronted with a problem of comparability. For example there are Brazilians with a *café-au-lait* complexion who can find themselves classed as 'black' in the United States when they would never be so classified in their own country. Visitors to Brazil from the United States may perceive racial categories where Brazilians see only a series of differences between individuals. The social scientist needs concepts which are independent of the culturally-conditioned perceptions of persons from particular societies. When 'race' is used as a social construct it is the basis for a small number of categories, perhaps only two. The number of categories does not correspond with the reality of phenotypical variation which includes a gradual shading of colour from dark to light with no clear dividing lines. When ethnicity is used as a social construct it may become the basis for a large number of categories, but since some individuals have multiple ethnic origins assignment to ethnic categories may also depend upon individual choice.

Since the words 'race' and 'ethnicity' have so many strong associations in the practical language, it may never be possible to use them as names for theoretical concepts within social science. Max Weber was inclined to this conclusion, for he wrote that 'the notion of "ethnically" determined social action subsumes phenomena that a rigorous sociological analysis – as we do not attempt it here – would have to distinguish carefully . . . It is certain that in this process the collective term "ethnic" would be abandoned' (Weber, 1968: 395). To supersede the concept of race in the study of social relations it will probably be necessary to supersede the concept of ethnicity at the same time. This can be done, and in a manner faithful to the Weberian tradition, by showing the significance for group formation and maintenance of the processes of social exclusion and inclusion (Barnes, 1992). Ideas of race have mostly been used to exclude others from privilege whereas a shared sense of common ethnic origin has been used as a basis for the creation of an inclusive group (though a group will be the more strongly constructed when it is based on several kinds of social distinctiveness and not on ethnic origin alone). Ethnic groups are created when a consciousness of shared ethnic origin is the primary basis for the creation of an inclusive group. Racial categories are created when beliefs about biological differences are used to exclude persons from equal relations.

An earlier formulation of this statement was discussed by Alan Carling (1991: 330–1) who observed that it read like a definition of two kinds of group. He maintained that when individuals created an inclusive group this almost inevitably evoked exclusive reactions from others and that as a definition the distinction was therefore untenable. In his view the proposition was more plausibly regarded as an empirical generalisation about differences between two kinds of group, but this is subject to the same objection as the one he identified. For this reason the author presents it as a distinction between two kinds of social process, not between two kinds of group.

Collective action

In the course of their socialisation individuals develop tastes or preferences which they may or may not share with their peers. They also acquire longer-term goals or ambitions. Some such goals they can pursue by individual action. For example, some may want to accumulate wealth for themselves, though even this goal may operate only in a social context, since many people's desire for wealth incorporates a desire to display their success to others. Other goals can be pursued effectively only by collective action, either of a voluntary character – as by forming or joining an association – or of a coercive character. The coercion may pass unnoticed. For example, nearly all humans grow up as citizens of a state which provides them with a variety of services. The defence of the state usually requires an army and a body of state representatives (like ambassadors) to represent the state's interests to the representatives of other states. Such services, which are called public goods, can be provided only by coercive collective action to which every member of the state is forced to contribute. In certain other circumstances, however, individuals may be free to decide whether to pursue their goals by individual or collective action.

The theory used here relies on the axiom that individuals optimise – that is, that they seek to maximise their net advantages, both material, and immaterial (or psychological). This is a presupposition of much economic theory and is the basis of rational choice theories. That name has misled some into thinking that they are theories only of rational choices and that some other kind of theory is needed in order to account for irrational choices, or choices which do not produce the greatest material gain. Yet the name is used simply to indicate that a theory is a member of a family of theories which start from a view of social action as the allocation of scarce means to competing ends. Optimisation is an axiom, not a proposition that can be proved. If a person works extra hours of overtime, that is taken to indicate a revealed preference for extra income by comparison with the leisure time that is forgone. If the same person took the opposite decision, that would be taken as revealing a greater preference for leisure. Revealed preferences are contrasted with positive preferences ascertained by independent inquiry. Yet if someone acts in a manner inconsistent with a stated positive preference, this is not an empirical falsification if no one can be sure that the person's preference had not changed by the time of the action. What the theory does is to specify the costs that have to be borne, or the benefits that are forgone, when someone fails to reach the optimal decision.

Immaterial or emotional preferences may sometimes be more important than material ones. During the course of socialisation an individual learns that he or she has obligations to fellow group members in accordance with what Meyer Fortes (1983: 23) named the principle of prescriptive altruism. Humans become psychologically dependent upon their identification with particular groups and upon receiving approval from those who represent them. Thus, when an individual optimises he or she may regard it as more important to conform to a group norm than to obtain maximum material advantage. A group's norms can sometimes run counter to its material interests.

Underlying the theory is a conception of procedural rationality. In industrial societies many consumers take pains to try to ascertain what will be the 'best buy'. Yet after making a purchase they may conclude that they have failed to allocate means to ends in the optimal manner; if so, they seek to learn from that experience so that next time they may make a better buy. Just because the purchase turns out to have been a 'bad buy' does not mean that it was the result of an irrational choice. Consumers are impelled in this way to rationalise their purchasing. Therefore the rationality in question is not a property of some actions rather than others, but a criterion for examining behaviour over time. Such an approach breaks away from Max Weber's attempted distinction between rational and non-rational action and links instead with his discussion of the process of rationalisation (Banton, 1985). As Weber argued, in every kind of society, capitalist, socialist, Islamic or Hindu, there are pressures making for the reduction of inconsistencies. People share common ultimate ends (even if these are changing) and over the course of time they rationalise their lives in terms of these values.

The theory allows for the possibility that individuals may revise their personal goals or change the order of priority in which they rank their goals, especially if one goal proves difficult or costly to attain. Large sums of money are spent on advertising that is designed to persuade people to acquire new tastes or goals and to change their priorities. This includes both personal goals (as when someone decides to start or to give up smoking) and shared goals (such as support for political movements to promote equality of opportunity). No new generation is socialised in exactly the same way as its predecessor because the societies themselves are changing. Nor is socialisation ever completely effective, because each new generation has ideas of its own which are likely to be regarded as deviant. Though the adjective 'deviant' is often used to designate anti-social behaviour in breach of the law, not all deviance can be accounted undesirable. New philosophies and social practices usually appear first as forms of deviance. For example, in many western societies the new generation of the 1960s challenged prevailing norms of gender differentiation; their ideas appeared perverse to their seniors but as time has passed the tables have been turned and the old expectations have come to be seen as deviant. More recently a new generation has shown heightened concern for the rights of animals and more individuals avoid meat-eating.

The belief that racial discrimination is morally wrong has become more widespread.

Deviance has also to be considered in relation to social divisions. The parental generation rewards the new generation for conforming to its expectations, but in many schools pupils do not perceive these rewards to be as attractive as the thrills they can get from challenging their elders' expectations. If the esteem which their peers accord them for ability on the sports field or for participating in gang activities can outweigh the rewards the school can give for success in examinations, then the young people may be more anxious not to deviate from the norms of their peers than from those of their teachers. The recent rise of Neo-Nazism in some European countries may to some extent be fed by the reaction of some young people against the pressures of a competitive society and against the expectations of the parental generation: they develop a counter-culture.

Socialisation is of particular relevance to the maintenance of national and ethnic identities. At school, pupils learn to identify with the history and the heroes of their country, which reinforces the sense of primary ethnicity. Growing up with coethnics, individuals acquire the tastes that characterise their groups, whether primary or secondary. These may be tastes as to food, dress, pastimes and so on, or they may be tastes as to the persons with whom they prefer to associate or with whom they are content to be identified. Members of the older generation within indigenous peoples or immigrant minorities may be anxious that their children should maintain the group's distinctive language. Their children may be more inclined to speak the language of their classmates and to adopt the idioms of the mass media. Social scientists have developed special techniques for research into language maintenance and language shift in such groups (e.g. Fishman, 1990). Representatives of some such minorities fear that their groups will lose their distinctiveness by being assimilated into the surrounding society, but in other circumstances people may have little alternative to maintain their membership in a group (for example, few people find it worthwhile to give up their nationality and obtain another, while it may be impossible to change ascription to a racial category).

While some goals can be pursued only by collective action, a great many can be pursued by either individual or collective action. Wage-bargaining can serve as an example. One of the difficulties of trade union officials is that if, by bargaining with management, they secure a wage increase for all employees in a particular category, the benefits are enjoyed by union members and non-members alike. A male non-union employee who set out to calculate whether it was worthwhile joining the union would ascertain the costs of the subscriptions or dues of membership. Then he would work out the extent to which the union's power to win a wage rise would be increased by his joining. Next he would compare the likely benefit of his joining with the cost incurred. Usually he would be led to the conclusion that his economic interest was not to join but instead to take a 'free-ride' at the expense of his fellow employees who bore the costs of union representation. Mancur Olsen (1965) generalised this by showing that in a whole range of situations rational self-interested individuals will not engage in collective action to advance their interests, particularly when others are doing so.

If a bargaining agency is to get maximum benefit for those who support it, the agency has to represent all beneficiaries. A trade union seeks to become a monopoly (one seller of labour, many buyers). An employers' agency seeks to become a monopsony (one supplier of jobs, many applicants for them). Such agencies can exert maximum bargaining power. They can draw up and enforce rules binding upon their members. Here there is a parallel with the distinction in philosophy between act utilitarianism and rule utilitarianism. In philosophical discussion this is a distinction between two sets of criteria for judging the goodness or badness of actions, but in social science it can be used to differentiate two kinds of assumption in the interpretation of behaviour. Act utilitarianism is the assumption that actions are intended to maximise net advantages. Rule utilitarianism envisages a two-step process. It seeks to formulate rules so as to maximise net advantages for those bound by them. Individual members of a bargaining agency are then expected to observe group rules, though they may calculate their individual costs and benefits of observance and comply with the rules only to the extent that maximises individual net advantages.

Some benefits can be enjoyed by a single person, but others have to be shared. This leads to the concept of public goods, which in economic theory are things like clean air, protection from foreign enemies, a system of highways and (a favourite example!) lighthouses. If the air is clean for one person it is clean for all others. If one person is protected from foreign attack by the national army, so are all the others. If there is a road for one driver or a lighthouse for one ship, it is equally available to others. No taxpayer has a private right to the air he wants to breathe, to the services of the artillery, or to the roadway outside his or her house. Thus public goods are characterised by jointness of supply: once the good is produced for one person, it can be made available to others at little or no extra cost. Such goods are also characterised by the way that they are external to ordinary market transactions. They make trading possible, and increase national wealth, but those who produce them cannot charge users as they might charge them for private services. (Of course there are schemes for charging road users proportionate to use, as with differential licence fees for heavy vehicles, but these are as yet of a limited character.) The same kind of analysis can also be applied in wage-bargaining when others will benefit from the outcome even if they are only a small section of the general public.

Racial discrimination can be seen as the opposite of a public good, as a public bad, corresponding to atmospheric pollution. In neither case are the negative consequences evenly distributed, but the overall effect of both is to reduce the welfare of the society as a whole. The equivalent of clean air is then racial harmony, though this is not a very good name since grossly unfair relations may for a time appear harmonious. Just as it is difficult to agree a positive definition of freedom, as a freedom *to* things, and more satisfactory to define freedom in terms of freedom *from* various kinds of oppression, so it is better to define racial harmony as an absence of discrimination and other features which embitter social relations, or may come to do so.

If an individual can be expected to join in collective action only when he or she expects the benefits of so doing to exceed the costs, how are these to be calculated? Michael Hechter *et al.* (1982) proposed a theorem designed to specify the basic factors determining the individual's net benefit from participation in the action under consideration. They are (1), the portion of the shared good he or she expects to obtain if the action succeeds; plus (2), the amount of the private reward; these together are then multiplied by (3), the person's estimate of the probability of success; to this is added (4), the amount of private reward expected for participation regardless of the probable outcome; then subtractions are made to allow for (5), the amount of private punishment if the action fails; and (6), the cost of injury; these last two are then multiplied by (7), their likelihood; to this is added (8), the amount of private punishment the individual expects to receive if he or she does not join the collective action. This equation predicts when collective action is likely to take place; it also has implications as to the likely form of such action – predicting, for example, that forms which entail fewer personal costs for individuals will occur with greater relative frequency. It further implies that the position of an ethnic group in the stratification system has no direct bearing either on a member's decision to participate or on the group's propensity to engage in collective action.

The likelihood of success will depend upon how well the action is organised. Hechter *et al.* explain how a group that supplies private goods to its members can prevent free-riding, and can control the information available to members, and more easily persuade them that collective action has some prospect of success. Sometimes organisations are set up to secure public goods for members of an ethnic group. Sometimes organisations which already exist for the purpose of supplying private goods to members (like churches and social clubs) can be redirected to seek political or economic benefits for the group as a whole (i.e. public goods). Ethnic mobilisation may then be a by-product of activity originally oriented towards some other goal.

This notion of a capacity for collective action as a by-product is important. It also points to a major limitation on the applicability of rational choice theory, namely the extent to which present possibilities are always constrained by the products and by-products of past activities. Any theory has to start somewhere, so that some social scientists think it only reasonable that they should start at one point in time and take for granted the effect of previous history in producing groups that have developed distinctive cultures, created social institutions and acquired particular positions in structures of power. If it turns out that they have not started far enough back in time, they can always move back their point of departure. While rational choice theory does not account for the values that people place upon their likes and dislikes, it can help explain the patterns of behaviour of aggregates and why those patterns change in particular ways. It assumes, for example, that physical features have a given social significance, but critics ask how it was that the features in question came to be used in that way in the first place? This question can be dismissed on the same grounds as people dismiss the question about whether the chicken came before the egg, but on the empirical level the problem is not always so easily side-stepped. Several of the factors in the Hechter *et al.* theorem depend very much upon the individual's assessment of how others may react and of the kind of relationship in which the parties are involved. They may be more anxious to prevent their rivals obtaining a benefit than to obtain one for themselves. Some of these problems may be elucidated by using a very elementary application of the theory of games described later in the section on inter-group bargaining (pp. 220–2). Relations between groups are then seen to result from implicit processes of bargaining for collective benefit.

The calculation of possible benefit may depend upon whether someone takes a short- or long-term view. An elderly person might believe that a change in the social order could be only beneficial in the longer term but fear that it would be painful and dangerous in the short term. Readiness to take the long-term view might depend upon that person's age, occupation, number of children and group identification. When it is very difficult for anyone to calculate the likely risks and possible benefits, much may depend upon the ability of political activists to persuade their fellows that the net benefits would be greater and the chances of success high (factor (3) in the Hechter *et al.* equation). Activists or entrepreneurs will differ from ordinary members in drawing much more private benefit from the satisfaction of serving what they see as the group cause.

The Hechter *et al.* theorem has been criticised for underestimating ideological influences. For example, at a time during the Second World War when the German army was retreating on the eastern front and there was a desperate need for railway equipment to support the troops, some of that scarce stock was being used to transport Jews to the extermination camps. In the words of Heribert Adam (1983: 379–80) groups have held to their ideological commitments even when their construction of reality has become so dysfunctional that it endangers the very survival of the collectivity. Furthermore, 'the history of nationalism everywhere seems to show that a conflict is much more intense when it expresses itself in terms of symbolic resources than in competition over mere material rewards'. Hechter and Friedman (1983: 384) replied 'We do not deny the existence of non-material rewards, only their relevance for predicting collective action.' The word 'predicting' merits emphasis. Sometimes it appears after the event that ideological forces (such as those of nationalism) must have outweighed material interest. The theory can be buttressed by contending that activists can persuade their fellow group members to set much more store upon factor (4) in the equation – the amount of private reward they experience from supporting the cause irrespective of whether or not it succeeds. If the activists gain support they may be able to change the balance between the alternatives open to group members by threatening them with greater punishments for any failure to join in. Support for the movement may then gather strength like a snowball being rolled down a hill. However, to defend the theory by stressing factor (5) is to admit that it is more difficult to test than Hechter *et al.* would like to believe.

The Hechter theorem also needs some augmentation to take account of the differences between visible groups or categories (males, females; blacks, whites) and invisible ones (gays and communists have been taken as examples, but membership of an ethnic group is often not outwardly visible). According to the theory as it was originally proposed by Olson, collective action will be highly unusual as everyone will try to free-ride. More recent analysis (Gartner and Segura, 1997: 150–1) suggests that there are two steps in the process of collective action. The first is identification, the second mobilisation. Members of visible groups identify with the groups more readily because however they themselves feel about it, others assign them to these categories. Members of invisible groups (or categories) may calculate that it is not in their interest to identify themselves as members (to 'come out'); therefore it is easy to under-estimate how many of them there are, and it is for this reason that collective action seems more frequent than the theory might predict. Some members of invisible ethnic groups may acknowledge their membership if asked, but others may display their membership by voluntarily wearing a distinctive item of costume like a Sikh turban in order to make a public commitment to a particular identity.

Choosing between alternatives

Actions undertaken at one moment in time influence and restrict the alternatives available to individuals at later moments of time. In circumstances of group oppression it may appear as if a member of the oppressed group has no alternative but to behave in the manner required by a member of the oppressing group, but humans are not all the same. Some have valued their dignity so highly that they have refused to submit to unjust demands and have sometimes lost their lives in consequence. There is always some alternative even if it is so unattractive that almost everyone will reject it.

A child will be subject to great pressure to identify himself or herself as male or female on the basis of physical characteristics, to identify as a member of the same nation and perhaps the same class and race as others in the family, though there may be some variability in the number of class and race categories from which a choice can be made. As he or she grows up, that child will have some freedom to decide to what extent he or she is willing to conform to others' expectations of each of the categories to which he or she is assigned. There will be a great range of alternatives when it comes to decisions about engaging in collective action, and with which other persons to combine.

The alternatives between which a person has to choose may be much more complicated than those facing a consumer in a supermarket. A more realistic analogy may be that of competition between a small company that can easily be forced into bankruptcy and a big company able to place a massive order. The latter has greater resources and can get better terms when purchasing from a supplier, it can induce the supplier to stop supplying goods to its competitor or, by temporarily reducing selling prices, force the small firm to cease trading. Like the big company, members of a dominant racial group may be able to select between many alternatives, while limiting those available to the minority; members of that group may feel that they must take what is on offer because the only alternative is a rebellion that has little chance of changing the social order.

Why an individual will be confronted with one particular set of alternatives (or social constructs) leads back to the problem of a starting point in time. Alan Carling has queried whether individuals are ever in a position to 'create groups and categories', in the sense imagined. To account for the range of alternatives available at one moment requires an incursion into history. One response, to repeat an argument of chapter 5, is that a historical interpretation cannot offer the sort of explanation needed to build a social science. The other response, as advocated by Carling and the authors whose work was discussed in chapter 6, is to maintain that a theory must account for the alternatives as well as the choices, and that a social science must account for historical developments. The theory must comprehend 'the determinants of the European explosion which has dominated the history of the last 1000 years' (Carling, 1991: 329, 1996: 60–6).

In an earlier formulation of this theory (Banton, 1983: 125–6) the author made use of the concept of group boundary (discussed in chapter 5) to suggest that racial and ethnic groups could usefully be differentiated along two dimensions reflecting the hardness of their boundaries and the relative privileges of membership. A hard boundary was one that was difficult to cross; usually it would be a question of someone's wanting to cross the boundary in order to become a member, but groups that were hard to join were often hard to leave. The significance of racial differences was that they could be used to draw a very hard boundary and it was usually difficult for a person of inappropriate characteristics either to join or leave a racial category. The greater the privileges of membership, the more incentive there would be for people to seek to join. Carling (1991: 302–13) objected that it was too great a simplification to say that groups that were hard to join were often hard to leave. He detected an ambiguity in that whereas the diagram in the text appeared to represent relations between a group and an individual who might be an applicant to join the group, the individual would probably be a member of some group already. A more complicated diagram was needed to represent the relations between groups with respect to possible movement across boundaries. Besides representing encapsulating, excluding and incorporating groups, it had to allow for the possibility of coexisting groups such that no one had any incentive to change group membership. Other analysts would want to take this further and try to specify the entry and exit costs for the individual who joined or left a group.

The most crucial proposition in the earlier formulation was the one which held that when groups interact, processes of change affect their boundaries in ways determined by the form and intensity of competition. In particular, when people compete as individuals, this tends to dissolve the boundaries that define the groups; when they compete as groups, this reinforces those boundaries. It has been asked whether competition

among individual persons which is affected by the group memberships of
the persons concerned would count as individual or group competition
(Carling 1991: 332–40). The intention was that it should count as
individual competition, though clearly this entails some judgement about
the degree to which, in any particular instance, individual action is
constrained by group demands. To support the claim that once individuals start to trade goods and services with members of another group they
will create ties across the group boundary that will weaken it, reference
was made to Max Gluckman's (1955: 140–52) provocative argument
about the 'bonds in the colour bar' in South Africa. It was based on an
account of the developments in Zululand after the imposition of direct
control by the British in 1887. The Zulu themselves were divided and this
facilitated the growth of alignments that crossed the colour line. With the
Zulu king in exile, some members of the royalist section asked a British
Native Commissioner to adjudicate between them. Royalist chiefs who,
to start with, had refused government stipends, decided to accept them.
Some chiefs thought it advantageous to align themselves with the new
government while the commissioners tried to make use of them in their
administrations. In tax collection, control of hunting, pass laws and like
matters, a steadily increasing minimum of allegiance to the Commissioner was enforced. Thus 'desire for peace, for White technical assistance, and for White money and goods, introduced conflicts in Zulu
allegiance, and thus led some Zulu – eventually almost all Zulu – into
cooperation with Whites'. Nor were the whites without their divisions.
'Missionaries who wanted to evangelize, educate, and improve Zulu
approached them with interests very different from Boer farmers; churches of Zulu and Whites worshipping together arose. Traders and [labour]
recruiters had other interests.' In pursuit of various, and often conflicting,
ends in the new social system, bonds were created between sections on
opposite sides of the colour line which enabled that system to work and to
expand as a way of integrating economic and social activity. Within it
there was a deep cleavage, but in the late nineteenth century there were
many situations in which the black–white conflict was not obtrusive.
Under a different regime cross-cutting ties of class and religion could
have strengthened until they balanced the opposition between black and
white. Gluckman's study was also important as a technique for resolving
the 'micro–macro problem'. He demonstrated that macro-sociological
influences could be seen at work in micro-sociological situations if only
the observer looked for them, and in this way showed how misleading it
can be to differentiate levels of social reality.

In the last ten years there have been developments in ethnic relations
which underline the urgency of the search for better explanations of the

processes which weaken and strengthen racial and ethnic boundaries. The release from prison of Nelson Mandela in 1990 and the establishment of democratic rule based on universal suffrage, with remarkably few moves by blacks to revenge themselves upon whites, shows that even extremely hard racial boundaries enforcing strict segregation and huge inequalities need not prevent the recognition of shared national values and interests. This may be contrasted with events in Rwanda and Burundi, two adjacent countries inhabited principally by the same two ethnic groups, Hutu and Tutsi, speaking the same language and living together in the same settlements. Though Tutsi are often taller than Hutu, members of the two groups cannot reliably be distinguished on the basis of appearance and intermarriage used to be common. Hutu domination of the Rwandan state was challenged by a Tutsi invasion in 1990 and led to a genocide conducted by Hutu militia groups. In Burundi a democratic government was overthrown in 1993 by the Tutsi-dominated army and genocidal atrocities have ensued. The South African experience can also be contrasted with events in the former Federal Republic of Yugoslavia with its political structure designed to allow Serbs, Slovenes, Croats, Bosnians, Montenegrins and Macedonians to share power. Most of its citizens spoke Serbo-Croat; divisions between Catholics, Greek Orthodox and Muslims were important, but in many parts of the country members of the various groups lived intermingled with little regard for differences of ethnic origin, and intermarriage had been common. In 1991 Croatia and Slovenia declared their independence. Serbs and Croats then fought over the territory in Croatia occupied by a long-standing Serb minority. Serbs, Croats and Muslims fought over territory in Bosnia-Herzegovina. Serb forces, and others, embarked on policies of 'ethnic cleansing' in order to enforce residential segregation. Genocidal atrocities were committed. How was it that in Rwanda–Burundi and the former Yugoslavia processes of integration could be put into reverse? Until the conflicts erupted these societies had been characterised by individual rather than group competition and rational choice theory would have predicted that participation in collective ethnic action would have been contrary to the interest of nearly everybody.

Part of the answer must be that the parties to a bargaining relationship often have insufficient information about the likely consequences of their following certain of the alternatives open to them. The parties to the conflict in South Africa exercised good judgement when many observers were expecting the worst. In the former Yugoslavia and in Rwanda political leaders made important decisions which may have seemed likely to bring them individual reward but which turned out to be serious misjudgements; all the parties then found themselves worse off as a result.

Another part of the answer must be that political judgements can be influenced more by the internal dynamics of the group than by any dispassionate assessment of the other party's strength and of the likely outcome of conflict.

It should also be noted that most versions of economic theory, and of theories which derive from economic reasoning, assume that the state will maintain the public order which is essential if market processes are to operate. The order maintained by the state may be unfair in that it serves the interests of some groups more than others, but an unfair order is better than no order at all. In both Rwanda–Burundi and the former Yugoslavia armed force was used to coerce people into obedience. Thousands who had lived in peace with their neighbours without worrying about their ethnic origin were forced to identify themselves ethnically. Circumstances were so changed that they could feel secure only when they were with their co-ethnics.

Policies of segregation or ethnic cleansing depend upon the availability of signs by which individuals can be identified as belonging in particular categories. The process is the same as that employed when persons are ranked as being of higher or lower status within a category except that its consequences are different. Some signs are adopted to mislead: the man in the expensive suit may not be as wealthy as he pretends. Some signs are adopted voluntarily to signal commitment to a distinctive identity, like the Jewish skull cap, the Sikh turban, the 'Afro' hairstyle, the Rasta 'locks' or 'tam' in its red, green, and black colours. An individual who publicly commits himself or herself to a group or a course of action takes a decision which has the effect of reducing future options. It can be important to group mobilisation. Some of the things that people say and do may be read for their significance by fellow group members as well as by members of an outside group. What interests fellow members can be an indicator of the nature of the group. A religious group may be intolerant of theological idiosyncrasies (reading them as signs that a member's commitment to the group is questionable), but be uninterested in a member's political opinions, whereas a political group will see things the other way round. A racial, ethnic or linguistic group will have a conception of deviance only in so far as it is also a political group.

Some characteristics are taken by others as signs of a person's social origin. Research into discrimination in the process of recruitment to employment has shown that accent, address and birthplace may be taken as signs that an applicant belongs to a minority. Studies in Belfast have also illuminated the process of 'telling', the ways in which people 'tell' whether someone else is Protestant or Catholic (Burton, 1978: 37–67; Jenkins, 1982: 30–1). It was reported that when travellers were stopped at road blocks in Yugoslavia at the beginning of the conflict they might be asked to recite the Lord's Prayer, because although they spoke a common language Serbs and Croats tended to use different words for 'bread' in the plea 'give us this day our daily bread'. In Rwanda people were required to carry an identity card which specified their ethnic group; this could be examined, though it seems clear that many persons were killed simply on the suspicion that they belonged to the opposed group. It scarcely needs saying that physical differences, such as those of skin colour, can constitute signs of group belonging that are extremely difficult to modify, ignore or counterbalance. Signs that are transmitted genetically bind parents and their children into the same category. Though they may be called 'racial' it is not 'race' but phenotypical features which indicate assignment to a social category. Race is a second-order abstraction.

Having established the nature and function of signs, the theory incorporates at this point the theory of discrimination as this was described in chapter 5. Pierre van den Berghe (1997) has elaborated it in his discussion of stereotypes as 'guidelines in making statistical discriminations in situations of imperfect competition'. This leads him to five conclusions: that

1. The criterion of discrimination [that which has sign-value] or the object of the stereotype must have an external and pre-existing test of validity, a grain of truth, which permits predictions beyond chance.
2. The criterion of discrimination must carry a low information cost to the discriminator, that is, its presence or absence must be easily, quickly, cheaply and reliably ascertained.
3. The poorer the level of information and the costlier information gathering are, the more likely discrimination will be.
4. It follows from 3 above that stereotypy and discrimination will be most prevalent in large-scale, urban, impersonal, transient, non-repeated situations where encounters with strangers are common and inevitable.
5. As an extreme special case of 4 above, ethnic and racial stereotypy and discrimination are most likely to thrive in culturally and structurally heterogeneous societies where multiple barriers of religion, language, caste, class or race impede communication (and thus raise information costs), and where spatial segregation reinforces social segmentation.

Such considerations decide whether or not two individuals ever enter into a relationship in which they can trade goods and services.

The terms on which they trade may depend upon the power of groups to set limits to prices. If the parties cannot agree upon a price, one of them may either withdraw from exchange or utilise political resources to change market conditions. After a period of conflict, exchange may start again on new terms. In the Weberian tradition power is defined as a potential, an ability to influence others or to get them to do what they would not otherwise do. Blalock (1967: 110) rejects this kind of definition. He notes that in the study of physics power is defined as work/time, so that if two agents perform the same amount of work in different lengths of time, the one who does it quicker exercises more power. Perhaps influenced by the parallel, Blalock defines power as the actual overcoming of resistance in a standard period of time, while admitting that it may be difficult to tell when it has actually been exercised. The definitions of both Weber and Blalock conceive of power as the securing of submission or compliance, but sociologists have to study power as exercised within social relationships and therefore as involved in transactions over time. When the superior party exercises power he or she does so in order to obtain a service, and if the inferior party is reluctant to perform the service he or she may attempt to change the relationship so as to reduce the disadvantage. This may well succeed, for in the long run even the most brutal forms of slavery and subjection have been brought to an end. To study the exercise of power in respect of one action only is to overlook important features of its social character.

According to Anthony Heath (1976: 25–6) the great advantage of the rational choice theory of power is that it can be measured by the price it enables a man to secure for his services:

> To use the theory we have to know about the alternatives open to men and their valuation of them, and we can then make predictions about the consequential rate of exchange. *But we do not actually need to measure power itself directly.* Since power seems to be just about the most difficult thing to measure in social science this must be counted a notable success for rational choice theory.

Power derives from such things as money, property, physical strength, knowledge, and the expectations others have about the sanctions that could be brought into play. These can all be considered as resources, indeed Blalock (1967: 113) defines resources as 'the actual sources of power, or those properties of the individual or group that provide the power potential or ability to exercise power'. Resources can lie unutilised; they contribute to power only when they are mobilised, so Blalock regards power as a multiplicative function of resources and the degree to which they are mobilised in the service of those exercising the power. While an individual can mobilise power in seeking his or her goals, a more important circumstance arises when individuals mobilise their *collective* resources to improve their collective position in relation to another group.

The effect of group power at one point in time then influences the alternatives open in future periods of time.

A political theorist (Hardin, 1995: 37) has commented feelingly on 'the vast and vastly disagreeable "power is . . ." literature'. He contends that one reason for its being so unsatisfactory is its failure to distinguish the dual nature of the sources of power. It can be generated both by the coordination of action and by the exchange of goods and services. A simple example of coordination is observance of a convention that traffic shall keep to one side of the road. To the individual driver it matters little whether it is a 'keep left' or a 'keep right' convention. In international traffic, on sea or in the air, there has to be an international rule. There are comparable conventions for recording time. Once, each town or region used to set its clocks by the sun; then national conventions standardised the setting of clocks and now there are international time zones. Such conventions are the more influential because they come to be taken for granted. They increase the returns to effort and they generate power to sanction violators. The more extensive they are, the less will authorities use force in order to regulate behaviour. Coordination then facilitates exchange, because individuals who coordinate their behaviour can engage in wider systems of exchange (such as markets).

The power of the whites in the Deep South stemmed partly from the coordination of their actions around the convention that whites were superior to blacks, and partly on their ability to decide the terms on which rewards would be exchanged for labour. The differential between the higher wages and better conditions for whites and the lower wages and poorer conditions for blacks measured that power. Since blacks as a category were disadvantaged this constituted categorical discrimination. However, there were tensions within the white category. Some had a greater interest than others in the defence of the established order, because it protected them from black competition. Some believed that whatever might be their short-term interest, their long-term individual interest, or the long-term collective interest of their group, pointed towards the elimination of racial inequality. Yet even people who had an individual interest in promoting fair competition would not act to advance that interest if they believed that their family might suffer as a result. The structure of white society in the Deep South, and the strength of its justifying ideology, were such that it was risky for individuals to break ranks. The whites were in a state of continuous mobilisation, ready to defend their privileges. Blalock (1967: 126) defined degree of mobilisation as the proportion of total resources actually utilised or expended to achieve a given objective. Thus in the electoral field mobilisation could be measured as the proportion of eligible voters who had registered and had cast their votes. Since in the Deep South the whites allowed only a token few blacks to register as voters they prevented blacks from mobilising their electoral potential.

In the 1960s, that started to change. The convention of white superiority was undermined by federal legislation, so that in more and more fields of life behaviour came to be coordinated around the convention of legal equality. The power of the local white elite to determine the terms of exchange was reduced.

The argument so far has outlined a rational choice theory which explains aggregate behaviour. Just as Durkheim's celebrated theory of suicide demonstrated that even if every single suicide results from an autonomous decision, there are nevertheless aggregate patterns which can be explained sociologically, so this theory explains patterns of discrimination. A given change in, say, the penalties for discrimination may not predict whether a particular person will stop discriminating, but if data are available on the effects of previous changes it should be able to predict what percentage will stop because of a 20 per cent increase in the probability of being taken to court (see also Little, 1991: 42–66). This same kind of calculation of likely costs and benefits can similarly predict the likelihood that individuals will join in collective action. The theory then moves up a step, and the complexity increases, as it tries to predict or explain the behaviour of collective actors as well as individuals. It begins with the study of ethnic alignment, for which straightforward research techniques can be devised, and then moves on to that section of the theory which deals with intergroup bargaining.

Ethnic alignment

A good indicator of ethnic alignment is a measure of a subject's readiness to join with co-ethnics in the course either of individual goal-seeking or in collaboration to secure shared goals. For such a purpose, few countries can be as rewarding of study as Malaysia. That country has a population fairly evenly divided between ethnic Malays, the traditional inhabitants, and the descendants of Chinese who have dominated the economic sphere. After the elections in May 1969, there was rioting in which many people lost their lives. The Malays then used their political power to attain economic parity with the Chinese-Malaysians (as by joint ventures, licensing quotas and preferential policies in education). As the national wealth was increasing rapidly, benefits could be channelled toward the Malays without reducing the income received by the Chinese-Malaysians. Malays came increasingly to identify themselves as Muslims, but a Malay middle class emerged together with a mass consumer market, so that in daily life Malay ethnic preferences can conflict with religious duty, with class or status identifications, with financial interest, or with the personal obligations stemming from new social bonds generated in ethnically mixed work organisations. It therefore becomes possible to investigate the price Malays or Chinese-Malaysians put on any preference for dealing with their co-ethnics.

In a first study (1981), Sanusi Osman asked a sample of subjects about an imagined conflict between a Chinese employer and his Malay employees. It could be predicted that Chinese subjects with high incomes would side with the actions of the employer, while Malays of low income would side with the workers. But how would a Chinese worker align himself? Would a Malay employer side with his fellow employer or with his fellow Malays? A second study (1992), in which the fieldwork was carried out by Mohd-Noor Mansor, compared the priority which a subject attached to alignment with co-ethnics to action reflecting self-interest (of either a monetary character or of association with persons of higher social status), and with action reflecting a sense of personal obligation to a co-worker or neighbour.

In the second study, subjects were told about an imaginary individual, Husin Ali, a clerk working in 1989 for a multinational engineering firm in Petalingjaya, a suburb of Kuala Lumpur (Banton and Mansor, 1992). A sample of residents in that locality was told that Husin Ali had been patronising Mr Ah Kow's grocery shop, noted for its cheapness and near to his house. He had been told that someone called Ahmad was about to open a second grocery shop in the same neighbourhood. Respondents were asked whether they thought that Husin Ali would transfer his custom to the new shop. The research assumed that the names of the three individuals would be taken as signs that Husin Ali and Ahmad were Malays and Ah Kow a Chinese Malaysian. Some respondents, so it was thought, would expect that Husin Ali would want to shop with Ahmad because he was a fellow Malay, while others would expect him to shop wherever the goods were cheapest.

There were two main reasons for expecting Husin Ali to change to Ahmad. Firstly, the possibility that the personal satisfaction he would derive from helping a co-ethnic would outweigh any greater price of the goods bought. Secondly, the possibility that he would be influenced by a concern for the judgement of his peers, who would approve his patronising a co-ethnic and disapprove of his shopping with a Chinese when he could quite easily have helped Ahmad.

There are some circumstances in which virtually all Malays will feel bound to align themselves with their co-ethnics in dealing with Chinese-Malaysians, such as in situations of political competition, and some circumstances in which an individual will have an unconstrained choice whether or not to interpret the situation in ethnic terms. This points to the existence in Malaysia of ethnic roles – that is, of relationships in which the parties' conduct is governed by shared beliefs about their mutual rights and obligations. As hypothesised, respondents were found to be divided in their predictions about whether Husin Ali would see shopping for groceries as a relationship governed by ethnic roles. One finding was that ethnic preferences were less important as determinants of Malay ethnic alignment than the Malay research worker had predicted. At a time when ethnic nationalism is often interpreted as a living force, it is important to note the finding that self-interest in saving money or gaining social status, and sentiments of obligation to a friend, neighbour or fellow-worker, were often more influential than ethnic identification.

The research in Petalingjaya was primarily concerned with variations in Malay ethnic alignment *vis-à-vis* Chinese Malaysians. It did not examine Chinese alignment *vis-à-vis* Malays, but this has now been the subject of a third study utilising the same research technique (Mariappam, 1996). The research could also have been extended so as to throw light on Malaysian alignment *vis-à-vis* other nationalities by asking respondents how Husin Ali would choose between alternatives involving, say, Chinese Malaysians and Indonesian immigrant workers. Malays and Indonesians are physically and culturally similar. Many earlier Indonesian immigrants have become Malays but in the late 1970s illegal immigration from Indonesia increased appreciably. Restrictions were imposed, but they were ineffective. Opinion within Malaysia was divided. The wealthier section of the Malaysian population – plantation-owners, businessmen and middle-class housewives – welcomed the availability of cheap labour. The trade unions and the political parties dominated by Chinese interests demanded the immediate deportation of illegal immigrants. It should therefore have been possible to draft a question about the employment at a cheaper rate of a person with an Indonesian-sounding name that would have evoked different responses from different subsamples and could have provided a measure of the significance attached to nationality relative to self-interest. Another kind of question might have measured willingness to join with a non-national in pursuit of a shared interest. In such ways it might have been possible to discover any differences in the significance that Malaysians attached to nationality when pursuing their individual interests, and the significance they attached to nationality compared to ethnicity when engaging in collective action.

This example points to the dangers in working with assumptions from outside about how people will perceive alternatives and how signs may be

read. No research worker could tell *a priori* whether residents in Petalingjaya would take the names Husin Ali and Ah Kow as signs of ethnic,
national, religious or any other kind of role. How the respondents perceived and categorised them was an empirical issue. How well their
categorisations corresponded to those that would have been employed by
a British or a US sociologist is then a second issue. The resident of
Petalingjaya rarely employed any concept of ethnicity. He or she used a
practical language embodying proper names, such as Malay, Chinese and
Indian. Anyone who spoke this language knew that persons assigned to
these categories varied in their cultural distinctiveness. In the languages
they used, the costume they wore, the use they made of their leisure, etc.
some were more culturally distinctive, and in this sense more 'ethnic',
than many of the adolescents who listened to the same pop music, ate
similar foods and mixed readily with members of other groups. Some
Malays may have perceived certain Chinese as being more oriented
towards China, and in this sense more 'national'. Some Malays, too, were
more concerned with the promotion of Islam, and might consider a
difference in ethnic origins unimportant by comparison with profession
of the faith.

Young Malaysians, whether Malay or Chinese, might have had a lower
preference for associating with co-ethnics than their parents' generation,
though their own preference might change as they grew older (the
Petalingjaya research found Malay ethnic preferences to be slightly
weaker among subjects aged less than 30 than among their seniors:
Mansor, 1992: 214–19). Variations in preferences for 'ethnic mix' can be
noted in North America and western Europe, among both the majority
and the minority groups.

This technique enables a research worker to compare the strength of
ethnic or national ties with the strength either of individual interest or that
of some alternative basis for collective action. Malaysia is a more interesting location for such research because political power has been shared,
within the governing coalition, between Malay and Chinese elites. In a
manner that is reminiscent of rule utilitarianism, a party can go to the
electorate with a platform of ethnic cooperation as the best framework for
the pursuit of sectional and selfish interests as well as for the promotion of
the national interest. The results of Mansor's research suggested that the
measures adopted by the government during the 1970s created the conditions for the members of both major ethnic groups to develop common
loyalties to the political settlement agreed by their representatives. Each
group had changed more than the other group yet recognised. When
asked, for example, about people who failed to stand respectfully for the
national anthem, the Chinese in the area studied were as disapproving as

the Malays. The Malays overwhelmingly endorsed the proposition that Malaysia belongs to all its citizens equally, even if not so strongly as did the Chinese respondents. Malaysia's policies have been more successful in developing common loyalties than those pursued in the republics of the former Soviet Union. Economic growth seems to have played an important part in distracting attention from inter-group jealousies and allowing space for toleration. People may disapprove of the presence of a group of different ethnicity or religion, and perhaps wish they would go away, yet tolerate their presence because their suppression or expulsion would conflict with higher priorities. There has been a trade-off between the priority they attach to their individual advancement and their belief that members of the other group are entitled to lesser rewards. This makes it appear as if the parties have struck a bargain with one another.

Mobilisation

The concept of mobilisation was developed in the 1950s by Karl Deutsch and other political scientists, but it is of very wide application to groups of all sises. To take an example from the author's own earlier work in Sierra Leone, immigrants from the hinterland settling in the city of Freetown found that ethnic groups were ranked in an order of prestige. The majority group were the Temne; they regarded the city as situated within their territory and thought they should therefore rank high, but such was not their experience. One of their leaders described the way in which his co-ethnics were identifying themselves with higher status groups when he wrote:

The Temnes in the City were moving rapidly towards detribalization, some becoming Creoles and others Akus and Mandingoes. The first were the educated ones in English and others who were not educated but have come to Freetown to seek jobs. The reason for the exodus was the backwardness of the Temnes socially and economically. To be considered favourably was to call yourself a Mandingo, Creole, or Aku. This protective measure was adopted in many forms, dress, language, and in joining foreign dances. Consequently every bright looking young Temne is lost to the other tribes and the word Temne is associated with the uncivilized people. (quoted Banton, 1957: 165)

This writer was a schoolteacher who formed a new voluntary association for ambitious young Temne, appealing to ethnic pride. It was very successful and was widely copied. With this organisational base he had himself elected Tribal Headman for the Temne in Freetown and, being active in the main political party, he became Deputy Prime Minister after independence. By this time the young men's associations, so active in the pre-independence phase had faded away (confirming a hypothesis of

Immanuel Wallerstein who had studied similar associations in the city of Abidjan further along the coast).

This little history highlights the importance of the boundary processes discussed by Barth. When they were in their rural homelands to the north, the Temne migrants had not needed to take action to maintain their ethnic identity, but in the city they had to act to prevent a loss of members. Their leader persuaded them to prioritise a collective goal relative to their individual goals. The sequence also illustrates Wallman's thesis that a shared ethnic origin (and all the cultural features that go with it) is a resource which people use in some circumstances but not others. Much may depend upon the initiative of individual leaders or entrepreneurs. Furthermore it suggests that though the young men's associations were not manifestly political in the sense in which that word is conventionally used in the West, they had a political dimension. They were competing with the associations of other ethnic groups for allegiance and repute. After the growth of party politics and then independence for Sierra Leone, political action ran in other channels.

The connection between ethnicity and party politics can be important, but before turning to this it may be helpful to indicate how some elementary concepts borrowed from the theory of games can illuminate the way in which the framework of group competition influences the outcome. Some struggles are 'zero sum' because the net gains of the two sides, if added together, total zero; the two sides dispute over the division of a fixed quantity of goods. Other struggles lead to the production of more goods and are therefore 'positive sum'. Still others damage the whole framework of interaction by reducing the quantity available for division and are therefore 'negative sum'. As was noted earlier in this chapter, when this approach is applied to racial and ethnic relations, the elimination of racial discrimination may be seen as a public good. Struggles between groups that result in better measures for the reduction of discrimination therefore have a positive outcome.

For examples of highly institutionalised zero-sum struggles it can be interesting to consider inter-caste relations in Hindu India. Members of one caste group may maintain that because of past misfortune they have been forced into a lower rank in the caste hierarchy than they once occupied. They mobilise to try to have this alleged injustice rectified. Success would entail their moving up the scale and therefore forcing some other groups to move down, so that the first group's gain would be others' loss; if the gains and losses are added up they total zero. A hierarchical system of ranking necessarily generates tensions about the justice of relative positions and threatens social tranquillity, but in the Indian system its divisive implications have been counterbalanced by the division of labour which gives each caste group a monopoly upon some trade. Since each group needs the other's economic services they do not usually push very far their disagreements about rank. Less usually, one instance has been described in which a dissatisfied group refused any longer to provide services for the Brahmins and therefore could not call upon them to officiate at marriages. They carried their resistance to a point at which an increasing number were not marrying at all (Harper, 1968). In such circumstances one group may be worse off and no other group may derive any benefit; this is a negative-sum game. It can be contrasted with the sort of change in which members of all castes are allowed to follow any occupation they wish; the result is likely to be an increase in the total welfare of the society, so that if everyone's gains and losses are added up the result is a positive sum.

Intergroup competition is most fierce, and collective action most easily organised, when the parties believe they are involved in zero-sum relations; a gain by one group is seen by another as necessarily a loss on their part and each individual's consciousness of his or her group identity is constantly reinforced. The struggles between blacks and whites in the Deep South during the 1930s for shares in a declining job market appear to have been zero sum in character. When one group seeks to retain a monopoly power, it has to exert control over members who can make a greater profit by defecting from the group norm (Banton, 1983: 118–19). In the Deep South, informal controls upon white as well as black deviance could be as powerful as formal controls elsewhere. Zero-sum perceptions can influence national politics. There have been times when, for example, the government of Malaysia knew that if it made a concession to the Chinese population it would be pressed to give some corresponding benefit to the Malays. Zero-sum tension can be most effectively resolved when energies are redirected into positive-sum competition. This in turn may depend upon acceptance of the view that the public interest requires action against discrimination.

Once a group is mobilised, then, consciously or unconsciously, it will bargain with other groups. Sometimes this changes the nature of the groups. The most developed studies of inter-group bargaining are those developed by economists in application to wage and tariff negotiations, imperfect competition, settlements out of court and real estate transactions. It has also been applied to the bargaining between the superpowers over the construction of missile systems, 'star wars' technology, and nuclear disarmament (Schelling, 1963: 21–52). Bargaining over armaments is conducted between the agents of states. The citizens of each state share long-term interests and cannot opt out of the bargains that are struck on their behalf.

Ethnic conflicts can sometimes constitute a kind of implicit bargaining, even if the participants do not think of their actions in such terms. In what are seen as situations of zero-sum competition (as in the Deep South earlier and Northern Ireland more recently, but also in several African states such as Rwanda and Burundi in recent years), individuals are highly conscious of their group identity because it is seen as relevant to behaviour in so many situations. The groups are in a state of almost continuous mobilisation. In other circumstances, it may be more difficult for leaders to get their fellow members to act together. Tensions may build up gradually until some form of public disorder causes polarisation. Members of a more powerful group may conduct a pogrom (in the Deep South a lynching was a disorder of this kind). Members of a less powerful group may riot and destroy property. In each case the lower class and younger elements of the group may be more prominent, sometimes believing that they will have the support of the higher class and older elements of their group; even if they do not have this support at the start, the logic of the confrontation is such that these others may be obliged to support them later. Disorders may be influenced by the desire to teach the other side a lesson; those staged by members of the superordinate group may serve to keep the others in what is thought to be their place. Disorders by members of the subordinate group may damage the reputation of the state, city or locality and destroy some of its wealth; in some circumstances they have been a preliminary to revolution.

Where, as a result of immigration, ethnic minority groups have become established in industrial societies, their collective action may be aimed at (a) influencing events in the sending society; (b) creating a cultural community within the receiving society; and (c) bargaining with the receiving society to change the conditions of minority–majority interaction. One institution may attempt to do all three. Action of the kind envisaged in (b) is likely to be action that provides members with private goods. A recognition of common ethnicity may lead to the formation of either a personal network or a voluntary association with its own rules and arrangements for the payment of subscriptions. Members will gather for calendar and life-cycle ceremonies, helping one another and sustaining a distinctive identity. Action of the kind envisaged in (c) can include disorders stimulated by the hostility of young males towards the police. These may have their origins in particular local dissatisfactions, but any riot attracts attention and argument about underlying causes. The steps taken to avoid repetition may include action to remedy the dissatisfactions and, in this way, to improve the position of members of the minority relative to the majority. The threat of riot can secure concessions in the processes of bargaining that characterise all political relations. In a comparable manner, some members of the black minority in Britain have during the recent past sought to encourage a 'culture of resistance' to the demands of white society. This can be seen as a refusal of incorporation on unfavourable terms. Ethnic bargaining in industrial societies can scarcely ever be as clear-cut as in industrial relations, and it has always to be remembered that some people who have the qualifications for ethnic group membership may not identify themselves ethnically or be ready to commit themselves to group actions when, perhaps because of differences in socio-economic status, they can identify themselves with group members only in particular circumstances. Those who seek to lead ethnic minorities may have difficulty mobilising others whom they regard as group members. It may not be easy to persuade them to put collective goals before individual ones.

Some ethnic minorities in Britain have engaged in collective action more often than others. Some are more oriented towards the societies from which their groups originate, but this is not related to collective action in any simple manner. The Polish minority, for example, has organised to influence events in Poland and to bring up children to have a consciousness of Polish origin. By contrast, the Italian minority in the western part of England has been described as one in which people maintain ties with their separate kin and former neighbours in Italy and are too individualistic to organise associations in England unless the priest or an official from the consulate takes the lead. The Maltese were at one time described as positively preferring not to come together because they wished to make their own way in British society as individuals. The first generation of West Indian settlers has also been described as individualistic except that consciousness of white racial prejudice evokes powerful feelings of solidarity. There are epithets such as 'coconut' used to describe somebody allegedly brown outside but white inside that have a power both to wound and to control. Settlers from South Asia have shown a greater capacity for collective action. Middle-class Indians and Pakistanis could often attain their ends individually by working and maintaining social ties with their professional associates but the working-class Asians who followed in their wake were more homeland-oriented. Some remained committed to the politics of the subcontinent, but rather more directed a significant proportion of their income into the opening of places of worship and into the recreation of forms of collective life known in their countries of origin. New associations provided arenas in which homeland distinctions could be rehearsed and would-be leaders could compete for status. Those migrants who brought with them a set of expectations about community life and a power to sanction deviance were more easily able to mobilise for a wide variety of ends in their new

country. Seen comparatively, no minority has been more successful than
the Jews in maintaining a distinctive identity despite the loss of potential
members who, particularly in twentieth-century Western societies, have
stopped identifying as Jewish and have passed into the majority population.

The sociologist who examines ethnic mobilisation from a top-down (or
katascopic) rather than a bottom-up (or anascopic) perspective, can
discern some more general patterns, such as the four propositions advanced by Susan Olzak and Joane Nagel (1986: 3–4):

1. Urbanisation accelerates levels of ethnic mobilisation and collective action
   because it initiates contact and competition between ethnic populations.
2. Expansion of industrial and service sectors of the economy increases rates of
   ethnic mobilisation and collective action because it increases competition
   among ethnic groups for jobs. Ethnic competition within labour markets
   intensifies when ethnic segregation diminishes. Ethnic segregation declines
   when (a) differences in wage levels between ethnic groups decline or (b)
   barriers between jobs filled by ethnic groups recede.
3. Development of peripheral regions or the discovery of resources in a periphery
   occupied by an ethnic population increases the probability of mobilisation by
   the ethnic population. These changes create the potential for the emergence of
   subnationalist movements, ethnic political parties, and ethnic elite movements.
4. Processes of state-building (including those following colonial independence)
   that implement policies targeting specific ethnic populations increase the
   likelihood of ethnic collective action. Policy changes (such as instituting ethnic
   and racial civil rights laws, designating official lands, or implementing language rules) increase ethnic awareness and the likelihood of ethnic movements.

Using US data, it is not difficult to find support for such propositions, but
they need to be heavily qualified if they are to be tested at ground level in
other countries. Sandra Wallman (1996), for example, gave a very different picture when she came to compare the results of fieldwork in three
urban locations, two in London and one in Kampala, Uganda. The inner
London areas of Battersea and Bow were both low-income and multiethnic. Yet in the former the various boundaries of difference did not
overlap, the structure was relatively open and organisation was heterogeneous. The latter was tightly-bounded, relatively closed, consistently
homogeneous. When it came to identity options and resource management, people in the first area were disposed to mobilise on a local basis,
those in the second area to mobilise on an ethnic basis. In the Kampala
neighbourhood there had been a nearly total collapse of the formal
economy and a consequent intensification of attempts to 'get by' in the
cracks and niches of informal economic activity. As a result, there was no

consistency of association between kinds of difference – ethnic, occupational, neighbouring and so on. For example, while some of the men's football teams were composed of players of the same ethnic origin who drank local beer together, players and supporters of other teams could be recruited on the basis of residence or friendship. In the national election one candidate pressed his claims as a member of the same ethnic group as 60 per cent of the neighbourhood's residents and insulted his opponent as a half-caste and the bastard son of a prostitute. This cost him the election. The male voters perceived the second candidate as one who would protect their occupational interests; the females identified with his mother and defined the situation in terms of a responsibility to help others who struggled with problems that resembled their own.

The Kampala example recapitulates the findings of studies in the Zambian Copperbelt during the 1950s, in showing that attempts to organise on an ethnic basis may be trumped by class-based collective action. Left-wing political parties in Europe have appealed to minority voters on a class basis, but with less than total success. The main alternatives to class interest are those of action based upon shared culture or shared religious faith. Which of these becomes the most important in the countries of immigration will be decided by the results of implicit bargaining between three main groups. Firstly, there is that of the receiving society, its structure and self-conception (as described for France, Germany and Britain in chapter 5). France, expecting immigrants to join its political community, will make it difficult for them to organise as ethnic minorities. Germany expects non-German immigrants, like the Turks, to remain foreigners. Britain expects the immigrants to fulfil their duties as citisens and is tolerant of ethnic association. All three countries regard religious observance as a private matter. Secondly, many members of the older immigrant generations remain oriented to the sending societies and encourage their children to maintain some at least of these societies' customs, especially those touching on religion. Thirdly, members of the younger immigrant generations assess what the receiving society can offer them and identify what appears to them the best alternative. Much depends upon whether they are able to keep in touch with their communities of origin and see a future for themselves there; whether they can see a future in a distinctive minority community within the receiving society; or whether they believe they will have to make their way within the receiving society, perhaps on their own. If they engage in collective action, it will be as part of such a general strategy. Almost certainly, there will be a scatter of individual decisions, and this will be important to the distinction between cultural groups and religious groups. In industrial societies culture is constantly changing, being subject to a constant barrage from the mass media, from new technology and from the stress on consumption; these all make for ever greater uniformity. The component that changes least, and demands most by way of individual choice, is that of religious identification. It may be that in the early stages of immigrant settlement cultural differences define what people think of as ethnic groups, but that with the passage of time religious differences define the main social divisions. The receiving societies cannot deny the legitimacy of religious association or the demand that religious faith be respected. Because religion has been defined as a private matter, it is easier for the state to recognise a person or a council that represents a religious association than someone or somebody representing a cultural community. So the descendants of immigrants may prefer to be identified by a distinctive religion. Such considerations underline the argument for a bottom-up approach to theory construction in this field.

Ethnicity and politics

At the level of state organisation, there are some striking examples of political frameworks that proved too weak to contain ethnic bargaining. The problem can be summarised quite briefly. Social and economic development leads to a widening of horizons and is facilitated by such widening. This constitutes an upward movement in the scale of social living, which is met by another in the opposite direction. Especially since 1945, the organisation of world trade and of international politics has required the division of the globe into less than 200 sovereign states, each of which is expected to cooperate with others in accordance with the Charter of the United Nations. According to the 1970 UN Declaration concerning Friendly Relations and Cooperation among States, each state is expected to be 'possessed of a government representing the whole people belonging to the territory without distinction as to race, creed or colour'. In practice, many governments have difficulty holding together a fissiparous population. Their states have not come into existence as a result of an upward movement, but because other and more powerful states have drawn their boundaries.

In all societies humans recognise obligations to their kin and to close associates, exemplifying the principle of prescriptive altruism (or possibly the socio-biological determinants of kin-selection). The belief that a person has a duty to his or her neighbour may not change, but the conception of who is a neighbour has extended to include, in particular circumstances, members of ever-widening circles. An expanding sense of fellowship and shared interest facilitates an expanding political organisation because it makes trust possible. Relations can be much more productive when a person can make the first move in the belief that the other party will reciprocate; as Durkheim wrote, contractual relations are not sufficient in themselves, since every contract depends upon some external framework that will keep the parties to their bargain.

The psychological dimensions of the upward process can be discerned and generate hypotheses capable of empirical examination. Two have been advanced by Sun-Ki Chai (1996:291):

1. Large scale ethnic groups will first form in societies where the majority of the population still resides in small, stable and relatively self-sufficient communities, but where modernising structural change has proceeded to the point where many individuals will migrate from these communities to larger population centres in their lifetime.
2. Where such groups are formed, their boundaries will be based upon a relatively simple set of criteria that meets the following conditions:
2.1 It generates a group of sufficient size to comprise a substantial proportion of the population within the population centre, but not significantly more than half the entire population.
2.2 It aligns with a common position in the population centre's division of labour.
2.3 It encompasses communities of origin rather than cross-cutting them.

What are described as 'the four most notable examples of "ethnicity construction" that have occurred during this century' (located in Nigeria, Zaire, Malaysia and Pakistan) give support to these generalisations.

As a theory of group formation, this underplays the importance of two dimensions: reaction to perceived discrimination and political entrepreneurship. Many communities have formed as a result of oppression or subordination, including the African-American and others inspired by liberation movements. They may not all have been considered ethnic groups but they shared common features. An explanation of ethnic group formation should invoke causes of a kind which can help explain why the women's movement of the 1960s took hold where and when it did, because gender consciousness also shares common features with ethnic consciousness. Such an explanation should be able to incorporate Ernest Gellner's (1983: 43) conclusion that in recent European history there has been only one effective nationalism for every ten cases in which, had things been in some way different, comparable developments could well have occurred. The strength of ethnic and nationalist movements often depends upon the kinds of experience that can be turned to use (for example, as grievances) and the commitment of ideologists of all kinds with the talents and ability to highlight them. Poets, novelists, and now film directors, develop the myths that shape group self-conceptions; social activists change them into the currency of politics.

Nineteenth-century racial theories represented racial assignment as an objective process, while allowing for the possibility that individuals could come to a consciousness of where they belonged in the natural scheme. No one makes a comparable claim for ethnicity, which is usually regarded as a consciousness of shared culture related to a common ethnic origin. Ethnic origin is thought to be objective, but the strength of the shared sentiment is highly variable, being the product of an interaction between within-group feeling and the degree of institutional recognition accorded by the political environment. The highest degree of recognition is that given to the sovereign nation-state. At the other end of the scale are situations such as those in which members of minorities ask for public recognition and the right of association but for no special privileges, and then those such as that in France where the constitution of the republic permits no recognition of minorities at all.

In between come constitutional arrangements allowing various degrees of ethnic autonomy. A favourite example for students of international law is that of the Åland Islands, lying in the Baltic sea between the coasts of Finland and Sweden. When in 1917 Finland became independent from Russia the population wanted the islands to become part of Sweden, but under an arrangement negotiated by the League of Nations they were instead given cultural autonomy within the Finnish state. The Swedish language was accorded a special status and the rights of persons from outside the islands to purchase real estate were restricted. It has been more difficult to achieve this sort of compromise in the case of other disputed territories (like the Falkland Islands) or in situations in which ethnic groups have insisted upon a greater degree of autonomy within states (like Quebec, Scotland, and the movement in favour of a separate Sikh state of Khalistan within the Republic of India). The success of international diplomacy after the First World War in respect of the Åland Islands was not repeated in the division of the former Ottoman empire into states; the claims of the Kurds were passed over, but Kuwait, which was a small and ethnically undistinctive unit, was elevated to statehood. More recently, the United Nations refused to support the attempted secession of Katanga (from what was then the Congo) or Biafra (from Nigeria), and agreed only reluctantly to the recognition of Bangladesh. Other countries, and particularly the most powerful, arbitrate the claims that are made in the names of ethnic and national character.

The feeling of identification that people express when arguing for a greater degree of autonomy, or demanding outright independence, or when identifying with an existing status, is a compound of many different kinds of alignment and emotion. The mixture varies from case to case. Political, religious, linguistic and other elements may be mixed up with remembered grievances. The sorts of feeling that are called racial, ethnic, national and nationalist may be inseparable. These feelings are expressed with reference to the circumstances in which the members of the group find themselves and cannot be abstracted from their context. The sentiment of group identification that is called nationalism has different effects when it is expressed in a movement demanding a nation-state from when it expressed in a movement within such a state, but is not useful to try to distinguish two different sentiments.

Ethnic sentiment may inspire political activity, but this is not a one-way relationship. Politicians and governments may intentionally or unintentionally encourage ethnic bonding. The earlier discussion of Furnivall's (1948) concept of the plural society served as a reminder of the tendency for imperial governments to permit and at times reinforce ethnic occupational monopolies, giving credence to the belief that they acted on the basis of the maxim 'divide and rule'. This inference has been questioned (Horowitz, 1985: 66–8, 75–6, 149–60). Furnivall's study also provided many examples of colonial governments' taking steps to bring benefits to native populations (such as health and educational services) well in advance of any demand for these services. Economic growth offered opportunities for individual goal-seeking which could weaken the motivations for collective action along ethnic lines. Yet greater wealth also permitted an expansion in governmental activity, an increase in the power of the state, and the growth in size of the public sector within the national economy. A private economic sector can exist only within a political unit that regulates markets, and the working of this sector is greatly facilitated when government regulation permits the establishment of banks and systems of credit. Given such institutions, however, the private sector is self-regulating to the extent that labour is rewarded according to the marginal value of its productivity. The public sector is different, in that within this sector resources are allocated by more subjective criteria. Governments decide what customs duties and taxes they will impose, and upon whom; they decide where the roads, schools and hospitals will be built, who will get the contracts, who will be employed in the civil service, and what their salaries will be. Control of the state's powers has always been a glittering prize and the value of that prize does not diminish with economic growth. These powers are not subject to the discipline of competition, so that public sector rewards may bear no relation to productivity.

The desire for national independence was given a moral priority in the era of decolonisation. It became one of the values which individuals sought to maximise, though the costs to minorities of such preferences rarely entered into the majority members' implicit calculations of net benefit. When ethnic nationalists have campaigned for the creation of a state in accordance with their ideological self-conception, they have regularly neglected the interests of other ethnic groups within the boundaries they claimed for themselves, as can be illustrated by the blindness of Ataturk with respect to the Kurds, the Zionists regarding the Palestinians, and the leaders of some of the new republics in the Caucasus, Moldova and the Baltic. By comparison with imperial or theocratic rule in which ultimate authority is independent of the contending parties, the nation-state with its doctrine of 'one person, one vote' suffers from inherent disadvantages in the promotion of inter-group harmony. When popular majorities prevail, it is easy for an ethnic group with 55 per cent of the vote to insist upon policies unacceptable to another group with 45 per cent of the vote, so that the latter group is then tempted to secede.

It should surprise no one that many of the African political parties since independence have had an ethnic basis, because constituencies based upon ethnicity do not rise and decline as readily as those which respond to class interest. A would-be leader could appeal for the votes of his or her co-ethnics in their own language, and this made it easier to win their trust. An ethnically-based political party can form part of either a ranked or an unranked social system. According to Horowitz (1985: 36), in a ranked system, like that of apartheid South Africa, the boundaries of ethnic groups tend to coincide with the boundaries of class; conflict between these groups then points in the direction of revolution. Unranked systems, like that of Nigeria, are made up of groups which try to act like mini-states; their conflicts are more likely to result in the partition of the state or the attempt of groups to secede from it. This simple picture has then to be qualified, for some groups may be ranked in relation to each other but not in relation to further groups. In apartheid South Africa Afrikaners were ranked in relation to Zulus, but not necessarily in relation to English-speaking whites; nor were Zulus ranked in relation to Xhosas. In a generally unranked political system like that of Nigeria, one group may be more than proportionately represented in the elite, or may control a state government and rank above the members of minorities from other ethnic groups. There are therefore two dimensions to ethnic interaction: one that stems from differences of rank and power, another that arises from expectations associated with cultural differences. The first is evident in conflicts over material resources, the second in conflicts motivated by group pride.

After independence, new governments could remunerate their supporters through the public sector where the costs of discrimination in employment were less evident. Members of the minorities have therefore been more inclined to rely on the private sector where they have more opportunity to compete as individuals. Any tendency to regard the state as a cow to be milked invites, firstly, divisiveness and corruption and, secondly, military intervention. An army exists to serve the state; soldiers can be very critical of politicians for failing to display the sense of service which is their ideal, and so they have often seized power in the name of national salvation. It rarely seems to bridge the gap between the upward movement of community spirit and the downward imperative of national unity.

Governments are now expected to represent the whole people of the territory without distinction as to race or ethnic origin, but what happened in several parts of the world was that, with the approach of independence, or shortly afterwards, different ethnic groups struggled either for the control of the apparatus of the new nation-state or to improve their share of the power. Under British rule, Asian immigration into East Africa, Fiji, Guyana and Malaysia was encouraged to promote economic development. Indians and Chinese came from competitive cultures that had developed an entrepreneurial spirit and achievement motivation. After independence their relative prosperity was a source of strain. Asians were expelled from East Africa, though it is conceivable that, had there been more time, a better structure for group bargaining, and a willingness on each side to adjust to the other in the interests of the whole, their expulsion might have been avoided. That some have since returned, so that there are now said to be more Asians in Kenya than there were before, suggests that Africans there have come to believe that they are better off because of the Asians' contributions to their economies. In countries like Rwanda, Burundi, Zanzibar and Sri Lanka the use of state power to further ethnic interests led to terrible massacres. Elsewhere the processes of ethnic polarisation led to the expulsion of a minority or genocidal attack (Burma, Uganda, Indonesia), or contributed to partition.

The political framework developed by the British for the government of the Indian subcontinent was not strong enough to withstand the pressures that led to its partition in 1947. The power of the state was insufficient to prevent the partition of Cyprus, Bangladesh's secession from Pakistan, Slovenia's and Croatia's secession from Yugoslavia, the separation of the Czech and Slovak republics and the independence of the republics of the Soviet Union. Many of the states whose population and frontiers were established under imperial rule now face serious challenges because of what they may perceive as ethnic separatism, though observers may maintain that the tensions stem from the politicians' own ethnic nationalism.

Like others, Alvin Rabushka (1974: 98) has observed that in multiethnic societies the introduction of electoral politics has caused candidates for office to appeal to ethnic constituencies; the need to form winning coalitions, whether by ballots or by rifles, converts communities of individuals into competing groups. The conclusion he has drawn is that

> those who desire racial harmony should support the development and expansion of a free market economy in which the government's role is restricted to providing the institutional framework within which market exchange can take place, and to defend that market system from those who seek to destroy it.

This formulation assigns extensive and active functions to governments, even if Rabushka chooses not to acknowledge this when he says that the closer any society approximates perfect competition then the more likely is it that government intervention will cause racial tension. It was said long ago that all men would be monopolists if they could. Even in countries committed to the ideal of a free market economy, like the United States, many markets are so heavily influenced by monopoly power that governmental enforcement of anti-trust legislation is essential. In other parts of the world there is little chance of free market economies being established without government regulation, for if the governments of under-developed countries were to allow powerful overseas companies to control their manufacturing industry this could be exposed to sudden collapse were cheaper labour to become available elsewhere. For lack of any countervailing power to balance that of the overseas company, the prices given for products would reflect conditions in the low-wage economy and not the prices those goods could command in the high-wage economy. Dissatisfaction in the former country would lead to a change of regime and the adoption of another trading policy. Furnivall referred to one consequence of such an imbalance when he observed that British rule opened up Burma to the world but not the world to Burma; the government of Burma (now called Myanmar) indeed attempted for a significant period of time to exclude foreign economic interests. Governmental intervention in economic activity can be productive of ethnic tension, but it can equally be essential to the promotion of ethnic harmony. Only if there were a truly competitive market able to maintain itself (which would surely be remarkable) might it be reasonable to prescribe non-intervention by the government.

The theory outlined in these pages attempts to resolve the 'micro–macro problem' by starting from individual behaviour and introducing into the analysis components which recognise the constraints to which individual actors are subject and the ways in which individuals are organised in collectivities. It does not treat groups as if they had a life of their own but shows how they are constituted from individual behaviour and are subject to continual alteration as individuals respond to changes in their circumstances. Seen in historical perspective, it synthesises components of previous theories but its explanatory power is still limited. All that this author would claim is that it can hold out a prospect of answers to certain kinds of question.

In his *Autobiography*, R. G. Collingwood (1939: 22, 28) presented Bacon and Descartes as having asserted that knowledge comes only by asking questions, and that 'when Kant said that it takes a wise man to know what questions he can reasonably ask, he was in effect repudiating a merely propositional logic and demanding a logic of question and answer'. If old racial theories are to be superseded, wise social scientists will concentrate upon the strategic questions that can open up theoretical advances. Questions which lead to interpretations of history will produce answers that appeal only to those who share their authors' values. Other kinds of question can lead to answers that compel acceptance from every student of the subject, including those who hold very different views of society and politics. Social science will progress most rapidly if it concentrates on questions of this second sort.

Conclusion

In chapter 1 it was suggested that those who use the English language have got into a muddle in the way that they use the word 'race' to designate groups. The origins of the muddle lay in mistaken theories which brought together elements of what would now be seen as biological science and of social science, though at that time there was little separation of the language of science from the practical language of everyday life. Since then, biological knowledge about human variation has grown enormously and developed its own theoretical language. Social science has been more closely involved with everyday language, both for good and for ill, but it too has grown very greatly and is opening up new ways of understanding the social consequences of physical differences between individuals. An appreciation of how knowledge has grown may help both social scientists in their work and those who worry about the ways in which slack definitions of important variables can hamper attempts to address practical problems.

The racial theories formulated in Europe and North America over the last two centuries were embedded in the political and social life of the societies to which their authors and their readers have belonged. Perhaps the central question that interested theorists and members of the public alike was: why are they not like us? To begin with, those who asked the question may have identified the particular 'they' as a group of whom they had only limited or inaccurate knowledge. The question became more interesting once it was possible to treat the 'they-group' as one among many others, and to accept that the questioners themselves belonged to another such group whose peculiarities had to be explained by reference to the same principles.

The first comprehensive answer was one which conceptualised race as lineage. It said that 'they' were not like 'us' because 'they' belonged to a genealogical group which had acquired special characteristics either because of divine intervention or because of its distinctive environmental experience. The weakness of this answer was that it could not satisfactorily explain how environment affected the transmission of inherited characters.

A second answer was that people were different because they represented different racial types. The differences had existed either since the creation of the earth or for as long as there was reliable evidence. This argument smuggled in a significant change in the meaning of the word 'race'. Previously race was not a label for a class in a classification, like species, but a name for a line of descent. Since, however, the differences to be classified derived from descent, the implications of the shift in meaning were not properly appreciated. The weakness of this answer was that it failed to account for evolution.

The third answer replied that other peoples were different because they were separate subspecies. Because of genetic variability, mutation, genetic drift and natural selection, regular differences could appear and subspecies could in time become separate species. To say that a set of individuals constituted a subspecies was therefore like a snapshot classification at a particular moment in time. It did not reflect the significance of their shared history or the relations between them. To refer to racial groups as populations was an improvement because it represented them as more than the results of a snapshot classification. However, this was still an answer to only half the question. The conceptualisations of race as lineage and race as type attempted to explain why people were both physically different and culturally different. Race as population offered a satisfactory explanation of physical differentiation but it could interpret cultural differentiation only by analogy, on the assumption that the ecological processes governing unconscious behaviour could explain as much about humans as they could about animals.

The ecological theory enabled the sociologist to reply that they were not like us because of the positions we occupied and the nature of the relations between us and them, but ecological factors alone could not account for the differences in wealth, power and social position of racial groups which formed parts of the same society. So it was said that racial minorities differed because they were of unequal social status; this was the outcome of an interaction between their own preferences and skills, and the ways in which they were regarded by others. The physical difference served as a social sign, indicating to people whether another person was a fellow group member or an outsider. The significance of such an assessment varied, of course, from one place, one time, and one social setting to another. Those who see behind this the influence of racism as a historical phenomenon claim that it is possible to account for those variations of place, time and social setting by elaborating a broad top-down and historical perspective. What they offer is an interpretation of trends pointing to political prescriptions rather than a social science explanation pointing to theory-testing. In recent years the class perspective has been the inspiration for a constructive and necessary critique of the status perspective.

If those who use the English language have indeed got into a muddle in the way they use 'race', how can they escape from it? The word is now so securely established in the practical language that for the foreseeable future English-speakers will continue to talk of racial groups and to draw upon the idiom of race when punishing racial discrimination, even if they talk more often of ethnicity in other contexts. Superseding 'race' in the theoretical language of social science will depend upon the development of a better theory of group formation and dissolution. Improving concepts is not just a matter of scholarly reflection, important as that always is. Concepts are refined in the process of answering well defined questions.

In the latter part of the twentieth century the vast improvements in communications and transport together with the creation of global markets have brought the peoples of the earth more together and, in some respects, have jumbled them up so that the old boundaries between groups are no longer so distinct. As the frameworks have weakened, individuals have become more interested in questions of racial and ethnic identity and the ways in which their subjective experience does not accord with the assumptions of others in their own milieu. These trends should increase interest in a bottom-up approach to questions of racial and ethnic relations, but the validity of such an approach is not dependent upon such circumstances. Though theories which start from the individual making choices from among a restricted range of alternatives have been much improved during the past thirty years, they have a long history. This concluding chapter has tried to indicate their potential, and to outline an agenda for the twenty-first century.

Bibliography

Adam, Heribert (1983) 'Rational Choice in Ethnic Mobilization: A Critique', *International Migration Review*, 18: 377–81

Anthias, Floya and Nina Yuval-Davis (1992) *Racialized Boundaries: Race, Nation, Gender, Colour and Class and the Anti-Racist Struggle*, London: Routledge

Augstein, Hannah Franziska (ed.) (1996) *Race. The Origins of an Idea, 1760–1850*, Bristol: Thoemmes Press

Banks, Marcus (1996) *Ethnicity: Anthropological Constructions*, London: Routledge

Bannister, Robert C. (1979) *Social Darwinism: Science and Myth in Anglo-American Social Thought*, Philadelphia: Temple University Press

Banton, Michael (1957) *West African City: A Study of Tribal Life in Freetown*, London: Oxford University Press

   (1967) *Race Relations*, London: Tavistock

   (1977) *The Idea of Race*, London: Tavistock

   (1983) *Racial and Ethnic Competition*, Cambridge: Cambridge University Press (reprinted 1992, Aldershot: Gregg Revivals)

   (1985) 'Mixed Motives and the Processes of Rationalization'. *Ethnic and Racial Studies*, 8:534–47

   (1986) 'Epistemological Assumptions in the Study of Racial Differentiation', in John Rex and David Mason (eds.), *Theories of Race and Ethnic Relations*, Cambridge: Cambridge University Press: 42–63

   (1993) 'Galton's Conception of Race in Historical Perspective', in Milo Keynes (ed.), *Sir Francis Galton, FRS: The Legacy of his Ideas*, London: Macmillan: 170–9

Banton, Michael and Mohd-Noor Mansor (1992) 'The Study of Ethnic Alignment: A New Technique and an Application in Malaysia', *Ethnic and Racial Studies*, 15:599–613

Barkan, Elazar (1992) *The Retreat of Scientific Racism. Changing Concepts of Race in Britain and the United States*, Cambridge: Cambridge University Press

Barker, Anthony J. (1978) *The African Link: British Attitudes to the Negro in the Era of the Atlantic Slave Trade, 1550–1807*, London: Frank Cass

Barnes, Barry (1992) 'Status Groups and Collective Action', *Sociology*, 6: 259–70

Barth, Fredrik (ed.) (1969) *Ethnic Groups and Boundaries: The Social Organization of Cultural Difference*, London: Allen & Unwin

Becker, Gary S. (1957) *The Economics of Discrimination*, Chicago: University of Chicago Press

Beddoe, John (1885) *The Races of Britain*, Bristol: Arrowsmith

(1912) *The Anthropological History of Europe* (revised edn, originally 1891, Paisley: Gardner)

Bendyshe, T. (1865) 'The History of Anthropology', *Memoirs read before the Anthropological Society of London*, 1:335–458

Biddiss, Michael D. (1970) *Father of Racist Ideology: The Social and Political Thought of Count Gobineau*, London: Weidenfeld & Nicolson

(1976) 'The Politics of Anatomy: Dr Robert Knox and Victorian Racism', *Proceedings of the Royal Society of Medicine*, 69:245–50

Blalock, Hubert M. (1967) *Toward a Theory of Minority Group Relations*, New York: Wiley

Blome, Hermann (1943) *Der Rassengedanke in den deutschen Romantik und seine Grundlagen im 18 Jahrhundert*, Munich and Berlin: Lehmann

Blumenbach, J. F. (1865) *The Anthropological Treatises of Johann Friedrich Blumenbach*, London: Anthropological Society of London

Blumer, Herbert (1958) 'United States of America', *International Social Science Bulletin*, 10:403–47 (reprinted in UNESCO, *Research on Racial Relations*, Paris: UNESCO, 1966: 87–133)

Blumer, Herbert and Troy Duster (1980) 'Theories of Race and Social Action', in UNESCO, *Sociological Theories: Race and Colonialism*, Paris: UNESCO: 211–38

Boas, Franz (1940) *Race, Language and Culture*, New York: Free Press

Boissel, Jean (1971) 'Un Théoricien des races, précurseur de Gobineau: Victor Courtet de l'Isle', *Études Gobiniènnes*: 203–14

(1972) *Victor Courtet 1813–1867. Premier théoricien de la hierarchie des races*, Paris: Presses Universitaires de France

Bonacich, Edna (1972) 'A Theory of Ethnic Antagonism: The Split Labour Market', *American Sociological Review*, 37:547–59

(1975) 'Abolition, the Extension of Slavery, and the Position of Free Blacks: 1830–1863', *American Journal of Sociology*, 81: 601–28

(1976) 'Advanced Capitalism and Black/White Relations in the United States: A Split Labour Market Interpretation', *American Sociological Review*, 41: 34–51

(1979) 'The Past, Present and Future of Split Labour Market Theory', *Research in Race and Ethnic Relations*, 1:17–64

(1981a) 'Capitalism and Race Relations in South Africa: A Split Labour Market Analysis', *Political Power and Social Theory*, 2:239–77

(1981b) 'Reply to Burawoy', *Political Power and Social Theory*, 2: 337–43

Boyd, William C. (1950) *Genetics and the Races of Man*, Boston: Little, Brown

Broca, Paul (1864) *On the Phenomenon of Hybridity in the Genus Homo*, London: Longman Green for Anthropological Society (originally 1859–60)

(1874) *Mémoires d'Anthropologie*, 5 vols., Paris: Reinwald

Buenzod, Janine (1967) *La Formation de la pensée de Gobineau et 'L'Essai sur l'inégalité des races humaines'*, Paris: Nizet

Burawoy, Michael (1981) 'The Capitalist State in South Africa: Marxist and Sociological Perspectives on Race and Class', *Political Power and Social Theory*, 2:279–335

Burton, Frank (1978) *The Politics of Legitimacy: Struggles in a Belfast Community*,

London: Routledge

Cairns, H. A. C. (1965) *Prelude to Imperialism: British Reactions to Central African Society, 1840–90*, London: Routledge

Carey, A. T. (1956) *Colonial Students*, London: Secker & Warburg

Carling, Alan H. (1991) *Social Division*, London: Verso
(1996) 'Michael Banton's Twins: Affiliation and Formation in the Rational Choice Theory of Racial and Ethnic Relations', in Rohit Barot (ed.), *The Racism Problematic: Contemporary Sociological Debates on Race and Ethnicity*, Lampeter: Edwin Mellen Press: 44–68

Carmichael, Stokely and Charles V. Hamilton (1967) *Black Power: The Politics of Liberation in America* (Harmondsworth: Penguin, 1968)

Carus, Carl Gustav (1849) *Denkschrift zum hundertjährigen Geburtsfeste Goethes: Über ungleiche Befähigung der verschiedenen Menschheitstämme für höhre geistige Entwickelung*, Leipzig: Brockhaus

Chadwick, H. Munro (1945) *The Nationalities of Europe and the Growth of National Ideologies*, Cambridge: Cambridge University Press

Chai, Sun-Ki (1996) 'A Theory of Ethnic Group Boundaries', *Nations and Nationalism*, 2:281–307

Chakravati, Nalini Ranjan (1971) *The Indian Minority in Burma: The Rise and Decline of an Immigrant Community*, London: Oxford University Press

Chambers, Robert (1844) *Vestiges of the Natural History of Creation*, London: Churchill (reprinted Leicester University Press, 1979)

Chiswick, Barry R. (1988) 'Differences in Education and Earnings Across Racial and Ethnic Groups: Tastes, Discrimination, and Investments in Child Quality', *Quarterly Journal of Economics*, 103:571–97

Coleman, William (1964) *Georges Cuvier, Zoologist: A Study in the History of Evolution Theory*, Cambridge, MA: Harvard University Press

Collingwood, R. G. (1939) *An Autobiography*, Oxford: Oxford University Press (Harmondsworth: Penguin, 1944)

Coppel, Charles A. (1997) 'Revisiting Furnivall's "Plural Society": Colonial Java as a Mestizo Society?', *Ethnic and Racial Studies*, 20:562–79

Cox, Oliver C. (1948) *Caste, Class and Race: A Study in Social Dynamics*, New York: Monthly Review Press

Crook, John Hurrell (1980) *The Evolution of Human Consciousness*, Oxford: Clarendon Press

Curtin, Philip D. (1964) *The Image of Africa: British Ideas and Action, 1780–1850*, Madison: University of Wisconsin Press and London: Macmillan

Daniel, W. W. (1968) *Racial Discrimination in England*, Harmondsworth: Penguin

Darwin, Charles Robert (1871) *The Descent of Man, and Selection in Relation to Sex*, London: Murray

Davis, Allison, Burleigh B. Gardner and Mary R. Gardner (1941) *Deep South: A Social Anthropological Study of Caste and Class*, Chicago: University of Chicago Press

Davis, Kingsley (1948) *Human Society*, New York: Macmillan

Dawkins, Richard (1976) *The Selfish Gene* (2nd edn, 1989) Oxford: Oxford University Press

Dennett, Daniel C. (1995) *Darwin's Dangerous Idea. Evolution and the Meanings of Life*, Harmondsworth: Penguin

Desmoulins, A. (1826) *Histoire Naturelle des races humaines*, Paris

van Dijk, Teun A. (1991) *Racism and the Press*, London: Routledge

Dikötter, Frank (1992) *The Discourse of Race in Modern China*, London: Hurst

Dollard, John (1937) *Caste and Class in a Southern Town*, New York: Doubleday Anchor

—— (1938) 'Hostility and Fear in Social Life', *Social Forces*, 17:15–26

Dover, Cedric (1952) 'The Racial Philosophy of Johann Herder', *British Journal of Sociology*, 3:124–33

Down, John Langdon (1866) 'Observations on an Ethnic Classification of Idiots', *Clinical Lectures and Reports of the London Hospital*, 3: 259–62

—— (1887) *On Some of the Mental Affections of Childhood and Youth*, London: Churchill

Drake, St Clair and Horace R. Cayton (1945) *Black Metropolis*, New York: Harcourt Brace (the London edn was published with the authors' names in reverse order)

Dubow, Saul (1995) *Scientific Racism in Modern South Africa*, Cambridge: Cambridge University Press

Durkheim, Emile (1901) *Les Règles de la méthode sociologique*, Paris: Presses Universitaires de France (1950 edn)

Echevaria, Durand (1957) *Mirage in the West: A History of the French Image of American Society*, Princeton: Princeton University Press

Edwards, W. F. (1829) *Des Caractères physiologiques des races humaines, considerés dans leurs rapports avec l'histoire: lettre à M. Amédée Thierry*, Paris: Compère Jeune

Elster, Jon (1989) *The Cement of Society: A Study of Social Order*, Cambridge: Cambridge University Press

Erickson, Paul (1981) 'The Anthropology of Charles Caldwell, M.D.', *Isis*, 72: 252–6

Eze, Emmanuel Chukwudi (1997) *Race and the Enlightenment: A Reader*, Cambridge, MA: Blackwell

Fenton, C. Stephen (1980) 'Race, Class and Politics in the Work of Emile Durkheim', in UNESCO, *Sociological Theories: Race and Colonialism*, Paris: UNESCO: 211–38

Fishman, J. A. (1990) *Reversing Language Shift*, Cleveden: Multilingual Matters

Fortes, Meyer (1983) 'Rules and the Emergence of Society', *Occasional Paper*, 39, London: Royal Anthropological Society

Frazier, E. Franklin (1957) *Race and Culture Contacts in the Modern World*, Boston: Beacon Press

Fredrickson, George M. (1971) *The Black Image in the White Mind: The Debate on Afro-American Character and Destiny, 1817–1914*, New York: Harper & Row

Freeman, Derek (1974) 'The Evolutionary Theories of Charles Darwin and Herbert Spencer', *Current Anthropology*, 15:211–37

Froude, James Anthony (1866) *Oceana, or England and her Colonies* (new edn, 1894), London: Longmans, Green

Fryer, Peter (1984) *Staying Power: The History of Black People in Britain*, London: Pluto

Furnivall, J. S. (1948) *Colonial Policy and Practice: A Comparative Study of Burma and Netherlands India*, Cambridge: Cambridge University Press

Gartner, Scott Sigmund and Gary M. Segura (1997) 'Appearances Can be Deceptive: Self-Selection, Social Group Identification, and Political Mobilization', *Rationality and Society*, 9:131–61

Geiger, Theodor (1962) *Arbeiten zur Soziologie*, Berlin: Neuwied

Gellner, Ernest (1983) *Nations and Nationalism*, Oxford: Blackwell

——— (1985) *Relativism and the Social Sciences*, Cambridge: Cambridge University Press

Ghiselin, Michael T. (1969) *The Triumph of the Darwinian Method*, Berkeley and Los Angeles: University of California Press

Gilroy, Paul (1987) *There Ain't No Black in the Union Jack: The Cultural Politics of Race and Nation*, London: Hutchinson

Glazer, Nathan and Daniel Patrick Moynihan (1975) *Ethnicity: Theory and Experience*, Cambridge, MA: Harvard University Press

Gluckman, Max (1955) *Custom and Conflict in Africa*, Oxford: Blackwell

Gobineau, A. de (1853–5) *Essai sur l'inégalité des Races humaines*, Paris: Firmin-Didot (page references are to the 1967 edn, Paris: Belfond)

——— (1915) *The Inequality of Human Races*, London: Heinemann (translation of vol. i of Gobineau, 1853–5)

Goering, John and Ron Wienk (eds.) (1996) *Mortgage Lending, Racial Discrimination, and Federal Policy*, Washington, DC: Urban Institute Press

Goldberg, David Theo (1993) *Racist Culture: Philosophy and the Politics of Meaning*, Oxford: Blackwell

Gould, Stephen Jay (1977) *Ontology and Phylogeny*, Cambridge, MA: Harvard University Press

——— (1978) 'Morton's Ranking of Races by Cranial Capacity', *Science*, 200: 503–9

——— (1981) *The Mismeasure of Man*, Harmondsworth: Penguin

Greene, John C. (1959) *The Death of Adam: Evolution and its Impact on Western Thought*, New York: Mentor Books

Gumplowicz, Ludwig (1875) *Rasse und Staat: Eine Untersuchung über das Gesetz der Staatenbildung*, Vienna: Verlag der Manzschen Buchhandlung

——— (1881) *Rechtsstaat und Socialismus*, Innsbruck: Verlag der Wagner'schen Universitäts-büchhandlung

——— (1883) *Der Rassenkampf: Sociologischen Untersuchungen*, Innsbruck: Verlag der Wagner'schen Universitäts-buchhandlung

Hall, Stuart (1980) 'Race, Articulation and Societies Structured in Dominance', in *Sociological Theories: Race and Colonialism*, Paris: UNESCO: 305–45

Halliday, R. J. (1971) 'Social Darwinism: A Definition', *Victorian Studies*, 14: 389–405

Hardin, Russell (1995) *One for All: The Logic of Group Conflict*, Princeton: Princeton University Press

Harper, Edward B. (1968) 'Social Consequences of an "Unsuccessful" Low Caste Movement', in James Silverberg (ed.), *Social Mobility in the Caste*

System in India, Comparative Studies in Society and History, supplement 3, The Hague: Mouton: 36–65

Heath, Anthony (1976) *Rational Choice and Social Exchange: A Critique of Exchange Theory*, Cambridge: Cambridge University Press

Hechter, Michael (1987) *Principles of Group Solidarity*, Berkeley: University of California Press

Hechter, Michael, and Debra Friedman (1983) 'Does Rational Choice Theory Suffice? Response to Adam', *International Migration Review*, 18:381–8

Hechter, Michael, Debra Friedman and Malka Appelbaum (1982) 'A Theory of Ethnic Collective Action', *International Migration Review*, 16:412–34

Hodson, H. V. (1950) 'Race Relations in the Commonwealth', *International Affairs*, 26:305–15

Hofstadter, Richard (1955) *Social Darwinism in American Thought* (revised edn), Boston: Beacon Press

Horowitz, Donald L. (1985) *Ethnic Groups in Conflict*, Berkeley: University of California Press

Horsman, Reginald (1981) *Race and Manifest Destiny: The Origins of American Racial Anglo-Saxonism*, Cambridge, MA: Harvard University Press

Hughes, Everett C. (1946) 'The Knitting of Racial Groups in Industry', *American Sociological Review*, 11: 512–19 (reprinted in Everett C. Hughes and Helen McGill Hughes, 1952, *Where Peoples Meet: Racial and Ethnic Frontiers*, Glencoe: Free Press: 175–88)

(1973) Personal communication (14 November)

Hunt, James (1865) 'On the Negro's Place in Nature', *Memoirs read before the Anthropological Society of London*, 1: 1–64

(1866) 'On the Application of the Principle of Natural Selection to Anthropology', *Anthropological Review*, 4: 320–40

(1870) 'On the Acclimatisation of Europeans in the United States of America', *Anthropological Review*, 8: 109–37

Huxley, Julian S. and A. C. Haddon (1935) *We Europeans: A Survey of 'Racial' Problems*, London: Jonathan Cape

Jenkins, Richard (1982) *Hightown Rules: Growing up in a Belfast Housing Estate*, Leicester: National Youth Bureau

(1994) 'Rethinking Ethnicity: Identity, Categorization and Power', *Ethnic and Racial Studies*, 17: 197–223

Jordan, Winthrop D. (1968) *White Over Black: American Attitudes Towards the Negro, 1550–1812*, Chapel Hill: University of North Carolina Press

Just, Roger (1989) 'Triumph of the Ethnos', in Elizabeth Tonkin, Maryon McDonald and Malcolm Chapman (eds.), *History and Ethnicity*, ASA monographs, 27, London: Routledge: 71–88

Keith, Sir Arthur (1931) *The Place of Prejudice in Modern Civilization*, London: Williams and Norgate

Kelley, Jonathan, and Ian McAllister (1984) 'The Genesis of Conflict: Religion and Status Attainment in Ulster, 1968', *Sociology*, 18: 171–87

Keynes, Milo (ed.), *Sir Francis Galton, FRS: The Legacy of his Ideas*, London: Macmillan

Killian, Lewis M. (1970) 'Herbert Blumer's Contribution to Race Relations', in Tamotsu Shibutani (ed.), *Human Nature and Collective Behavior: Papers in Honor of Herbert Blumer*, New Brunswick, NJ: Transaction Books: 179–90

Kiple, Kenneth F. and Virginia H. King (1981) *Another Dimension to the Black Diaspora: Diet, Disease and Death*, Cambridge: Cambridge University Press

Klemm, Gustav (1843–52) *Allegemeine Cultur-Geschichte der Menschheit*, 10 vols., Leipzig: Teubner

(1851) *Grundideen zu einen allegemeinen Cultur-Wissenschaft: Sitzundsberichte der philosophischen–historischen Classe der K. Akad. der Wissenschaft*, Wien

Knox, Robert (1850) *The Races of Men: A Fragment* (2nd edn, 1862), London: Renshaw

(1857) *Man: His Structure and Physiology: Popularly Explained and Demonstrated*, London: Ballière

(1863) 'Ethnological Inquiries and Observations', *Anthropological Review*, 1: 245–63

Krech, David and Richard S. Crutchfield (1948) *Theory and Problems of Social Psychology*, New York: McGraw-Hill

Kroeber, Alfred (1917) 'The Superorganic', *American Anthropologist*, 19: 163–213

Kuhn, Thomas S. (1962) *The Structure of Scientific Revolutions*, Chicago: University of Chicago Press

(1968) 'Science: History of', *International Encyclopedia of the Social Sciences*, vol. 14: 74–83

Kuper, Leo (1974) *Race, Class and Power: Ideology and Revolutionary Change in Plural Societies*, London: Duckworth

(1977) *The Pity of it All: Polarization of Racial and Ethnic Relations*, London: Duckworth

Lal, Barbara Ballis (1990) *The Romance of Culture in an Urban Civilization: Robert E. Park and Race and Ethnic Relations in Cities*, London: Routledge

Lapouge, Georges Vacher de (1887) 'L'Anthropologie et la science politique', *Revue d'Anthropologie* (15 May)

(1899) *L'Aryan: son rôle social*, Paris: Fontemoing

Lasker, Bruno (1929) *Race Attitudes in Children*, New York: Henry Holt

Latham, Robert Gordon (1850) *The Natural History of the Varieties of Man*, London: Van Voorst

Lee, Frank F. (1961) *Negro and White in Connecticut Town*, New York: Bookman Associates

Lewis, Sir W. Arthur (1985) *Racial Conflict and Economic Development*, Cambridge, MA: Harvard University Press

Lieberson, Stanley (1980) *A Piece of the Pie: Black and White Immigrants since 1880*, Berkeley: University of California Press

Lind, Andrew W. (ed.) (1955) *Race Relations in World Perspective*, Honolulu: University of Hawaii Press (reprinted, 1973, Westport, CT: Greenwood Press)

(1966) 'Race Relations in the Islands of the Pacific', in *Research in Racial Relations*, Paris: UNESCO: 229–48

Lipton, Merle (1985) *Capitalism and Apartheid: South Africa, 1910–1986*, Aldershot: Gower

Little, Daniel (1991) *Varieties of Social Explanation: An Introduction to the Philosophy of Social Science*, Boulder: Westview Press

Little, Kenneth L. (1948) *Negroes in Britain: A Study of Racial Relations in English Society*, London: Routledge

Lonsdale, Henry (1870) *A Sketch of the Life and Writings of Robert Know, the Anatomist*, London: Macmillan

Lorimer, Douglas A. (1978) *Colour, Class and Victorians: English Attitudes to the Negro in the Mid-Nineteenth Century*, Leicester: Leicester University Press

Lundahl, Mats and Eskil Wadensjö (1984) *Unequal Treatment: A Study in the Neo-Classical Theory of Discrimination*, London: Croom Helm

Lyman, Stanford M. (1972) *The Black American in Sociological Thought*, New York: Putnams

(1992) *Militarism, Imperialism, and Racial Accommodation. An Analysis and Interpretation of the Early Writings of Robert E. Park*, Fayetteville: University of Arkansas Press

Lyman, Stanford M. and Arthur J. Vidich (1988) *Social Order and the Public Philosophy: An Analysis and Interpretation of the Work of Herbert Blumer*, Fayetteville: University of Arkansas Press

Lyon, Michael H. (1972) 'Race and Ethnicity in Pluralistic Societies. A Comparison of Minorities in the USA and UK', *New Community*, 1:256–62

Makabe, Tomoko (1981) 'The Theory of the Split Labor Market: A Comparison of the Japanese Experience in Brazil and Canada', *Social Forces*, 59:786–809

Mansor, Mohd-Noor (1992) 'The Determinants of Malay Ethnic Alignment', PhD dissertation, University of Bristol

Mariappam, Kntayya (1996) 'Micro and Macro Ethnicity: Ethnic Preference and Structures in Malaysia', PhD dissertation, University of Bristol

Martinello, Marco (1996) 'The Existence of an Urban Underclass in Belgium', *New Community*, 22:655–69

Mason, David (1986) 'Introduction: Controversies and Continuities in Race and Ethnic Relations Theory', in John Rex and David Mason (eds.), *Theories of Race and Ethnic Relations*, Cambridge: Cambridge University Press: 1–19

(1994) 'On the Dangers of Disconnecting Race and Racism', *Sociology*, 28:845–58

Massey, Douglas S. and Nancy A. Denton (1993) *American Apartheid. Segregation and the Making of the Underclass*, Cambridge, MA: Harvard University Press

Mayr, Ernst (1982) *The Growth of Biological Thought: Diversity, Evolution, and Inheritance*, Cambridge, MA: Harvard University Press

Michael, John S. (1988) 'A New Look at Morton's Craniological Research', *Current Anthropology*, 29: 349–54

Miles, Robert (1980) 'Class, Race and Ethnicity: A Critique of Cox's Theory', *Ethnic and Racial Studies*, 3, 169–87

(1982) *Racism and Migrant Labour*, London: Routledge & Kegan Paul

(1989) *Racism*, London: Routledge

(1993) *Racism after 'Race Relations'*, London: Routledge

Mill, John Stuart (1843) *A System of Logic. Ratiocinative and Inductive* (London: Longmans Green, 1898)

Montagu, M. F. Ashley (ed.) (1964) *The Concept of Race*, London: Collier-

Macmillan

Morton, Samuel George (1839) *Crania Americana: or, A Comparative View of the Skulls of Various Aboriginal nations of North and South America, to which is prefixed an Essay on the Varieties of the Human Species*, Philadelphia and London

    (1844) *Crania Aegyptica: or, Observations on Egyptian Ethnography*, Philadelphia and London

Murray, Gilbert (1900) 'The Exploitation of Inferior Races in Ancient and Modern Times', in *Liberalism and the Empire*, three essays by Francis W. Hirst, Gilbert Murray and J. L. Hammond, London: Johnson: 118–57

Myrdal, Alva and Gunnar Myrdal (1941) *Kontakt med America*, Stockholm: Bonniers

Myrdal, Gunnar, with the assistance of Richard Sterner and Arnold Rose (1944) *An American Dilemma: The Negro Problem and Modern Democracy*, New York: Harper

North, Douglass C. (1983) 'A Theory of Institutional Change and the Economic History of the Western World', in Michael Hechter (ed.), *The Micofoundations of Macrosociology*, Philadelphia: Temple University Press: 190–215

Nott, J. C. and G. R. Gliddon (1854) *Types of Mankind: or Ethnological Researches* Philadelphia: Lippincott and London: Trubner

    (1857) *Indigenous Races, or New Chapters of Ethnological Enquiry*, Philadelphia: Lippincott and London: Trubner

Olsen, Mancur (1965) *The Logic of Collective Action: Public Goods and the Theory of Groups*, Cambridge, MA: Harvard University Press

Olzak, Susan (1993) *The Dynamics of Ethnic Competition and Conflict*, Stanford, CA: Stanford University Press

Olzak, Susan and Joane Nagel (1986) *Competitive Ethnic Relations*, Orlando, FL: Academic Press

Omi, Michael and Howard Winant (1994) *Racial Formation in the United States: from the 1960s to the 1990s* (2nd edn), London: Routledge

Osman, Sanusi (1981) 'The National Unity Policy and Ethnic Relations in Malaysia, with special reference to Malacca Town', PhD dissertation, University of Bristol

Owen, David (1996) 'Changes in the Spatial Distribution of People from Minority Ethnic Groups in England and Wales between 1981 and 1991', Seminar paper, Centre for Research in Ethnic Relations, University of Warwick

Papiha, S. S. (1987) 'Genetic Variation and Disease Susceptibility in NCWP [New Commonwealth with Pakistani] Groups in Britain', *New Community*, 13:373–83

Park, Robert E. (1950) *Race and Culture*, Glencoe: Free Press

Park, Robert E. and Ernest W. Burgess (1921) *Introduction to the Science of Sociology*, Chicago: University of Chicago Press

Patterson, Orlando (1975) 'Contest and Choice in Ethnic Allegiance: A Theoretical Framework and Caribbean Case Study', in Nathan Glazer and Daniel P. Moynihan (eds.), *Ethnicity: Theory and Experience*, Cambridge, MA: Harvard University Press: 305–49

Pearson, Veronica (1973) 'Telegony: A Study of this Belief and its Continued

Existence', MSc dissertation, University of Bristol

Perraton, H. D. (1967) 'British Attitudes towards East and West Africa, 1880–1914', *Race*, 8:223–46

Phelps, Edmund S. (1972) 'The Statistical Theory of Racism and Sexism', *American Economic Review*, 62:659–61

Pierson, Donald (1942) *Negroes in Brazil: A Study of Race Contact at Bahia*, Chicago: University of Chicago Press (reprinted, 1967, Carbondale: Southern Illinois University Press)

Poliakov, Léon (1974) *The Aryan Myth: A History of Racist and Nationalist Ideas in Europe*, London: Chatto, for Sussex University Press

Popper, Sir Karl Raimund (1945/66) *The Open Society and its Enemies*, 2 vols., London: Routledge

(1957) *The Poverty of Historicism*, London: Routledge and Kegan Paul

(1972) *Objective Knowledge: An Evolutionary Approach*, Oxford: Clarendon Press

(1974/76) *Unended Quest: An Intellectual Autobiography* (first published as 'Autobiography of Karl Popper' in *The Library of Living Philosphers*, (ed.) Paul Arthur Schilpp, IL: Open Court) revised edition, London: Fontana

Powdermaker, Hortense (1939) *After Freedom: A Cultural Study on the Deep South*, New York: Atheneum

Prichard, James Cowles (1826) *Researches into the Physical History of Mankind* (2nd edn 1826, 3rd edn 1836), London: Arch

(1843) *The Natural History of Man*, London: Ballière

Quatrefages, A. de (1879) *The Human Species* (2nd edn), London: Kegan Paul

Rabushka, Alvin (1974) *A Theory of Racial Harmony*, Studies in International Affairs, 11, Columbia, SC: University of South Carolina Press

Rattansi, Ali (1994) ' "Western" Racisms, Ethnicities and Identities in a "Postmodern" Frame', in Ali Rattansi and Sallie Westwood (eds.), *Racism, Modernity and Identity on the Western Front*, Oxford: Polity Press: 15–86

Rattansi, Ali and Sallie Westwood (1994) 'Modern Racisms, Racialized Identities', in Ali Rattansi and Sallie Westwood (eds.), *Racism, Modernity and Identity on the Western Front*, Oxford: Polity Press: 1–12

Rex, John (1970) 'The Concept of Race in Sociological Theory', in Sami Zubaida (ed.), *Race and Racialism*, London: Tavistock: 35–55

Rex, John and Robert Moore (1967) *Race, Community and Conflict: A Study of Sparkbrook*, London: Oxford University Press

Richards, Evelleen (1989) 'The Moral Anatomy of Robert Knox: The Interplay between Biological and Social Thought in Victorian Scientific Naturalism', *Journal of the History of Biology*, 20:373–436

Sauer, Norman J. (1992) 'Forensic Anthropology and the Concept of Race: If Races Don't Exist, Why are Forensic Anthropologists so Good at Identifying Them?', *Social Science and Medicine*, 34: 107–11

Schelling, Thomas C. (1963) *The Strategy of Conflict*, New York: Oxford University Press

(1978) *Micromotives and Macrobehavior*, New York: Norton

Sivanandan, A. (1976) 'Race, Class and the State: The Black Experience in Britain', *Race and Class*, 17:347–68

Sloan, Philip R. (1973) 'The Idea of Racial Degeneracy in Buffon's *Histoire Naturelle*', in Harold E. Pagliaro (ed.), *Racism in the Eighteenth Century*, Studies in Eighteenth-Century Culture, 3, Cleveland: Press of Case Western University: 293–321

Smith, Bernard (1960) *European Vision and the South Pacific 1768–1850: A Study in the History of Art and Ideas*, Oxford: Clarendon Press

Smith, Charles Hamilton (1848) *The Natural History of the Human Species*, Edinburgh: W. H. Lizars

Smith, Samuel Stanhope (1787) *An Essay on the Causes of the Variety of Complexion and Figure in the Human Species* (2nd edn, 1810) (Cambridge, MA: Harvard University Press, 1965)

Solomos, John and Les Back (1996) *Racism and Society*, London: Macmillan

Sorokin, Pitirim A. (1928) *Contemporary Sociological Theories*, New York: Harper

Sowell, Thomas (1981) *Markets and Minorities*, New York: Basic Books

(1983) *The Economics and Politics of Race: An International Perspective*, New York: William Morrow

(1994) *Race and Culture: A World View*, New York: Basic Books

Stanton, William (1960) *The Leopard's Spots: Scientific Attitudes Towards Race in America 1815–59*, Chicago: University of Chicago Press

Stocking, George W. (1968) *Race, Culture and Evolution: Essays in the History of Evolution*, New York: Free Press

(1971) 'What's in a Name? The Origins of the Royal Anthropological Institute', *Man*, 6:369–90

(1973) 'From Chronology to Ethnology: James Cowles Prichard and British Anthropology, 1800–1850', in J. C. Prichard, *Researches into the Physical History of Man*, Chicago: University of Chicago Press: ix–cx

(1987) *Victorian Anthropology*, New York: Free Press

Sumner, William Graham (1906) *Folkways: A Study of the Sociological Importance of Usages, Manners, Customs, Mores, and Morals*, New York: New American Library

Taguieff, Pierre-André (1988) *La Force du préjugé: Essai sur le racisme et ses doubles*, Paris: La Découverte

Temperley, Howard (1987) 'Eric Williams and Abolition: The Birth of a New Orthodoxy', in Barbara L. Solow and Stanley L. Engerman (eds.), *British Capitalism and Caribbean Slavery: The Legacy of Eric Williams*, Cambridge: Cambridge University Press: 229–57

Thierry, Augustin (1825) *History of the Conquest of England by the Normans* (London: Everyman's Library, no date)

Thomas, William I. (1904) 'The Psychology of Race Prejudice', *American Journal of Sociology*, 9:593–611

Thuillier, Guy (1977) 'Un anarchiste positiviste: Georges Vacher de Lapouge', in Pierre Guiral and Emile Temime (eds.), *L'idée de race dans la pensée politique française contemporaine*, Paris: Editions du Centre Nationale de la Recherche Scientifique: 48–65

Todd, Emmanuel (1994) *Le Destin des immigrés. Assimilation et ségrégation dans les démocraties occidentales*, Paris: Seuil

van den Berghe, Pierre L. (1967) *Race and Racism*, New York: Wiley (revised edn, 1978)

(1981) *The Ethnic Phenomenon*, New York: Elsevier

(1995) 'Does Race Matter?', *Nations and Nationalism*, 1:357–68

(1997) 'Rehabilitating Stereotypes', *Ethnic and Racial Studies*, 20:1–16

van den Berghe, Pierre L. and Peter Frost (1986) 'Skin Colour Preference, Sexual Dimorphism and Sexual Selection: A Case of Gene Culture Co-evolution?', *Ethnic and Racial Studies*, 9:87–113

Vincent, John (1990) *Disraeli*, Oxford: Oxford University Press

Vögelin, Erich (1933a) *Die Rassenidee in der Geistesgeschichte von Ray bis Carus*, Berlin: Junker and Dunnhaupt

(1933b) *Rasse und Staat*, Tübingen: Möhr

Vogt, Karl (1863) *Lectures on Man: His Place in Creation and in the History of the Earth* (ed. James Hunt) (London: Longmans Green for Anthropological Society, 1864)

Wallman, Sandra (1979) 'Foreword', in Sandra Wallman (ed.), *Ethnicity at Work*, London: Macmillan: ix–xii

(1996) 'Ethnicity, Work and Localism: Narratives of Difference in London and Kampala', *Ethnic and Racial Studies*, 19:1–28

Washburn, S. L. (1963) 'The Study of Race', *American Anthropologist*, 65: 521–31

Weber, Eugen (1976) *Peasants into Frenchmen: The Modernization of Rural France, 1870–1914*, Stanford, CA: Stanford University Press

Weber, Max (1922) *Economy and Society* (trans. and ed. G. Roth and C. Wittich) (New York: Bedminster, 1971)

Wieviorka, Michel (1991/5) *L'Espace du racisme*, Paris: Seuil (trans. 1995, *The Arena of Racism*, London: Sage)

(1994) 'Racism in Europe: Unity and Diversity', in Ali Rattansi and Sallie Westwood (eds.), *Racism, Modernity and Identity on the Western Front*, Oxford: Polity Press: 173–88

Williams, Eric E. (1944) *Capitalism and Slavery*, Chapel Hill, NC: University of North Carolina Press (New York: Harper Torchbooks, 1965)

Williams, Robin M., Jr. in collaboration with John P. Dean and Edward M. Suchman (1964) *Strangers Next Door: Ethnic Relations in American Communities*, Englewood Cliffs, NJ: Prentice-Hall

Wimmer, Andreas (1997) 'Explaining Xenophobia and Racism: A Critical Review of Current Research Approaches', *Ethnic and Racial Studies*, 20:17–41

Yinger, Milton (1994) *Ethnicity: Source of Strength? Source of Conflict?*, Albany: State University of New York Press

Index